M. Mauheim

– 1996 –

CHEKHOV'S PLAYS

CHEKHOV'S PLAYS

An Opening into Eternity

Richard Gilman

Yale University Press ▪ New Haven and London

Designed by Jill Breitbarth and set in Garamond type by
Keystone Typesetting, Inc., Orwigsburg, Pennsylvania.
Printed in the United States of America by BookCrafters, Inc.,
Chelsea, Michigan.

Library of Congress Cataloging-in-Publication Data
Gilman, Richard, 1925–
Chekhov's plays : an opening into eternity / Richard Gilman.
p.   cm.
Includes bibliographical references and index.
ISBN 0-300-06461-6
1. Chekhov, Anton Pavlovich, 1860–1904—Criticism and
interpretation.   I. Title.
PG3458.Z8G5   1995
891.72′3—dc20   95-10913
CIP

A catalogue record for this book is available from the
British Library.

The paper in this book meets the guidelines for permanence and
durability of the Committee on Production Guidelines for Book
Longevity of the Council on Library Resources.

10   9   8   7   6   5   4   3   2

For Yasuko Shiojiri, my wife

Contents

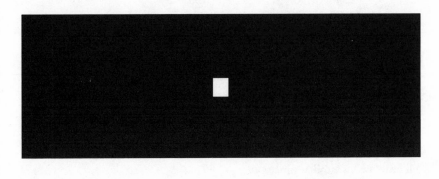

Preface

A respectable if rather drab and characterless district near the center of Moscow in March 1989. It's a gray Sunday morning and I'm standing with a talented young theater teacher and critic named Sergei and a friend of his, the sixteen-year-old daughter of a prominent professor of drama. We're in a side street called Sadovaya-Kudrinskaya off a wide boulevard down which we've just traveled on a clanking trolley, and we're waiting to be allowed into a small two-story house, which was once a private residence and is now a museum. The young woman calls my attention to a little metal plate on the wall near the front door on which is inscribed "A. P. Chekhov, Dr. of Medicine" in fading cursive Cyrillic script.

When my hosts for this trip had asked me for a list of the places I most wanted to visit in Moscow, I'd put this house near the top. Chekhov, my guidebook had told me in its sober and careful prose, had "resided and practiced medicine at this address" from 1886 to 1890 after getting his M.D. at the age of twenty-four in 1884. I know of two other Chekhov houses, one at Melikhovo, where he spent some summers and other periods in the late eighties and early nineties, and the other at Yalta, where he lived most of the time during his last years and which I'm going to visit later on.

We continue to wait outside the Moscow building, whose original red color is badly faded; Chekhov once described it as looking like "a chest of drawers."[1]

But after a while the museum opens and we go in, exchanging our presumably dirty shoes for the ill-fitting canvas slippers they always give you to wear in places like this.

Inside we walk at first among reminders of Chekhov's career as a physician, including a cracked brown leather doctor's satchel and a group photograph of his graduating class from Moscow University's Faculty of Medicine. Anton is one of the tallest among the two dozen or so earnest, somewhat stiffly or archly posing young men in black suits and white shirts, and he does not yet wear a full beard or his familiar pince-nez.

Chekhov several times referred to medicine as his "lawful"[2] or "legal" wife and to literature as his "mistress"; when he got tired of one, he said, he would go to the other. In fact, of course, the relationship was a good deal more complicated than that, and after I remember the quote and remind Sergei of it, I make a mental note to put the subject on some future agenda of Chekhov study. (One thing I will come upon is this variant concerning his writing: "Narrative is my legal wife and drama a flamboyant, rowdy, impudent, exhausting mistress."[3] That this description was accurate is borne out by the fact that Chekhov constantly complained about the difficulty—sometimes it seemed the impossibility—of writing plays, while writing fiction seems to have given him no such trouble.)

Along with the mementos of his "wife" in the first sense are some of his paramour, especially from the early years of their liaison: copies of a few of his first collections of stories; original issues of the weekly magazines in which he published his first humorous sketches under the noms de plume, among others, "A Physician without Patients" and "Antosha Chekhonte." (The latter name was given to him by one of his high school teachers in Taganrog, the nondescript little city on the Sea of Azov where he was born and lived until he was nineteen.) Some of the journals, which have names like *The Dragonfly, Alarm Clock,* and *Splinters,* are reminiscent of the old London *Punch,* with histrionic black-and-white illustrations on their covers.

In his small, rather dark study you can see his black wooden desk, his walking-stick, pens, a marble inkwell with two little pots flanking a metal horse, and the blotter he used. Here he wrote a number of stories and possibly worked on two plays, *Ivanov* and *The Wood Demon,* although he seems to have done a great deal of his writing during those years at the various weekend or summer homes he rented (and, in the case of Melikhovo, later bought) in the countryside around Moscow or a little further south. What look like galley proofs with corrections on them lie on the blotter, which impresses me as an astute note of realism, though I can't believe the proofs are authentic.

His bedroom and that of his sister Maria, who lived with him here and served as his assistant and hostess, are extremely small, with space enough only for narrow beds on which lie plump white comforters, for little marble wash-stands and, in Masha's room, for an easel. She was a rather talented artist several of whose paintings, most notably portraits of Anton and their older brother Alexander, hang on the walls of the main room. (Three of Chekhov's four brothers were also variously gifted; the youngest became a solid success as an educator.) Chekhov's mother, Yevgenia, and his younger brothers Mikhail (Misha) and Nikolai lived here too, the crowded household, for which Anton was the main, if not the only, economic support, being joined for a time by an aunt and a cousin; all their rooms were on the second floor, which isn't open to the public.

Two weeks later and seven hundred miles further south I'm at the Chekhov house in Yalta. Walking in the garden with my interpreter and guide, Nina, and the curator of the place—or, as everyone engaged in any of a wide range of formal cultural or intellectual activities in this country seems to be known, the resident "scholar"—I'm told that Chekhov himself carried up from the sea-shore, at least a couple of miles away down a winding road from the hillside where the house is perched, all the stones that cover the circling path, and planted many of the trees and shrubs we walk among, although he could scarcely have lived long enough to have seen more than a few of them grow to any size. And where could he have gotten the physical strength for it, I wonder.

Inside the museum, an oddly shaped three-story white structure about which Chekhov once said that it would make a perfect target if the British fleet were ever to bombard Yalta, I'm shown another cane, a pair of pince-nez that, placed on a shelf behind glass, looks like an artifact from some archeological dig, and another scruffy doctor's bag, which I didn't expect to see, since I hadn't thought he'd practiced medicine at all during those last few years.

An especially touching object in the dining room is an oblong of red cloth, like a shawl or banner, with a sewn inscription that reads: "To our dear Anton Pavlovich." This was a gift from the Moscow Art Theater; a number of the members, including Olga Knipper, the actress whom Chekhov married in 1901, arranged a Crimean tour in order to visit him at a time when his health made it more difficult than ever for him to travel up to Moscow.

A lovely photograph shows the group with him in the middle; from either side their heads are leaning toward him, most likely so they can all get into the frame of the picture, but looking as though they're propping him up with their love. On a wall covered with grey paper in a gold fleur-de-lis pattern I see an ancient telephone with a nearby slate for jotting down notes, and then I come upon another familiar photo, this one of Chekhov in a long black overcoat buttoned to the neck, wearing a black fedora and looking down at two small dogs at his feet. To see these well-known photos in the place where they were taken gives me a peculiarly strong sense of access to the past.

More paintings by Maria are on the walls. I'm told that she was the museum's curator for many years until her death in 1957 (fifty-three years after Chekhov's!) at the age of ninety-three. (Olga outlived him by an equally astonishing stretch; she continued to act nearly until her death in 1959, also at ninety-three.) I learn much later that Maria never married, having been fiercely—some would say excessively, even ruinously—devoted to her brother, first to his existence and then to his memory and name.

Earlier I went to the adjacent Conference Center, itself a minimuseum. There, by a most satisfying coincidence, the annual meeting of the Chekhov Society, with scholars from all over the Soviet Union, was holding its opening session. After Nina spoke to the chairman, I was summoned to the podium and graciously, if rather terrifyingly, invited to address the gathering—to talk about Chekhov from the point of view of an American admirer, it was suggested.

So I arranged myself at the lectern and ad libbed my way through fifteen or twenty minutes of an inevitably rambling and disjointed appreciation of Chekhov's distinctive genius. I remember saying something spirited in defense of his comic gifts, so often lost sight of, and I was thankful that I could recall some passages from the stories and especially bits of dialogue from the plays well enough to quote them. I ended with a gentle (if in retrospect rather banal) reminder that Chekhov belonged to all of us, having transcended national and cultural boundaries the way great artists always do.

Though I could see a frown here and there—a specialist's resentment of an amateur? a Russian chauvinist's of an American?—I was given a generous round of applause at the end, having evidently passed whatever test may have been implicit in my appearance. After that I sat down and listened to several other speeches, and as I sat there, with Nina whispering bits of translation into my ear and my own senses picking up other bits of meaning, there began to form in me the genesis of this book. I had already published a long essay on Chekhov in my book *The Making of Modern Drama*, and for years I had been toying with the idea of writing a thorough study of his full-length plays. Until now I had thought that my extravagant admiration for Chekhov as both a writer and a man didn't constitute a sufficient reason or qualification for writing a book about him. But it struck me now, as I listened to his Soviet enthusiasts, that it wasn't a disqualification either.

On the surface the talks resembled the sort of thing one hears at academic symposia and Modern Language Association conventions, though they were considerably less full of arid Talmudic inquiry, little strands of "significance" pursued to their most remote ends. ("All aesthetic discussions just exhaust me and seem like continuations of the scholastic disputes with which people wearied themselves during the Middle Ages," Chekhov once wrote.[4]) But there was a redeeming vein of personality and ardor on which I think he would have looked kindly had the conference been devoted to someone other than himself. It was a dimension of feeling unlike anything I'd ever come upon at gatherings devoted to intellectual or cultural proposals, a dimension that indeed has been all but banished at certain professional levels among us. It turned itself into a persistent theme or approach, something that went much beyond the technical or analytic or exegetical.

Again and again these Soviet critics and professors, men and women of a great range of age and, for all I knew, of personality and temperament, spoke of Chekhov's art and life as exemplary, as constituting a deep spiritual resource for human beings today. There hadn't been anything like this unanimity in his lifetime, I was thinking; alongside the admiration so many people expressed for him, savage attacks had been made on the political and ideological "neutrality" of his writing and on its artistic "inconclusiveness."

Even before the talks began you could feel his presence in the circumstances and the setting. In the side rooms off the small auditorium, more artifacts were on display—another of his desks, more manuscripts—and the meeting hall was presided over by a huge blown-up photograph of Chekhov wearing pince-nez and with one of his characteristically benign expressions, a look that belies the toughmindedness of his work. The poster, a smaller copy of which now covers a wall in my study at home, bore the legend "Chekhov: The Years at Yalta," the theme of this year's Chekhov Society meeting.

And now that presence, that tutelary spirit, was invoked as a criticism of and corrective to the actuality of these . . . "troubled" times, I was about to write, but as I remember the political atmosphere in which the talks took place, "desperate" would be more nearly true. The speakers kept bringing up Chekhov's "honesty," his "generosity" as both a man and a writer, the spaciousness of his "humanity" ("An author must be humane to his fingertips," he once wrote[5]), leaving little doubt that such qualities had been missing for generations from Soviet civic life.

How impressed I was by the way this writer, so lacking in the usual devices of literary seductiveness, so deliberately "small," unaggressive and ungodlike, continued to live so efficaciously in the minds of these people, how his stories and plays and the exemplary self that hovered behind their making went on animating and sustaining civilized men and women here. "Am I not fooling the reader, since I cannot answer the most important questions?" Chekhov wrote.[6] But like Thomas Mann—who years after Chekhov's death remarked in an appreciative essay that he hadn't answered any questions at all and thereby had kept to the proper role of the artist—these people weren't seeking any solutions from him, nothing like a literary package of aid and credits.

There wasn't a trace of anything cultic or runic about the proceedings, as there so often is in our own "higher" literary studies of a proprietary kind. Throughout the morning I felt a sense of intimacy, of unexploitative, non-professional possession, something I'd like to call "amorous" interchange between these scholars and teachers and a living body of work, a *living writer,* as indeed I usually felt whenever I talked about Chekhov to anyone in this highly literate country.

"Ah, he used to sit right there!" the curator of the Yermolova Museum in Moscow, my friend Sergei's mother, told me one afternoon as she pointed to a chair at one end of a large dining room table. It was as though she were literally recalling the scene instead of having simply assimilated handed-down remembrances. "He would always sit in that place, and he would give the most elegant toasts at dinner parties." Mariya Yermolova, the great turn-of-the-century Russian actress, never performed in a Chekhov play, but she cultivated his friendship.

And I remembered how at the Stanislavsky Museum a staff member had described to me some costumes from an early (could it have been the original?) production of *Three Sisters* with exclamations about Chekhov's taste: "He saw it that way—Irina in white, Masha in black. . . ."

Now I remembered that Chekhov, understandably unhappy at how, when he became well known as a playwright, people began using him as a guide to attitudes toward life, a source of quick wisdom or hints about "interesting" behavior, had once written that "everybody goes to the theater to see my [plays] to learn something instantly . . . to make some sort of profit, and I tell you I have not the time to bother about that *canaille*."[7] The uncharacteristic expletive rose from his wish to protect his art from all the reductive uses people sought to make of it, and that wish was protected at the conference. For I detected very little that was sentimental or utilitarian about the attitudes expressed in this forum, whose communal aspirations struck me as being directed toward the exactness of feeling, the daring and precision of honesty that had distinguished Chekhov, and no hints about behavior were being sought.

I walk along the seaside avenue called the Esplanade, in Yalta, the faded resort on the Black Sea whose reputedly salubrious climate at one time attracted many invalids and convalescents, along with a wealthy and, in their own minds at least, fashionable crowd. (The tsars kept a palatial winter home nearby; the Yalta Conference was held there in 1945, and you can see the places Roosevelt, Churchill, and Stalin occupied at the long table.) After several earlier visits, Chekhov settled here in 1898 to try to preserve the remnants of his shattered health. He could breathe a little better here, or so he thought, or so the doctors told him—how strange it was that he shied away from diagnosing his own tuberculosis. Yet for all its languid charm and the house on the hill with its grounds so lovingly laid out (Chekhov also bought another little piece of property just outside town), he could still call Yalta "a lousy dump."[8] He yearned for Moscow's pleasures and excitements and, most of all, for Olga, whose flourishing career with the Art Theater, which he fully encouraged, kept them so often apart during the few years of their marriage.

As I walk along under a pale April sky, I bring to mind Chekhov's immensely delicate sad story "The Lady with the Pet Dog" (variously translated as "The Lady with the Dog," "Lady with Lapdog," and "The Lady with a Small Dog"). Its central characters strolled this wide, once fashionable thoroughfare, now gone severely to seed. After many vicissitudes and much struggle, the adulterous yet strangely chaste and innocent lovers are temporarily reunited, although they are still legally barred from marrying. A long time ago I committed the story's last words to memory, and now I summon them up: "It seemed to them that in only a few more minutes a solution would be found and a new, beautiful life would begin; but both of them knew very well that the end was a long, long way away and that the most complicated and difficult part was only just beginning."

As I walk on, I think of the grave antiromanticism of this passage, its refusal of either consolation or despair, the sense it gives of existence as poised between fact and desire. *Fact* and *desire:* I turn the words over in my mind and can't think of a better, tighter formulation for the way Chekhov treats the tensions of ordinary experience in both his fiction and his plays.

The street has made me think of the story, and this adds to something I've gratefully noticed before: as I move around the country, I'm continually remembering Chekhov stories and plays, inspired by an incident, a face, a venue—some theater or other, this seaside resort—or even by an object such as a samovar, which always makes me think of *Uncle Vanya,* or an old clock, which brings to mind *Three Sisters.* This kind of evocation doesn't happen to me with Turgenev or Tolstoy or even Dostoevsky, who for all the admiration I have for him never gives me the sense of familiarity, the imaginative closeness I feel with Chekhov.

Two Soviet warships ride at anchor far out in the harbor on this afternoon that has suddenly turned sunny. People are lined up on a pier to buy tickets for what I guess are excursions on a newly spruced up coastal vessel. In how many Chekhov stories do people flee by water (on rivers, usually) from complicated love affairs or problematic selves? Taking me by surprise, several couples in warm-up suits jog by, like eerily transplanted yuppies.

Many people, almost all of them women, wait with disciplined resignation for the opening of shops which you can be sure have very little on their shelves. The street is full of soldiers, the way streets are everywhere in this country that seems to feel itself under perpetual siege. They're mostly army officers (and as such never fail to remind me of *Three Sisters*), the younger ones taller and leaner than those of the upper ranks, many of whom look like Marshal Zhukov of my World War II memories—square, barrel-chested, moving like a small tank. Unaccountably, I see very few navy men, just an occasional sailor swaying along with that universal peculiar rolling gait.

I sit down on a bench to rest and after a while a plainly dressed middle-aged man comes up and gently pats me on the shoulder. He saw me last night being interviewed about Chekhov on Crimean television, he says, and noticed my picture in the paper, accompanying a news story on my appearance at the scholarly conference. He hands me the paper; there I am, bearded, gesturing, a Chekhov fanatic described in the caption as a friendly visiting American scholar. I ask him if I might keep the paper, to which he assents by patting me on the shoulder once again.

In a plaza off the Esplanade a large flaking billboard displays heroic-sized workers with square jaws and flaxen hair. A mother, father, and two children; the parents thrust their fists into the future, as if heeding the sign's exhortation: "The motherland is calling you to new successes in labor."

At the Chekhov Memorial Theater in downtown Chekhov Square—both renamed some time after his death in 1904—a festival of his plays is going on in conjunction with the scholarly meetings. On successive evenings I see an elaborate, overwrought operetta made from his short farce, *The Wedding*; a plodding, laborious *Ivanov* performed by a visiting company from Poland; and a sparkling, enormously inventive *Uncle Vanya*, the work of a troupe called the Youth Theater of Lithuania, whose name derives not from the ages of its members but from its mission of bringing "good" theater to younger audiences. I can't remember a Chekhov production I've enjoyed more, even if my intimate knowledge of the text sometimes falters at the language barrier.

Chekhov is everywhere. Back in Moscow I go to see *Three Sisters* at the Art Theater, a revival of the famously far-out production by the famously far-out director Oleg Yefremov. Much as I detest this version's avant-garde tics, its insufferable artiness, just to see the familiar characters and the scenes I know so intimately is enough to give me pleasure.

I walk through the crowded, slush-filled streets of the capital, with its heavy, dour architecture; jostled by rude people with glum faces, I think of the half-dozen or more times in Chekhov's stories when someone is dreaming of Moscow or praying to be there, and of the supreme presence of Moscow-in-the-mind that runs through *Three Sisters*.

Chekhov has been around me from the beginning of my visit, even before I touched the ground of Russia more than a month ago. Several rows of birch trees rose from the flat, wintry earth surrounding Moscow's Sheremetivo Airport. "Dear, modest birches," Chekhov called his favorite tree, which is also my favorite. As we waited for the plane to taxi to a stop at the terminal, I looked out at my first horizon in this country I sometimes think I've known first and best through its writers, and especially Chekhov; I wanted to murmur, sentimentally it will be thought, but perhaps also as a talismanic exhalation, a "dear, modest birches" of my own.

Back in the familiar precincts of my life, I meditate for two or three months and then get ready to begin this book. First I catch up on the Chekhov literature, reading most of what I've missed that's been published since my *Making of Modern Drama* came out in 1974. The reading confirms me in a long-standing suspicion that there's still no fully satisfying book on the plays as a whole. (Robert Brustein's Chekhov chapter in his *Theater of Revolt* is full of useful material, while among the best of the more recent writers on Chekhov are Laurence Senelick and Richard Peace.) So I decide that I'm going to write this book for the same reason people write seriously on any subject—that they perceive a space waiting to be filled.

Time and again I've been struck by the thinness of so many explorations of Chekhov's work, the lack of sensibility exercised on a writer with perhaps the most exquisite sensibility of all. Apart from the dwindling but stubbornly persisting ideological interpretations and the more recent structural or deconstructionist assessments, one main deficiency of much writing about Chekhov is paradoxically due to the immense esteem nearly everyone else has for him, an admiration which unfortunately is most often nebulous and soft-minded in the extreme.

Because he has so largely been seen as a comparatively "unconscious" artist, an *artless* one, so to say, by temperament a realist for whom accurate perception was enough and by strategy a conservative in matters of technique, the revolutionary nature of his writing, particularly of his dramatic work, has seldom been noticed. He is considered "modern," all right, but hardly on the same level of originality and innovation as Joyce or Proust, Strindberg or Pirandello. This attitude is especially damaging to the criticism of his plays, no matter how otherwise astute. His seeming lack of sustained plots, conclusive dénouements, and, most of all, aggressive technical inventiveness has led to his often being spoken of as a playwright of "mood" and "atmosphere," a miniaturist of emotions, the serene recorder of the "bittersweet" minutiae of everyday life. These tiresome assertions are wholly wrong, and their effect is to reduce Chekhov's imaginative size and convert his radical orchestrations into a kind of high-level program music.

Apart from that, there exists a fairly widespread idea that for all the virtues of Chekhov's plays, his stories are superior. Ronald Hingley, a British translator and biographer, insists that of Chekhov's "mature stories" and "mature plays," the "former constitute by far the more significant body of work."[9] And V. S. Pritchett, who ought to know better, writes about Chekhov that "his genius . . . lies above all in his creative gifts as a writer of short stories . . . his plays derive directly from his stories, in which . . . the texture is far richer."[10] The texture of the stories is in no way "richer" than that of the plays, which, moreover, have connections to some of the stories (connections I intend to look into) but don't at all "derive" from them. To think that they do is to be blind in at least one important sector to both fiction and drama.

Chekhov's "genius" is found equally in the fiction and the plays, which Hingley and Pritchett might have seen if they didn't share that obstinate notion among literary people that theater is an inferior art—inferior, that is, to "creative" prose and poetry. It isn't inferior and Chekhov's pliant artistry is precisely the proof: no writer has ever surpassed him as a master of both fiction and drama, creating each with so nearly equal brilliance.

Without directly studying the fiction (which is beyond the scope of this book), I intend to trace some of the true connections between the stories and the plays. They exist, as we'll see, not so much in the realm of literal plots or subjects as in that of something much more subtle and delicate: what I'd like to call "imaginative ideas," a matter of webs and lacings of felt experience finding expression now in narrative prose and now in histrionic—dramatic—utterance.

It's not a question of richer or thinner texture but of different weaves, different ways of composition. As an example of what I mean, take this fragment from Chekhov's story "The Cossack": " 'You are not kind, you know . . . ,' said Maxim, looking into his wife's face. And for the first time since his marriage he perceived that his wife was not kind." The experience of such a birth of awareness about the deficiencies of a lover or a mate is to be found in Chekhov's plays, too: Nina's sudden revelation about Konstantin in *The Seagull*, Andrei's more gradual one about Natasha in *Three Sisters*. They don't "derive" from "The Cossack," they share its sensibility.

To go back to the Chekhov literature. There are some splendid essays on the individual plays, to which I'm much indebted—Francis Fergusson on *The Cherry Orchard*; Eric Bentley on *Uncle Vanya*; Robert Louis Jackson on *The Seagull*—but these pieces are thirty, forty, and nearly fifty years old. The single best study of the whole of Chekhov's dramatic work, by David Magarshack, was originally published in 1952 and wasn't entirely adequate to begin with. As I'll take up later in the book, Magarshack offered a valuable new perspective on Chekhov's growth as a dramatist by drawing a distinction between his early plays of "direct action" and the later "indirect" ones.

But this perspective doesn't go far or deep enough, and much less satisfying are thematic readings, some of them by Soviet scholar-apologists of various eras, with their ideological and quasipolitical axes grinding, and others by

Americans or Britons or Frenchmen who can't shake free from the idea that plays are really dramatized novels, with a story to tell rather than embody.

One more point. The argument has been made by scholars of the former Soviet Union and others that Chekhov's plays are solidly anchored in a native context and a particular time, not to be dislodged except at great and even mortal risk. I think the vision here is severely crimped. The modest, clear-eyed observer and elogist of his own culture, Chekhov is a poet of our lives too, an artist whose work doesn't simply survive but *continues,* moving most easily from the specificities of time and place to new ones, which it then makes its own; I find it impossible to separate most of what he wrote from the essential textures of life at this moment.

Of all writers I think him among the most readily transportable, the most able to transcend historical context and geographical limit, suffering the fewest losses along the way. And this is because I know of no writer who better exemplifies—radiates—the imperishable relationship between being and expression, the "universality" of which connection doesn't need to be demonstrated. It's the relationship that, I hope, will animate this book, in subtle, tacit ways usually, I suppose, but sometimes directly, as I try to trace Chekhov's nature and circumstances in his choice of forms, and to discover our own nature and human circumstances in the forms as he realized them in dramas.

Flannery O'Connor once wrote that "you use reality to make a different kind of reality."[11] I hope to show how those two kinds of reality—of being and expression, shall we call them?—stand in relation to each other in Anton Chekhov's plays.

A NOTE ON THE TRANSLATIONS

Translations or "adaptations" of most of Chekhov's full-length plays aren't in short supply; near my desk, for example, I have precisely a dozen English versions of *Three Sisters,* together with a batch of *Cherry Orchards,* and several *Uncle Vanyas* and *Seagulls. Ivanovs* and *Wood Demons* are scarcer, though, and as far as I know there is only one English rendering of the full text of *Platonov,* by David Magarshack, which I'm obviously compelled to use; fortunately, he does a more than serviceable job. When, however, we look at how the other plays have been turned into English, the range of integrity and accomplishment is remarkably wide, moving from the early mistake-ridden and awkward versions of Constance Garnett, through the more reliable yet uninspired work of Elizaveta Fen, to the more recent attempts by playwrights like Lanford Wilson, Brian Friel, David Mamet, and Jean-Claude Van Itallie, corrupted to one degree or another by flagrant omissions and even more flagrant additions, down to the calm, judicious, accurate, yet also, when necessary, lyrical versions of Paul Schmidt.

In the first stages of writing this book, I used the translations of Ronald Hingley, even though they left me vaguely (and sometimes sharply) dissatisfied. He seemed to me more reliable than most, but I was put off by his insistence on anglicizing everything, which resulted, among other sources of irritation, in characters with English names—Helen, Nicholas, Andrew, Paul—instead of the ones Chekhov gave them. Did Hingley think, I wondered, that we're all so provincial as to find Yelena, Nikolai, Andrei, and Pavel disconcertingly exotic?

Then a graduate student of mine at Yale, a brilliant scholar of both Russian and Russian theater named Kristin Johnsen-Neshati, completed a translation of *The Seagull* which I found so satisfying that I decided to use it, and shortly after that I discovered Schmidt, whose translations were slowly becoming known. His *Uncle Vanya, Three Sisters,* and *The Cherry Orchard* are the ones I draw upon in this book.

Both Johnsen-Neshati (who now teaches at George Mason University) and Schmidt (who is an actor and teacher as well as translator) were so gracious as to yield to me on the exceedingly few occasions when I found some word or phrase in their translations that didn't seem to me to do exact justice to the situation or context. I'm grateful to them for that. I'm grateful too for their having read my entire text in search of possible errors and potential improvements, Johnsen-Neshati having gone through it several times with never-flagging attentiveness.

For the rest, I use Magarshack's *Platonov,* as I said before, and Hingley's *Ivanov* and *Wood Demon.*

ACKNOWLEDGMENTS

Special thanks to Marshall Williams for his brilliant detective work in tracking down some very elusive sources. And a note of appreciation to my editors at Yale University Press, Jonathan Brent and Harry Haskell.

The Preface and the *Ivanov* chapters were published in somewhat different form in *Theater* magazine, as was the *Seagull* chapter in the *South Atlantic Quarterly*. A small section of the *Uncle Vanya* chapter appeared in *American Theater* magazine. And small sections of the "Chekhov: Truth, Moral Reality, Imagination," *Three Sisters*, and *Cherry Orchard* chapters were published in the *Village Voice*. Thanks herewith to the editors of those publications.

CHEKHOV
Truth, Moral Reality, Imagination

SAINT ANTON?

When in the early 1970s the translator Ronald Hingley went to work on a
biography of Anton Chekhov, he tells us that he was so acutely aware of his
subject's reputation for exemplary moral behavior and psychological good
health that in an effort to keep from composing a hagiography he found
himself going far out of his way to look for counterevidence. He didn't come up
with much—a couple of moral imperfections, a few instances of less than ideal
behavior, and, perhaps more substantial, something he interpreted as a coldness on Chekhov's part in erotic matters. But even these flaws came as a
surprise to almost everyone.

For Hingley was chipping against a formidable piece of moral statuary, a
monolith of goodness. Consider the person we'd all been presented with: a
dutiful son and affectionate sibling (he had four brothers and a sister); the
uncomplaining economic and emotional mainstay of his large and not always
uniformly appreciative family; an inventively loving husband for the extremely
short time he was given to be one; a conscientious and often self-sacrificing
physician; a warmly supportive literary colleague upon whom beginning writers in particular could count for advice and practical help; a public-spirited
citizen whose civic labors were entirely free of partisan political biases. And
then: a man blessed with the wryest sense of humor together with the most

delicate tact; lucidly honest, thoroughly self-deprecating, entirely without envy or airs; unprotesting about the torments and ravages of his incurable illness, the tuberculosis from which he would die at the age of forty-four; full of courage, full of light; the incarnation of professional conscience in everything he did. And on top of all that—how absurd to have it come like an afterthought!—a writer whose genius showed itself twice over, in fiction and in drama.

Anyone who gets to know Chekhov from the primary sources available to us, which are the usual and expected ones but especially ample in this case—his own letters and notebooks, the correspondence and reminiscences of his contemporaries, including members of his family—or from secondary sources—histories or biographies based, sometimes uncritically, on those documents—is sooner or later going to ask the sort of question Hingley no doubt posed for himself: Could so good a human being actually have existed?

The question is of course rhetorical; Chekhov as saint is a construct, although by no means entirely a piece of fiction. He was clearly a very decent and even—taking a good-sized step up from that rather bland adjective—a noble man, and by certain criteria, not all of them obvious, a very sound one; but he wasn't without faults, for which we can be grateful. Encased in those abstractions of impeccable virtue, he seems almost a fossilized freak.

Maxim Gorky was probably as responsible as anyone in Russia for turning Chekhov into an icon. Gorky, who turned out to be a notorious flatterer (of Stalin, among others) and whose grasp of Chekhov's work was erratic at best, told him that he was "the first free man I've ever seen: the first who never kowtows to anything,"[1] and told the world: "It seems to me that with Anton Pavlovich, everybody unwittingly felt an inner longing to be simpler, more truthful, to be more himself."[2] Gorky also reported that Leo Tolstoy, who was deaf to the music and moral reverberations of Chekhov's plays but had a fairly high opinion of some of the stories, gushed over the man himself: "Ah, what a dear beautiful man. He is modest and quiet, just like a girl! And he walks like a girl. He's simply wonderful!"[3] (In the usage and sensibility of the time, to be compared to a girl in this way didn't mean that Chekhov would be thought of as effeminate.)

At least in part, Gorky may have been flattering Chekhov to enhance his own literary status, but others had no reason to do so. Konstantin Korovin, the designer for Sergei Diaghilev and Anna Pavlova who had come to know Chekhov when they were both students in Moscow in the early 1880s and who left some charming memoirs, called him "simple and natural . . . unpretentious. . . .

It was as if he emanated waves of warmth and protection. Despite his youth, despite his adolescent appearance, he even then made you think of a kind old man whom you could approach and ask about the meaning of life, tell of your sorrows, and confess something very important, the kind of secret everyone has somewhere down deep."[4]

And, in a famous apostrophe delivered on the opening night of *The Cherry Orchard* in January 1904, the Moscow Art Theater's cofounder, Vladimir Nemirovich-Danchenko, spoke to the mortally ill Chekhov of "the limitless devotion which all Russian educated society has for you" and went on to talk of "your tender heart . . . your pure soul."[5]

Rhetoric like that, multiplied many times over and never likely to remain private, is hard to withstand. The fact that Chekhov was a doctor, especially self-abnegating, devoted, and generous to patients who lacked the means to pay him, naturally added to the mystique, as did his numerous philanthropic efforts, like helping to build schools and collecting and donating books for libraries (never well off, he gave a three-hundred-volume set of French classics to the public library of Taganrog, his home town), and, in some eyes, the romance of his fatal illness, his dying young. In the wake of all this, such flaws as might have pocked his image tended to be obliterated.

How much credence should we give to the strain of revisionism represented by Hingley? In particular, what are we to make of Chekhov's alleged sexual coldness, about which a few others besides Hingley have spoken? Most important, what was the real nature of the moral and psychic health Chekhov did possess? And how do those qualities or conditions of self show themselves in his writing, if they do?

Sometimes consciously and sometimes not, Chekhov revealed a good deal about himself in his large correspondence. Two manifestos or apologias stand out with special force and vivacity. They are both to be found in letters he wrote within a span of a little over three months in the fall of 1888 and the early winter of 1889. He would not reach thirty for another year or so, but while building up a medical practice he had already achieved a solid reputation as a writer of sketches and short stories and, with *Ivanov*, the beginnings of renown as a playwright.

The first letter, dated October 4, 1888, was to the well-known poet and critic Alexei Pleshcheyev, a much older man with whom Chekhov was on cordial if not intimate terms. In the course of a half-serious warning that a story he was about to publish might not be to Pleshcheyev's taste, Chekhov unexpectedly enunciated what Simon Karlinsky, the editor of a major collection of his letters, has rightly called his "great credo."[6]

"The people I am afraid of are the ones who look for tendentiousness between the lines and are determined to see me as either liberal or conservative," Chekhov began. "I am neither liberal, nor conservative, nor gradualist, nor monk. . . . I would like to be a free artist and nothing else and I regret God has not given me the strength to be one. I hate lies and violence in all of their forms. . . . Pharisaism, dullwittedness and tyranny reign not only in merchants' homes and police stations. I see them in science, in literature, among the younger generation. That is why I cultivate no particular predilection for policemen, butchers, scientists, writers, or the younger generation. I look upon tags and labels as prejudices. My holy of holies is the human body, health, intelligence, talent, inspiration, love, and the most absolute freedom imaginable—freedom from violence and lies no matter what form [they] . . . take. Such is the program I would adhere to if I were a major artist."[7]

The second letter, written on January 7, 1889, was to Alexei Suvorin, Chekhov's friend and publisher. Chekhov began by talking about *Ivanov*, which prompted some remarks about his recently having gained "a sense of personal freedom." This in turn led to the following tiny, scarcely disguised autobiography. After observing that "what aristocratic writers take from nature gratis, the less privileged must pay for with their youth"[8] (an uncharacteristically opaque sentence which would seem to be saying that writers from poor or nondescript families have a rougher early time of it), Chekhov went on to tell Suvorin: "Write a story . . . about a young man, the son of a serf, a former grocery boy, a choirsinger, a high school pupil and university student, brought up to respect rank, to kiss the hands of priests, to truckle to the ideas of others—a young man who expressed thanks for every piece of bread, who was whipped many times, who went without galoshes to do his tutoring, who used his fists, tortured animals, was fond of dining with rich relatives, was a hypocrite in his dealings with God and men, needlessly, solely out of a realization of his own insignificance—write how this young man squeezes the slave out of himself, drop by drop, and how, on awaking one fine morning, he finds that the blood coursing through his veins is no longer that of a slave, but that of a real human being."[9]

Not least among the many elements in this passage and in the aftermath of its composition that gleam with interest is something Karlinsky reports in his volume of Chekhov's selected letters: "The Soviet songwriter and underground poet Alexander Galich, who was expelled . . . in 1972 from the Soviet Writers' Union for writing and recording songs that extol personal freedom, incorporated a passage from this [letter of Chekhov's] into his best-known song, 'I Choose Freedom' ":

> I choose freedom
> Even if she's pockmarked and crude.
> And you go ahead and squeeze
> The slave out, drop by drop.[10]

To know anything about the predominant Soviet attitude toward Chekhov is to see at once how infuriating Galich's use of this quotation must have been to the literary commissars. Even the best of them—the ones least corrupted by ideology—had to some degree treated Chekhov in ways that did violence to his art. The worst of them had crudely put him to political use, forever invoking him as a forerunner of the Bolshevik utopia, a writer whose only real failing was that he hadn't supported his love of the "common people" with the proper political language. His critical intelligence, that acerbic glance of his, was ignored, except when it happened to fall on whatever could be identified and blamed as *tsarist* reality; his most subtle sense of the life of emotions was traduced into sentimentality. Even if they hadn't touched him, Chekhov almost certainly would have despised those who made up official Soviet literary circles, as he did the Marxists of his own time, with their fixed ideas and what he once described as "arrogant physiognomies."[11]

The letter to Suvorin contains another detail that leaps out of its immediate context to settle into broader literary and psychological annals. Chekhov's description of himself as the "son of a serf" should put us immediately in mind of the title of one of Strindberg's autobiographical books, *The Son of a Servant*. The two pieces of writing are immensely different in scope and intention, but it's legitimate to take note of how differently these writers, who were near contemporaries (Strindberg was about ten years older than Chekhov), responded to and expressed themselves about their respective family backgrounds.

Strindberg's book is as full of distortions and dubious assertions as Chekhov's little fictional life-sketch is of essentially accurate reminiscence. For rather esoteric reasons that had to do, I think, with a wish to construct a more "dramatic" background for himself, to create a more artistically useful, because more anxiety-ridden, family romance, Strindberg thoroughly distorted and obscured the truths of his lineage. The tale is a complicated one, but the thing to notice here is that the shame Strindberg tells us he felt about his origins and against which he summoned up so much psychic energy was partly invented, a literary conceit, as it were, from which were to flow many other singular autobiographical "facts." But that's another story, and telling this one isn't to say anything about Strindberg's ultimate worth as an artist, only to point out how far Chekhov was from the Swedish writer's need to agitate and "provoke" the materials of his own history.

In Chekhov's case, a background of serfdom or slavery was not an incurable psychic handicap or an ineradicable moral stain, and certainly not an artificial goad to creativity, but a situation whose consequences had to be worked through, and a metaphor for an internal condition that with effort could be transformed. And so the historical distortions he made were few and entirely forgivable. He was actually the *grandson* of a serf, his father's father, a self-educated man, having bought his own and his family's freedom about twenty years before Anton's birth in 1860, which was just a year before the serfs were officially emancipated by Tsar Alexander II. A few other details of the little autobiography were no doubt somewhat exaggerated or inexact—it's hard to imagine Chekhov, even as a small boy, "truckling to" other people's notions or being much of a torturer of animals, though he might have pulled the wings off a fly or two.

But everything else seems accurate enough, whether on the level of physical fact—he had indeed worked in a grocery store, sung in a church choir, been often whipped, and gone out *sans* galoshes in bad weather to pick up a few kopecks tutoring—or of spirit and attitude. He had certainly been "brought up to respect rank" and been taught to kiss the hands of priests, and we know that he and his brothers and sister were expected by their tight-fisted, tyrannical father to give "thanks for every piece of bread"; in the light of this it isn't surprising that he would have looked forward to dining with rich relatives and felt slightly guilty about the pleasure he got from it (we know that he had at least one well-off, generous uncle in Taganrog, his father's brother, Mitrofan).

What isn't susceptible of corroboration is Chekhov's remark about having been "a hypocrite in his dealings with God and men." He never confessed any other specific instances of hypocrisy, as far as we know, nor did anyone who knew him, even his worst enemies, ever make out a detailed case of this kind against him. Even so, let's accept his mea culpa and try to imagine what this teenage hypocrisy might have consisted in. What in particular could it have meant to be hypocritical in his relations with God? How could you hope to fool Him? And the "realization of his own insignificance"—what could that possibly mean?

If, as I think, Chekhov meant by hypocrisy in his dealings with God something more like hypocrisy *about* God, we can assume that he had pretended for a time to believe in a Supreme Being but in reality didn't. And this would accord with everything we can document or reasonably intuit about the place religion had in his mature life. He had an acute and sympathetic sense of spirituality, together with an extraordinarily detailed and sensuous understanding of the church, of Russian Orthodox practices and rituals; among his fictional characters are a number of shrewdly and sometimes affectionately seen priests, monks, and believers, including people on pilgrimage, and one of his last pieces of fiction, "The Bishop," hovers among his very greatest achievements, a triumph of perception about a spiritually childlike churchman but more broadly about death, ego, transience.

But he was not a believer. Throughout his letters and notebooks we find scattered comments which establish that he wasn't. A letter of March 9, 1892, to a friend, the writer Ivan Leontev (whose pen-name was Shcheglov), contains a flat declaration of his lack of formal faith, as well as the fullest description we have of what lay behind it. "In my childhood," he told Leontev, "I received a religious education and the same sort of upbringing—choir singing, reading the epistles and psalms in church, regular attendance at matins, altar boy and bell-ringing duty. And the result? When I think back on my childhood it all seems quite gloomy to me. I have no religion now."[12] And he told another correspondent that "I long since lost belief and can merely keep glancing in perplexity at every intellectual who is a believer."[13]

But something else he wrote toward the end of his life in a letter to still another friend is perhaps even more revealing of his ultimate spiritual condition or perspective. "One should believe in God," he told the singer and journalist Viktor Miroliubov in December 1901, "but if one does not have faith, then its place should not be taken by any hue and cry, but by seeking, seeking and seeking, alone and face to face with one's conscience."[14]

A key word in this passage is surely "should." Why does he say we *ought* to have faith? Well, if he wasn't a believer, neither was he anything like an adamant atheist. If it had been at all possible, he would have liked to believe, the passage tells us. On the one side are the usual attractions: bedrock, solace, a guide to behavior, a promise of beatitude; on the other the familiar sources of discontentment: constantly shifting ground, anxiety, with obliteration most likely at the end. But belief wasn't possible for him, nor, in his opinion, should it be for any other "intellectual," as we've seen. Yet that wasn't the end of it. Once again a letter keeps the question open.

Near the end of his life he engaged in a brief correspondence with Diaghilev. In a letter of December 30, 1902, he told the impresario: "Present-day culture is the beginning of work in the name of a great future, work which will perhaps continue for tens of thousands of years. . . . Finally . . . mankind will perceive the truth of the real God, that is, not make conjectures or search for Him in Dostoevsky, but perceive Him as clearly as they perceive that two times two is four."[15]

The real God would be obscured for a while. Chekhov doesn't say anything directly about the process, but at some point in his youth he must have broken away from the mechanical, unexamined acceptance of faith such as has always characterized communities of the orthodox; he would likely have followed the usual route, passing first into doubt and then into unbelief, becoming what in his narrowly traditional milieu would probably have been called a "freethinker." But a secret one, for if this reading is correct he continued to pretend, presumably out of habit, inertia. A greater factor may have been fear of his rigidly pious father and perhaps, peering over his old man's shoulder, society. But something else entered into it too: the "realization of his own insignificance."

What could that mean? And why did it lead to hypocrisy? We can find clues in still another letter, written nearly ten years earlier to his younger brother Mikhail, or Misha, in Moscow. In the middle of relating some chatty news of life in Taganrog and offering advice on books worth reading (he recommends *Don Quixote* as "a fine work"), Anton, soon to set off for Moscow and the real start of everything, and a little too soberly wise for his nineteen years, lectures Misha, then fourteen: "Why do you refer to yourself as my 'worthless, insignificant little brother'? So you are aware of your worthlessness, are you? . . . Do you know where you should be aware of your worthlessness? Before God, perhaps, or before human intelligence, before beauty or nature. But not before people. Among people you should be aware of your worth."[16]

The implication is that not believing in your own worth in relation to people can make for a perpetuation of the slave in yourself; in front of God, though, it's to be properly creaturely. But this would be true only if you really have belief. When Chekhov adds to God that qualifying "perhaps," and even more when he puts Him at the head of a series of secular values—intelligence, beauty, nature—we detect the beginnings of a loss of belief and consequently the arrival of a temptation to hypocrisy. We should remember that Chekhov said his hypocrisy was "needless," but it did have its reasons. Among them, as I've said, might have been a fear of being honest at so young and unarmed an age.

It seems to me that there might have been another, rather nobler motive. Chekhov might have been trying to create a defense against pride, or its beginnings, the sort of thing that might trouble a gifted youth who senses something special about himself but who has been brought up not to aspire beyond the most modest of futures. An intricate little game might have been going on in the psyche of the teenage boy. What better way to acknowledge your insignificance and so curb your ambition than to believe in—to submit to—God? And if you no longer believed, then you'd pretend to, practicing hypocrisy. But that might incite in you a memory of slavish origins, which might in turn stir ambition, and you'd keep on going round.

(So many "might"s in the last paragraph! But when biography enters the realm of interiority, syntax always has to use the conditional, and thought can only be speculative; in conjectures like these we're asked to stretch sympathy and shrink credence, to trust our intuition, sometimes against likelihood. What's being tested is our own originality against the pull of received wisdom.)

Ten years later, having long since acknowledged his lack of faith and so with no need to go on practicing hypocrisy, Chekhov says, Please, let's have no "hue and cry" about it (one translation renders it "sensationalism"[17]), which we can plausibly think means, Keep your spiritual condition to yourself; it's nobody else's business. (Questions of belief were notoriously public matters at the time, much argued over and much exploited in various ways.) His further recommendation is to go on "seeking," for God or whatever else might satisfy the longing, and to do it with only one ally or companion, your own conscience.

"My holy of holies is the human body, health, intelligence, talent, inspiration, love, and the most absolute freedom imaginable—freedom from violence and lies no matter what form [they] . . . take."

The following information appeared on Chekhov's internal passport, presumably one of the first to be issued to him: "Age: nineteen; Height: two arshins, nine vershoks [about five feet, eleven inches, or 181 centimeters]; Hair and Eyebrows: light brown; Eyes: brown; Nose, Mouth, Chin: average; Face: elongated; Complexion: fair; Distinguishing Features: scar on forehead under hair."[18]

He was tall for his day and age. He didn't begin to sport the famous moustache and Vandyke or wear the familiar pince-nez until some time after he got his medical degree in his middle twenties. Contemporary accounts agree that he was notably pleasing in appearance; many called him handsome, and all the photos and paintings we have of him, from every period, confirm it. Konstantin Korovin, the designer, wrote that Chekhov was "*extremely* handsome. He had a large, open face with kind . . . eyes . . . and . . . [a] special shy smile. His whole appearance—his open face, his broad chest—inspired in people a special sort of confidence."[19]

One observer described him as looking "Christ-like,"[20] a characterization that contributed to the myth but that in its excessiveness probably did him more harm than good in posterity's eyes. The most memorable image of him most of us have is likely to be that of the tall, fragile, slightly stooped figure in a long black overcoat buttoned to the neck, wearing a black, snap-brimmed fedora, with one hand holding a walking-stick and the other hand in his pocket; this photograph is an epiphany of the last years, the Yalta period, when he had turned the corner toward death and was engaging in a few delaying tactics.

To Chekhov the human body, his own and others', came of course under the particular scrutiny of that trained eye, the physician's. I say his own, but oddly enough for a doctor—disastrously, it might be thought—he persistently objected to looking at himself as a patient. "Medical treatment and anxiety about one's physical existence," he wrote to Suvorin, "arouse in me something close to revulsion. I will not be doctored."[21] The letter is dated November 18, 1891, long after he should have diagnosed in himself the tuberculosis that was consuming him.

He had doggedly refused to acknowledge it and only did so reluctantly in the end. When at twenty-four, in 1884, he first noticed blood coming from his throat, he ascribed it to "some broken blood vessel."[22] Later, he compared such blood to the "glow of a distant fire,"[23] and he continued to squirm and deny, though not often through such gorgeous literary evasions. The disease was incurable (in addition to his lungs, it eventually attacked his intestines and spinal cord), but it seems likely that a more "mature" attitude on Chekhov's part would have gained him an additional year or two of life and maybe even a little more comfort. He seldom complained, though, and he displayed a certain sense of humor about his general condition, which included excruciating sieges of hemorrhoids and periodic bouts of migraine; in 1898 he wrote to one of his brothers that "my health is such that it could only gratify you, my heirs."[24]

He also suffered from bouts of insomnia. In "A Boring Story" we find this sentence: "Not to sleep at night means to be conscious every minute that you are abnormal. . . ."

THE HUMAN BODY (2)

Chekhov died at the age of forty-four on July 2, 1904, during a heat wave, at a hotel in the German spa of Badenweiler in the west of the Black Forest, where Olga Knipper, whom he had married three years earlier, had taken him. She tells us that just after midnight he woke up and asked her to call a doctor, who, upon arriving, among other things ordered champagne from room service—to relieve Chekhov's breathing, Olga says, but also probably as a gesture toward his famous patient. She continues: "Chekhov sat up, and in a loud, emphatic voice said to the doctor in German (of which he knew very little): 'Ich sterbe' [I'm dying]. . . . Then he picked up the glass, turned to me, smiled his wonderful smile and said: 'It's been such a long time since I've had champagne.' He drank it all to the last drop, quietly lay on his left side and was soon silent forever. The . . . stillness . . . was broken only by a huge . . . moth which kept crashing . . . into the light bulbs" and then by "the cork [flying] out of the half-empty champagne bottle with a tremendous noise."[25]

There is a remarkable short story from the 1970s by Nathalie Sarraute (who was of Russian origin) entitled "Ich Sterbe." Using the materials Olga provided, she re-imagines Chekhov's death and meditates upon its place in both his and our consciousness. She writes about dying, about love, the void that overtakes us, language as immortality and failure, silence. From the story: "these words spoken on that bed, in that hotel room, already three quarters of a century ago come . . . borne on what wind? . . . come and alight here, a tiny ember, blackening, burning this white page . . . *Ich sterbe*. A signal . . . I am what I had to be."[26]

Chekhov's body arrived in Moscow in a refrigerated freight car marked "For Oysters." The body of a general named Keller happened to come in from Manchuria at about the same time. Part of the assemblage of mourners for Chekhov followed the wrong coffin to the cemetery and couldn't understand why he was being buried with military honors.

THE HUMAN BODY (3)

"A. P. Chekhov, Dr. of Medicine": so read the first shingle he hung out, the metal plate near the front door of the house I'd visited on Sadovaya-Kudrinskaya Street in Moscow. The celebrated remark that ties his two vocations together—"Medicine is my lawful wife and literature is my mistress; when I get tired of one I go to the other"[27]—was a jaunty way of putting it, but in actuality keeping it all going was never less than a huge strain. Writing provided by far the largest part of his income and indeed could be said to have subsidized his medical work. No small part of his reputation for selflessness came from the frequency with which he treated poor patients free of charge or for practically nothing. He was the most general of general practitioners; among his first patients were a "young lady with a toothache" and "a monk with dysentery,"[28] and early in his career he was called on to lend a hand at the autopsy of a murdered man.

There are doctors in all his full-length plays except *The Cherry Orchard*. All but Lvov of *Ivanov* are in one or another stage of withdrawal from conscientious practice. What are we to make of that?

In the realm of what we now call public health, he was involved with both the most physically intimate and the broadest and most abstract aspects of epidemics and famines—succor of individuals and strategies of public control—and did all he could to change what he considered disastrous policies and attitudes; he was especially scornful of the type of radical intellectual whose sentimentalization of the peasants encouraged the "people" in their ignorance of hygiene and sanitation.

Despite all his labors, he seems always to have felt a bit guilty about not having given enough to medicine, and it's possible that he decided on his famous journey in 1890 to the island of Sakhalin, the penal colony off the coast of Siberia, as a kind of reparation. No doubt he had other motives, too, among them probably a desire simply to get away from the rat-race for a while and, more seriously, a wish to take stock. ("I think that Chekhov needed to find the answer to the questions: 'What am I? Where and why am I moving forward?'"[29] Robert Louis Jackson told his fellow scholars when the centennial of the trip was celebrated on Sakhalin in 1990.) Then too he had a hope that he could collect enough material to work up into a doctoral dissertation.

He did a great deal of preparatory reading and even before he left Moscow had written to Suvorin: "Sakhalin is a place of unbearable suffering. . . . I'm sorry I'm not sentimental or I'd say that we ought to make pilgrimages to places like Sakhalin the way the Turks go to Mecca."[30] Everything he found there confirmed him in this. He spent three months on the island, chiefly conducting a census of its ten thousand convicts and settlers, and making notes on their wretched condition and that of the indigenous population, the Ainu and the Gilyak. *The Island: A Journey to Sakhalin*, the book he published a few years later, most of it dry and dispassionately informative but some of it a sharp evocation of suffering and despair, caused a considerable stir and resulted in measurable reforms of the appalling conditions. (It was, however, rejected out of hand as a doctoral dissertation by the unimaginative dean of Moscow University's medical school.)

For all his devotion to medicine, Chekhov was entirely unsentimental about it, keeping a clear-eyed view of the rigors and frequent ugliness of a doctor's life, which was considerably more strenuous and problematic and for most practitioners far less remunerative than in our own time. He addressed himself to some of these matters with special feeling in stories like "Ward No. Six" and "Enemies," and in an occasional letter. To Suvorin he wrote: "Physicians go through loathsome days and hours—May God withhold this from every man. True enough, ignoramuses and cads are no rarity among physicians, even as among writers, engineers, and people in general, but it is only physicians who go through those loathsome hours and days . . . and for that, in all conscience, much must be forgiven them."[31]

In 1899 in a letter to Dr. Grigory Rossolimo, who had been his fellow student in medical school and was now collecting material for a memorial album of their graduating class, he offered a rare estimate of the influence being a doctor had had on his writing. "There is no doubt in my mind that my study of medicine has had a serious impact on my literary activities," he told Rossolimo. "It significantly broadened the scope of my observations and enriched me with knowledge whose value for me as a writer only a doctor can appreciate. It also served as a guiding influence. . . . My familiarity with the natural sciences and the scientific method has always kept me on my guard. . . . I am not one of those writers who deny the value of science and would not wish to be one of those who believe they can figure out everything for themselves."[32]

As a man and a physician, he was considerably ahead of his time in the range and delicacy of his sympathies, and in his grasp of how the mind affects the body.

From a letter: Syphilis "isn't a vice, it isn't the product of ill will, but a disease, and the people who have it need warm, human care."[33]

From his notebooks: "He died from fear of cholera."[34]

Konstantin Korovin tells the following story. He was visiting Chekhov in Yalta a few months before his death. "Maria Pavlovna [Anton's sister] came into the room to say that the cook had fallen ill and was in bed. . . . At first Anton Pavlovich paid no attention, but then all of a sudden he stood up and said, 'Oh, I'd forgotten. I'm a doctor, aren't I? Of course I am. Let me go and see what is the matter with her.' "[35]

"HEALTH"

The second item on his list of holies is naturally inseparable from the first. He could have combined them: "the healthy human body," it would then have read. I have reverence for that, he might have said; lacking it myself, I posit it like any good doctor as the goal of my physicianship. But "health" for Chekhov surely spread beyond simple physicality toward *mens sana in corpore sano,* that august phrase he himself once used in a letter to his brother Nikolai in which he offered his prescription for a "well-bred"[36] person (the Russian word can also be translated as "cultivated"). And health in that psychological and spiritual sense leads us directly into intelligence and then into talent, inspiration, and the rest of his litany of what is to be sought for and admired in this life.

Like Socrates, whom he cites in the matter, Chekhov made a point of stressing how much he didn't know. There was nothing falsely modest about it. He admired keenness of thought and detested ignorance, but he wasn't sure he could always distinguish accurately between them. Especially was this true in the realm of matters of the spirit, of psychological nuance and moral discrimination. Devoted to scientific method, he could all the more deeply mistrust the power of the intellect to grasp the imperceptible (though to capture it was just what his art accomplished) or, in the same dimension of things, to solve dilemmas beyond the realm of the material. He sometimes feared he hadn't given answers to the big questions. But he knew better and once in a while said so. As he wrote to Suvorin in 1888, "Anyone who says the artist's field is all answers and no questions has never done any writing or had any dealings with imagery."[37]

The last phrase has a particular resonance. To "deal" with imagery is precisely to do the artist's work; it's to solicit the revelations of things seen newly, to "traffic" in forms. You don't *deal* with abstract knowledge, you wield it, especially in the shape of answers. In humanistic matters, the realm of the unverifiable and for that very reason, we can say, the poetic, I think Chekhov's true attitude was summed up in a remark such as this: "It's only fools and charlatans who know everything and understand everything."[38]

Notice he doesn't say that the fools and charlatans are those who *pretend* to universal knowledge; such a denunciation would be easy to make, and uninteresting besides. No, his objection is more daring; it's to the *idea* that anyone can escape having gaps and fissures in the mind; it's to the pretensions of certainty, the smugness of conviction. To be certain, to be convinced of anything beyond some physical facts is, in the present state of humankind (and, he rather thought, it would be so for some time to come), the very definition of foolishness and charlatanry. Intelligence, in the oldest, classical dispensation, consists to a great extent in knowing that we don't know.

And so, in an age of fierce political and social partisanship and of cultic wisdom, ideologues and sages dismayed him. He wrote to Suvorin that "the crowd thinks it knows and understands everything; the stupider it is, the broader it imagines its outlook. But, if a writer whom the crowd believes . . . declare[s] he understands nothing of what he sees, that . . . will constitute a major gain in the realm of thought."[39] (I find a related remark, more epigram-matic, and more enigmatic too, in his notebook: "The stars have gone out long ago, but they still shine for the crowd."[40]) About a writer who declared or let on that he understood *everything* of what he saw, Chekhov made some memorably sharp comments. He loved Tolstoy's spirit and much of his writing, but the great man's intellect in its prophetic mode was another matter; it came to represent everything Chekhov found deficient and dangerous in the way the mind works.

To Pleshcheyev he praised *The Kreutzer Sonata* but cited the "audacity with which Tolstoy treats topics of which he knows nothing";[41] in other letters he spoke of the "gelatinous"[42] image he got from Tolstoy's idea of immortality, and of the weary staleness of his preachings on art. To Suvorin he traced the course of his relations with Tolstoy as a thinker. After having been under his influence for many years, due in part to what was "probably a sort of hypno-tism," he had become disenchanted. "Now something in me protests," he wrote. "Prudence and justice tell me there is more love for mankind in elec-tricity and steam than in chastity and abstention from meat. War is an evil and the court system is an evil, but it doesn't follow that I should wear bast shoes and sleep on a stove alongside the hired hand and his wife."[43]

"To hell with the philosophy of the great men of this world!" he wrote on another occasion. "All great wise men are as despotic as generals."[44]

As much as he disliked the fiats of wise men, he was put off by a certain kind of flaccid amateur philosophizing. After quoting some statements by a contribu-tor to Suvorin's newspaper, *New Times*—"The aim of life is life itself . . . I believe in life, in its bright moments, for the sake of which one can, indeed one must, live; I believe in man, in that part of his soul which is good"—he commented, "Can all this be sincere and does it mean anything? This isn't an outlook, it's caramels."[45] I like to think that the intelligence he most esteemed was that which kept itself from hardening into cocksureness on the one hand or liquefying into sentimentality on the other.

"INTELLIGENCE" (2)

In the letter to Suvorin about Tolstoy, Chekhov cites "prudence and justice" as sources of his own sense of where love is likely to be found, and by extension his sense of things in general. These look like unexciting virtues, to be sure. In regard to how many other writers would we think of associating justice, and prudence even more, with genius? Can we imagine Dostoevsky, for example, exercising prudence and justice in arranging his plots, or his life for that matter? But this "reasonable" aspect of Chekhov, this matter-of-factness or groundedness, is the very principle of his creativity, as well as of his management of crises, and we ought never to be very far from that in thinking about him. Chekhov the sane, the lyricist of the prosaic.

The same letter to Suvorin contains more material for an understanding of Chekhov's qualities of mind, including an example of the gentle mockery with which he was so fond of treating the more horrendous or intractable aspects of existence generally or of his own history. In particular, he liked to relieve the ponderousness of general concepts by shrewdly whimsical logical constructions. "I acquired my belief in progress when still a child," he writes to Suvorin in this letter. "I couldn't help believing in it, because the difference between the period when they flogged me and the period when they stopped flogging me was enormous."[46]

But perhaps the most arresting clue to how he thought intelligence best operated and was most pertinent to his purposes as an artist comes right after that passage and deserves to be in italics: *"I've always loved intelligent people, heightened sensibilities, courtesy and wit."*[47]

At first glance there seems to be a diminuendo in this list, a trailing off. One might think that courtesy and wit are a long way beneath intelligence and sensibility in seriousness and importance. Yet to anyone who knows Chekhov the grouping has an unmistakable logic to it, an internal consistency and coherence, a special wit.

To begin with "courtesy." Chekhov no doubt used the word in the usual sense—to indicate politeness, civility, and so on—but I'm convinced he also meant by it something far more remarkable. Think of the luminous way Jean Genet defined talent—as "courtesy" in regard to matter—and of how this is so entirely applicable to Chekhov's practice as an artist. You give objects, beings, and persons their due, you pay your respects to phenomena, are *polite* to the outlines and definitions of things, their relationships, which means you acknowledge their integrity. From such recognitions you move to the center of Genet's idea, that the courtesy intrinsic to talent consists in "giving song to what was dumb." Such a fine notion of courtesy—giving the world more music! It isn't hard to see how all these things connect: intelligence is a kind of talent; heightened sensibilities are both the result of being more closely attuned to the distinctiveness and interplay of phenomena and a preparation for being so attuned; extending courtesy toward "dumb matter" brings everything into articulation.

And so we come to "wit." The *Oxford English Dictionary*'s "seat of consciousness . . . faculty of thinking" doesn't do anything for us here, but "quickness of intellect" is a help. Best of all is "speech or writing"—the definition doesn't extend to physicality; the *OED* isn't impressed by Charlie Chaplin's gestures—"calculated to surprise and delight by its unexpectedness." Let's go further, keeping Chekhov in mind. Wit as a tool of intelligence? Wit's unexpectedness as a relief from seemingly foregone conclusions? Wit as a means of atoning through certain deft motions of the mind or body for the ordinary world's dumb thickness? As liberation through the recognition of incongruity?

Out of the abundance of Chekhov's . . . I was about to say "witticisms" when I remembered that he himself had deftly marked out that word as a pejorative, because it implies strain and artificiality; so I'll say his wit, then, of which there are two examples I've been carrying around for just such an opportunity as this. One is from a story called "Talent" (a nice title for this stage of our investigation): "People who know nothing about life usually picture life from books, but Yegor Savvitch knew no books either." The other is from a letter to Maxim Gorky: "It is usual not to like a play while writing it, and it is usual not to like it afterward either."[48]

"TALENT" AND "INSPIRATION"

A tandem, certainly. "Talent" was one of Chekhov's words of highest praise, along with "culture" and "humane." He tended to use it sparingly and sometimes in the ordinary sense—as an asset we possess, something usable. For example, in 1886 he wrote to his older brother Nikolai (a gifted artist whose career, though, would come to nothing and who would drink himself to death at thirty-one) that "your talent sets you apart: even if you were a toad or a tarantula, you would be respected, for to talent everything is forgiven."[49] But he also seems to have meant by it what Genet did: an attitude issuing in a ceremonious action by which we confer some benefit or blessing. One of the very few times he spoke directly of his own talent (except for those intermittent grumblings about his lack of capacity to be a playwright) was in a letter to Suvorin of 1888, where he disavowed "drawing conclusions" for his readers and then wrote: "My only job is to be talented, that is, to know how to distinguish important testimony from unimportant, to place my characters in the proper light and speak their language."[50] How impressive this definition of talent is, in all its parts!

At the time of this letter Chekhov was still somewhat under the influence of an idea of the writer as a species of scientist: "The writer should be just as objective as the chemist," he had written in a letter of 1887.[51] This would account for the rather dry and unemotional quality of a word like "testimony." Yet I feel sure that he gives it a large poetic function too: testimony of this kind is evidence from all the human spheres; it's the self's experience, what the imagination has turned up. Years ago David Magarshack accounted in part for Chekhov's blossoming as a playwright (and by implication as a fiction writer too) by his abandonment of the canon of strict objectivity and his consequent adoption of more involved, relaxed, and "humanistic" criteria such as I've just sketched.

Magarshack's theory was certainly useful, but, like his related notion of Chekhov's having moved from "direct" action to "indirect" in his plays, it has always seemed to me a little too programmatic, a bit too crisp. I don't think Chekhov was ever quite so detached or objective as some of his own comments might make it appear, and so I don't think he moved so abruptly from aloofness toward a supposed "involvement"; there was never so clear a bifurcation in his attitude. It seems more likely that as his life increased in complexity and depth of experience in the 1880s, and as he gained confidence, his artistic and intellectual aims changed and deepened—"Everything I've written to date is nonsense compared with what I would like to have written,"[52] he told Suvorin in the letter in which he'd spoken of dealing with imagery—and he took on more formidable imaginative tasks; brilliant maker that he was becoming, he would discover the necessary aesthetic means.

He still collected "testimony," evidence, discriminating like any artist (or scientist too, for that matter) among its levels of pertinence and value. But that was just the point: his early humorous fictional pieces ("my literary excrement," he would later call some of them[53]), his theater skits, and that one huge, clumsy, derivative melodrama *Platonov* weren't "important" enough testimony. He became more serious; his talent was now an extension of courtesy to worthier objects, which is to say, to more complex and fugitive matters, secrets more difficult to pry open. He would remain on his guard; one of the things he'd told Rossolimo his medical training had done for him was to keep him alert as a writer. He would maintain a certain kind of distance, refrain from interfering in his characters' affairs. That, after all, is one of the things he became known for: authorial absence, which we can confidently ascribe to the modesty—a "fierce modesty," Nathalie Sarraute called it in his case[54]—that anyone practicing the scientific method ought to possess. But there was nothing like a "chemist's" cold, dispassionate eye or attitude; there were only alertness to deception and deceit, and dispassionate means, the unpolemical, nondidactic, uncoercive measures of his craft.

Again, it all fits—talent, sensibility, courtesy, wit. To speak his characters' language! What other writer would put it that way? Here's the truest modesty and the greatest creative mystery: he felt he had to be open to the nature of his characters, listening, absorbing, intuiting, weighing, before he gave them the lineaments of fictive existence. He owed them their own truth. And in return they told him what language he needed to speak.

There isn't much more to quote about his ideas on "talent." He once said that "when I write, I rely fully on the reader, on the assumption that he himself will add the subjective elements that are lacking in the story,"[55] which strikes a very "modern" note. Another time he said that "I can write only by thinking back; I have never written straight from nature. I need to let a subject strain through my memory until only what is important or typical remains as on a filter."[56] At an early stage of his career, in 1886, he told his brother Alexander what would be necessary for something Alexander was writing to be a work of art: "(1) no politico-economico-social verbal effusions; (2) objectivity throughout; (3) truth in the description of characters and things; (4) extreme brevity; (5) audacity and originality—eschew clichés; (6) warmheartedness."[57] Yes, he said "warmheartedness."

Once he gave this compact formula: "the artist observes, selects, surmises, composes."[58] Are there any objections to my nomination of surmising as by far the most arresting action in the series?

As for *inspiration,* he never did say how it came to him, only that it was one of the things he held sacred. One of the definitions I find in the *OED,* "a breathing or infusion into the mind or soul," has his recommended virtues of brevity and warmth.

LOVE (1)

In his notebook Chekhov once made a remark that can't be ignored in any consideration of how love—eros, sexual desire, romantic attraction—figures in his work and in some sense, we have reason to think, in his life as well. "Either it is a remnant of something degenerating," he wrote about love, "something which once had been immense, or it is a particle of what will in the future develop into something immense, but at the present it is unsatisfying, it gives much less than one expects."[59]

This is indeed what so many of his characters are brought to: romantic or erotic expectations that go unfulfilled, hopes that go awry; one of his persistent themes is that love isn't the "answer" to civilization's dilemmas and disconsolateness, any more than "work" is. And for himself? What did he expect and what in fact happened? Can we trace the course of eros in his life?

Before we even try, it might be useful to record what some *others* thought its course and status were.

The idea that Chekhov's erotic disposition wasn't all it should have been, and that his attitude toward women wasn't all *it* should have been either, an aspect of that slight wind of revisionism that has gusted at times in recent years, actually began with the memories and observations of a few of his contemporaries and has been promulgated most actively by some of his recent biographers and a putative scholar or two. They have found "evidence" in Chekhov's own letters, in the "facts" of his life, and in his obiter dicta, such as the comment quoted above. I don't mean to give the impression that the people I refer to as "revisionists" have mounted any sort of full-scale campaign; not at all. Nearly all of them enclose their criticisms of Chekhov as a lover within contexts of one degree or another of general praise and appreciation. Still, those criticisms—highly dubious theories, really—need to be addressed.

Ivan Bunin, the well-known novelist, late in his long life (he died in 1953) wrote a generally engaging memoir of his friendship with Chekhov and made this statement: "No one, not even those who were closest to him, knew what went on deep inside him. His self-control never deserted him, even during our most intimate conversations. . . . Had he ever had a passionate, blind, romantic love in his life? I don't believe so."[60] And Ignaty Potapenko, a minor writer and friend who had an affair with Lydia Mizinova, a woman Chekhov was thought by some to have been seriously involved with, in another memoir said of

Chekhov that "he resisted leading a private existence. He felt it robbed the creator in him of too much strength and concentration."[61]

In his assembly-line biography of Chekhov (he has also turned out lives of Dostoevsky, Tolstoy, Pushkin, and Catherine the Great, among others,) Henri Troyat quotes both Bunin and Potapenko as though they were gospel, and offers some observations of his own that might charitably be called intellectually undistinguished. Discussing Chekhov's fending off of Mizinova, he writes: "He would do everything possible to maintain the privacy, the inner solitude he needed for his work. What was a woman to him, no matter how desirable, when his life was all pen and paper?"[62]

Ronald Hingley, without citing any sources but with the same obnoxious claim as Troyat's to be a mind-reader, flatly asserts that "Chekhov lacked, even in his fantasies, the element of male aggressiveness,"[63] and on another occasion warns that "no sane reader would want to *model* [italics Hingley's] his sex life on that of Chekhov or of a typical Chekhovian character."[64] And in his peculiar, alternately brilliant and obtuse book on Chekhov, half biography and half study of the fiction, V. S. Pritchett—not usually one to parrot an opinion but doing it in this case, I think—rather halfheartedly announces that "we have to suppose that his sexual temperature was low."[65]

Why do we have to suppose it? And what, if we do suppose it, follows from that? Now, there seems to be a small cluster of grounds on which the theory of Chekhov's erotic deficiencies has been based: that he didn't marry until he was forty-one (and to some minds nothing about the union with Olga Knipper lightens the onus of belatedness; they see the marriage's strains but none of its beauties); that up to then we have no certified instances of his having had sexual relations and few pointers to any such consummations; that he almost never talked about sex; and, most important to critics looking to find fault, that a disproportionate number of the love affairs and erotic enterprises in his plays and stories turn out badly.

How difficult it is to refute such accusations! For all their veneer of seriously arrived-at conclusions, at bottom they're the products of radical failures of understanding, deficiencies of sensibility; they feel as though they've been delivered by a certain type of Chekhov character, a Lvov, a Solyony (to stick to the plays)—full of opinions or of a sense of the necessity to *have* opinions; blind to psychological and aesthetic nuance; above all lacking in "the tact, the delicacy which are so essential when you have to do with a fellow-creature's soul," a line from Chekhov's "An Anonymous Story."

The missing tact and delicacy I'm speaking of here have nothing to do with anything so obvious as an invasion of privacy, but with getting right the reasons for actions or for refraining from them, or at least not getting them flagrantly wrong, understanding the internal climate in which behavior prepares to become actual or to remain latent. Motives have always been the weakest area of biography, and is it any wonder? We have the hardest time ascertaining why we ourselves do what we do; how can it be expected that without great perceptiveness—and the greatest delicacy of inquiry—we should be able to know about other people? The weakest aspect of the biographies of artists has precisely been artistic understanding, and biographies of Chekhov are especially deficient. Ernest Simmons, Hingley, Troyat, the Soviet chronicler Vladimir Yermilov—there are no Richard Ellmanns or Leon Edels in those ranks.

I want just to touch on one more commentator on Chekhov before turning to the erotic history we do possess of him and offering as much of a corrective as I can to the inadequacies—and excesses—of revisionism. In 1973, in a book called *Anton Chekhov and the Lady with the Dog*, Virginia Llewellen Smith argued that Chekhov was close to being a misogynist, that he had a "gloomy view of heterosexual relationships,"[66] and that his writing about such relationships was characterized by a "distasteful undertone of uneasy salacity."[67]

There's no way to refute these accusations because they issue from what I consider a thoroughly and systematically obtuse reading of Chekhov's life and stories—Llewellen Smith doesn't discuss the plays. I don't want to pay much attention to her book, but to alert any prospective readers to the level on which her critical powers operate, I will quote a representative sentence: "A full appreciation of Chekhov's work requires of the reader a certain degree of involvement, a response intellectual, or, as in the case of his love-stories, emotional."[68]

LOVE (2)

Eroticism in Chekhov's life makes up a thin record in part because of the age's prohibition on direct references to what we ourselves talk about without hesitation—or scruples—and in part because of his own natural reticence and, we have reason for thinking, his delicacy. In his biography, Ernest Simmons quotes the mature Chekhov as having written to a friend, "I was initiated into the secret of love at the age of thirteen," but Simmons is sceptical, and the event would be hotly denied by Troyat, who cocksurely wrote, in the manner of recent biographers, that at sixteen "Anton's crushes were more a matter of admiration and affection than of sensuality. His feelings were skin-deep. . . . Perhaps he was still too young to feel a desire for carnal union."[69]

There's no real gossip to report until he reaches the age of twenty-six, when he writes to a friend that he has found a prospective wife. "My one and only is Jewish. If the rich young Jewess has enough courage to convert to Orthodoxy with all that this entails, fine. If not, that's fine too."[70] The marriage didn't come off. Most observers think the woman was Dunya Efros, a school friend of Chekhov's sister. It's quite possible that the relationship gave him ideas he would use a year or so later for the character of Anna in *Ivanov*.

Such affairs as he might have had after that are impossible to pin down as real liaisons. Most of the data is in letters characterized by banter which either masked deep passion or, perhaps more frequently, substituted for its lack. He addressed Lydia (Lika) Mizinova, whom he'd also met through his sister, as "darling little blonde,"[71] signed himself off as "Yours from head to heels, with all my soul and all my heart, until my tombstone, to the point of self-oblivion, of stupefaction, of frenzy,"[72] and pleaded with her to "allow my head to turn dizzy from your perfume and help me to tighten the loop of the lasso you have already thrown around my neck."[73] It's almost certain that their relationship never went beyond such verbal play.

Nor was Chekhov likely to have gone beyond it with Tatyana Shchepkina-Kupernik, to whom he wrote in November 1894, "I shall be ecstatic when you come to me, but I am afraid that your delicious cartilages and little bones will be dislocated. The road is terrible. The *tarantas,* in agonizing pain, keeps leaping up and loses wheels at every step. The last time that I was driving from the station, because of the jolting ride my heart was torn from its moorings, so that I am now incapable of love."[74]

He was thought by some to have had affairs of varying intensity with quite a few other women; if he did have, he appears not to have initiated or consummated any of them. Most notable among these presences or figments were Lydia Yavorskaya, a beautiful, blonde, untalented actress, and Lydia Avilova, the would-be writer who sent him a medallion engraved with a quotation from one of his stories—he would use the idea in *The Seagull*—and who after his death published a book about a love affair between them which an overwhelming weight of evidence indicates was a product of her wishful fantasizing.

From time to time he gave little hints or indications of his fundamental attitude toward women and of his erotic history and disposition, some of them charming and "literary" and a few of them likely to be dismaying to someone who still treasures the myth of his perfection. In 1886 he told a friend, Maria Kiseleva, "You have a completely masculine manner of writing . . . this should flatter your self-esteem, for, speaking generally, men are a thousand times superior to and more accomplished than women."[75] It doesn't take an effort to imagine that he was teasing her. But rare as it was in his utterance, for both its idea of women and its general cynicism, a remark like this—"Neither women nor men are worth a brass farthing, but man is more intelligent and more just"—is harder to overlook.

Still, here are a couple of possibly offsetting entries in his notebook: "When a woman destroys things like a man, people think it natural and everybody understands it; but when, like a man, she wishes or tries to create, people think it unnatural and cannot reconcile themselves to it."[76] "Women deprived of the company of men pine, men deprived of the company of women become stupid."[77]

In a different vein, on a train trip in 1887 he wrote to his sister, Maria: "At the last window of the second floor of the station house sits a girl (or a married woman, the devil knows which) in a white blouse, languid, beautiful. I look at her, she looks at me. . . . I put on my pince-nez, she puts on hers. Oh, wonderful vision! I contracted inflammation of the heart, and rode on."[78] To Maria Kiseleva, he wrote from Rome in 1891: "I dine at a *table d'hote* . . . sitting opposite me are two darling Dutch girls. . . . I keep looking at them . . . and in my imagination I see a tidy little white house with a turret, excellent butter, superb Holland cheese, Holland herrings, a benignly visaged pastor, a sedate teacher—and I want to marry a darling Dutch girl, and I want to be depicted on a serving tray with her near the tidy little house."[79] And to Suvorin he wrote in 1891, "Alas, I shall never be a Tolstoyan! In women what I like above all is beauty, and in the history of humanity, culture, which finds its expression in rugs, carriages on springs, and keenness of thought."[80]

He could boast playfully: "When I have children, I'll say to them, not without pride, 'Why, you sons of bitches, I've had relations in my day with a black-eyed

Hindu girl, and guess where? In a coconut grove, on a moonlit night!' "[81] And boast with sly playfulness: on his trip to Sakhalin he reported meeting "Japanese women . . . diminutive brunettes with oversized, ingenious coiffures, with beautiful torsos and, as it seemed to me, with short thighs. They dress beautifully."[82] As has been pointed out, how would he know about the thighs under those long straight kimonos?

(On the same trip he spoke of Siberian women as resembling frozen fish: "You'd have to be a walrus or a seal to have an affair with them."[83])

He once wrote in his notebook that "when I become rich, I shall have a harem in which I shall keep fat naked women, with their buttocks painted green."[84]

But other things he said struck a different note. To Suvorin he once wrote, "I have had few romantic affairs. . . . I do feel predisposed to comfort, but debauchery does not entice me."[85] When Suvorin pressed him to get married, he replied in March 1895, "Very well. . . . But my conditions are: everything must be as it had been before this . . . she will have to live in Moscow, while I'll live in the country and will make trips to see her."[86] Some time later he told Suvorin that "I am afraid of a wife and family routine, which would hinder me and which, I imagine, does not jibe, somehow, with my disorderliness."[87] "Still," he added, "this is better than bobbing about in the sea of life" (he meant alone, presumably).

Nearly two years later he gave the architect Franz Schechtel a more detailed, plausible, and wistful explanation for not getting married: "I cannot marry at the present time because, first of all, I have bacilli squatting in me, which are very disreputable tenants [he had finally accepted the diagnosis of tuberculosis]; secondly, I haven't a cent, and, thirdly, it still seems to me that I am very young. [He was about to be thirty-seven.] Allow me to kick up my heels for just two or three years more, and then we shall see—perhaps I really will get married."[88]

Anyone looking to bolster the theory of Chekhov's weak sexuality will cheer this piece of evidence from a letter to Suvorin of November 11, 1893: "Is potency a sign of true life and health? Is screwing the only thing that makes one a real person? All thinkers are impotent at forty, while ninety-year-old savages keep ninety wives apiece."[89] Then what about this from a letter to his brother Misha: "The most important nut in married life is love, sexual attraction, one flesh; all the rest is unreliable and dull, no matter how wisely we calculate"?[90]

That the letter was dated October 26, 1898, mustn't be lost on us, for a little less than two months before that he had met Olga Knipper, with whom we can confidently say he was in love, no matter how we choose to define that.

LOVE (3)

Chekhov first met Knipper on September 9, 1898, at a rehearsal by the Moscow Art Theater of *The Seagull,* in which she was playing Arkadina. (She would also play Yelena in *Uncle Vanya,* Masha in *Three Sisters,* and Liubov in *The Cherry Orchard.*) Of German-Russian descent, she came from a cultivated family and was eight years younger than he. By all accounts she was a highly gifted actress and had an astonishingly long career with the Art Theater, working until well past the middle of the twentieth century.

Less than two weeks after Chekhov and Knipper met, he wrote to Lydia Mizinova that "Nemirovich and Stanislavsky have a very interesting theater company. Beautiful little actresses."[91] And two weeks after that he told Suvorin, "If I had remained in Moscow I would have fallen in love with this Irina";[92] Knipper was playing a character of that name in *Fyodor Ioannovich,* by Alexei Tolstoy.

Chekhov left Moscow and fell in love with her anyway, although it took some time for their relationship to form. His first letter to her, dated June 16, 1899, is innocuous enough: a complaint that she hasn't been in touch, a mild joke or two, and his usual closing, "Your A. Chekhov."[93] But things picked up quickly. By September he was writing to her in this fashion: "Dear, wonderful actress, remarkable woman, if you only knew what joy your letter gave me! I make so low an obeisance to you that my forehead touches the bottom of my well . . . to the depth of 55 feet."[94]

From then on they grew toward each other at a steady pace, accumulating a relationship, both before and after their marriage (which took place on May 25, 1901), in large part through letters. For it was to be a source of conflict and unhappiness that they had to spend so much time apart, because of her career with the Art Theater and because he was mostly confined to the warmth of Yalta and for a stretch the Riviera, for the sake of the remnants of his health. I said they had to be apart, but of course there was no absolute necessity. Olga kept moving between love of acting and spasms of guilt over being away from Chekhov, together with desire for him, while he, much as he missed his "extraordinary, wonderful, proper, intelligent, rare wife,"[95] insisted that she continue her career. The strain of this led to misunderstandings, which caused them grief from time to time.

Surrounding their fallings-out and mock fallings-out—on January 11, 1901, he wrote from Nice: "Cruel, ferocious woman, for a century I haven't had any letters from you";[96] in less than a month she had sent him eighteen—was an affair and then a marriage sustained as far as we can tell by great esteem on both sides, by delight and desire as well. On his part there was perhaps rather more of a sense of having found an emotional home and refuge, but if so it was probably a matter of his shorter perspective on life. They had to deal with constant anxiety over his health, which steadily deteriorated through the three years of their marriage, and they did so mainly by suppressing full or active knowledge that he was fatally ill: he would exaggerate his moments of relative well-being and grumble humorously over the rest, and she would fuss maternally: Take your medicine, remember your galoshes.

They made as much as they could out of the periods they did have together. Several times he wrote to her after she'd left that he was having difficulty in sleeping without her lying beside him. The evidence is that they both wanted a child. On New Year's Day 1903 he wrote to her: "I wish you everything you need and deserve, and chiefly I wish you a little half-German who would rummage in your wardrobe and smudge my desk with ink, much to your delight."[97] She became pregnant at least once that we know of, but it resulted in a miscarriage that was a painful disappointment for them both.

He had an extraordinary variety of pet names for her: Knipshitz, little German, nincompoop, granny, booby, dumpling and—in a real burst of zoology—dog, doggie, puppy, little bug, perch, heron, dachshund, little mongrel, pony, dove, linnet. I like to think that the sheer number and exuberance of these appellations testifies to his having long had to suppress the impulse to bestow them, until she came along. (She, by the way, moved by rather less urgency if no less love, mostly called him simply Anton.)

Browsing almost at random through his letters to her, I find this sequence:

But darling . . . there is no sadness in me, there never was; most of the time life is bearable and when you are with me things are really fine. (August 24, 1901)[98]

It seems to me that I have become a regular Philistine and cannot live without a spouse. (August 28, 1901)[99]

I love you—you have known this for a long time. I kiss you 1,013,212 times. (November 7, 1901)[100]

I take my dog by the tail, swing her several times, then stroke and pet her. (August 29, 1902)[101]

Greetings my angry dog, my ferocious doggie! (December 4, 1902)[102]

I love you, you know, I love your letters, your acting, your manner of walking. The only thing I don't like is when you dawdle over the wash-stand. (April 15, 1904)[103]

How I long for you! I embrace and kiss you. . . . Christ be with you, my joy. (April 22, 1904)[104]

This letter, from Yalta, was his last to her. A little later he joined her in Moscow, and then they went on that final trip to Germany.

So was he disappointed? Did love with the lineaments of Olga Knipper give "much less than one expects"? Well, the statement had been a large general observation; he might have come to revise it. And anyway, who knows what he specifically had hoped for? What he found would seem to have been gratifying enough, though cynics are free to argue that his last five or six years, when he knew Olga, were so distorted by illness and fatigue as to make any authentic emotional experience highly doubtful. And his having written *Three Sisters* and *The Cherry Orchard* during this period, along with three or four of his most consummately realized stories, leaves us free to argue otherwise.

LOVE (4)

Here are some possible alternative ways of looking at the "evidence" that Chekhov was sexually ill adjusted, or anyhow not up to par. He consummated no, or very few, love affairs because he had only so much physical energy to give and was burdened by a great weight of responsibility: to his family, his medical practice, and his literary work; it wasn't because "his life was all pen and paper," whatever that silly phrase might mean. He didn't marry until late for pretty much the reasons he gave: he didn't want to present a potential bride with a landscape of infection and a ripe opportunity for widowhood; he never had much money; and because he didn't meet Olga sooner. The letter to Suvorin about "screwing" not being the test of a "real person" is a counterstatement to his friend's occasional macho posturings. The letter to his brother Misha about sexual love as the "nut" of marriage has a ring of authentic feeling about it. He didn't talk much more than this about sex because he was an extremely discreet man, with a highly developed sense of the appropriate.

We have no way of knowing what his "sexual temperature" was or, God help us, about his erotic fantasies. But we do know that love—as sensual desire or romantic longing, usually the two entwined—has a whole series of births in his consciousness, undergoes his artistic "surmises," and emerges in the forms and textures of his work; we have the stories and the plays.

Throughout this book I intend to talk about those forms and textures; here I only want to set down a few general remarks about the plays and a word or two about the stories. It's in the great female characters of the plays—Nina, Sonya and Yelena, the three Prozorov sisters, Ranevskaya and Anya—that are located the most central modes of feeling, the most luminous of meanings. In these women Chekhov moves closer even than in his men to the centrality of experience, those noncontingent states of being—the how-it-is of *Uncle Vanya,* the living-in-time of *Three Sisters*—whose rendering on stage in their smallest but most suggestive patterns is the secret of his art.

These women incarnate the very principle of stamina—getting through, going on—those "undramatic" progressions that, again, make up the secret of Chekhov's drama. It seems to me that only a writer, and a man, deeply, unerringly attuned to the women in his experience, and to the femaleness in himself, could have been capable of that.

Love in Chekhov is usually grave—consequential, a site of actual or potential pain—though not very often grim; in love his characters are tested in their capacity to understand, and when they can't, when circumstances are too inimical or the playing field is too distorted, it's we who understand on their behalf. Simon Karlinsky has written about how Chekhov so often "showed . . . female characters robbed of their individuality by the traditional roles society forces upon them."[105] And he showed still others battling to hold on to or win through to some elements of their selfhood. This is what happens to a number of his female characters, who struggle—again, more keenly often than men—against the way "things" are set up, and who therefore make up a disproportionate number of the participants in those "failures" of love to which some revisionists have pointed. But of course what such people can't recognize is that "success" and "failure" have no status as imaginative categories; or, to put it another way, on the level of literary creation material failures can be rich occasions for the "successes" of the art.

Chekhov himself made a point of condemning our hunger for dividing things into winning and losing, failure and success. An aspect of that was his refusal to condemn. Has there ever been a less judgmental writer, about sex or anything else? This capacity to keep from judging sexual behavior shows itself throughout his writing but most pointedly, in the plays, in his attitude toward Nina's affair with Trigorin, Masha's with Vershinin, and Liubov's with her Paris lover; and in such earlier stories as "Agafya," "The Chorus Girl," "Anyuta," and "A Calamity," and such later ones as "The Grasshopper," "The Duel," and "The Lady with the Dog," a masterpiece about love as inescapability, fatality, and hope.

Of all the witnesses I might call on to testify for Chekhov in this matter, I'll settle for just one, Eudora Welty, whose essay "Reality in Chekhov's Stories" is the wisest and most affecting of its kind that I know. "Chekhov wrote of sex," she said, "with honesty and lack of fuss as he wrote of all human experience. As always, it is a character's feelings that give it its meaning. Much ahead of his time, and perhaps of ours, in 'The Duel' he treated with candor and seriousness a young woman of compelling sexuality. 'The Lady with the Pet Dog' is a compassionate study of a cynical middle-aged man surprised when, almost against his will and against his belief, his sexual worldliness turns into the honesty and difficulty of belated love."[106]

And, Welty said, "success and defeat are aspects of the same thing. In the human being, as this great artist spent his short life showing us, anything is possible."[107]

FREEDOM FROM VIOLENCE AND LIES

In her essay, Welty speaks of the "abhorrence [Chekhov] felt toward coercion in human affairs" and makes the remarkably interesting point that this "must have played its part in" his rejection of "arbitrary plot, manipulated characters."[108] The linkage is one of those persuasive strokes of thought whereby diverse realms are brought together; a question of technique and construction from the side of art is brought together with a question of moral behavior from the side of life. Welty is saying that in this case at least innovation in literature was to some degree the result of a moral stance originally taken outside it.

It hardly needs to be announced that Chekhov was profoundly opposed to the wielding of physical force and saw the potential for it in all sorts of spiritual afflictions (in regard to the Dreyfus case, for instance, he said that anti-Semitism "reeks of the slaughterhouse"[109]). But violence takes more subtle forms, of course; verbal abuse is one of them, lying and ignorance are others—both of those being injuries done to truth. In what Chekhov said about these matters we mustn't lose sight of how his thoughts on "real" human behavior were related to the behavior that he caused to unfold in that dominion of aesthetic "unreality" of which the great director Vsevolod Meyerhold was to speak.

Chekhov is tirelessly concerned with finding the means to guard against violence (his well-known dictum that "writers and artists should engage in politics only enough to protect themselves from it"[110] is addressed to that, as is his constant struggle against the censors), and he denounces it in areas where his own times, and ours as well, are almost entirely complacent. In 1893 he writes to Suvorin on the subject of literary quarrels and feuds: "I am physically repelled by abuse no matter at whom it is aimed. . . . Why must they write in a tone fit for judging criminals rather than artists and writers? I just can't stand it, I simply can't."[111] Those last words and his general tone here are sharply reminiscent of Olga's reaction to Natasha's abuse of the maid Anfisa in *Three Sisters*.

Instead of "freedom from violence and lies" for his holy of holies, Chekhov might equally well or better have said "freedom from doing violence and lying," for it was the zone of personal responsibility that concerned him most. This is always a complex region full of intricate connections among ethical phenomena, the site of perpetual moral maneuvers and jostling of values. In Chekhov's case it was always intimately bound up with his work.

One time he wrote to Pleshcheyev: "You once told me that my stories lack an element of protest, that they have neither sympathies nor antipathies. But doesn't the story ["The Name-Day Party," which Pleshcheyev had criticized] protest against lying from start to finish? Isn't that an ideology? It isn't? Well, I guess that means either I don't know how to bite or I'm a flea."[112] In the same letter he wrote that "it seems to me I could be more readily accused of gluttony, of drunkenness, of frivolity, of indifference, of whatever you like . . . [but] never of a desire to seem or not to seem to be something—I never concealed myself."

We know that he almost never boasted; when he did, it would come out as a charming joke or he would neutralize the effect by a quick jab of humorous deprecation. But on at least one occasion he asked for recognition of his own moral record without his usual charm; that he didn't lie was a central element of his claim.

In April 1890 he sent to Vukol Lavrov, the owner and editor of the leftist literary journal *Russian Thought*—which had described him as an "unprincipled" writer—a spirited protest, probably the most elaborate he ever composed against that sort of attack. "True," he said, "my literary career has consisted of an uninterrupted series of errors, sometimes flagrant errors, but that can be explained by the dimensions of my talent, not by whether I am a good or bad person. I have never gone in for blackmail, I have never written lampoons or denunciations, I have never toadied, nor lied, nor insulted. In short, I have written many stories and editorials that I would be only too glad to throw out because of their worthlessness, but I have never written a single line I am ashamed of today."[113]

In an important letter to Pleshcheyev in May 1889, he goes deep into the nature of moral reality in relation to artistic creation. He has been working on a novel (which he never finished) and now brings Pleshcheyev in on his hopes for it. He begins routinely enough: "My aim is to . . . depict life truthfully and . . . show to what extent this life deviates from the norm." But suddenly everything becomes surprising, mysterious: "The norm is not known to me, just as it is not known to any one of us. All of us know what a dishonorable act is, but just what honor is we do not know. I'll keep to the framework which is nearer the heart and which has already been tested by people stronger and more intelligent than I. This framework is man's absolute freedom—freedom from coercion, from prejudices, ignorance, the devil; freedom from passions and so forth."[114]

A framework nearer the heart. A few months earlier, Pleshcheyev had been the recipient of the letter in which Chekhov described what he called his "holy of holies"; maybe that was what inspired its partial recapitulation here.

He once wrote: "One fine feature of art is that it doesn't let you lie. You can lie in love, politics, and medicine, you can fool people and even God—such cases do exist—but you can't lie in art."[115]

In his notebook he set this down: "He alone is all right and can repent who feels himself to be wrong."[116]

FAULTS

I said at the beginning of this chapter that we should be grateful Chekhov wasn't without flaws, and now as I come to the end I see that I seem to have recorded scarcely any. All right: if you look through the available sources you'll find an occasional lapse from full candor, a trace of ill temper at long intervals, an instance or two of resentment, bits of selfishness here and there, a couple of incidents where generosity may have been wanting. He was also accused of having exploited his friends' lives for a few of his stories, something he strongly denied. I see no reason to think he was lying, though he might have done it unconsciously.

The most serious charge that can be brought against him concerns an event all his biographers mention. In 1892 his sister, Maria, who as we know was fiercely devoted to him, received a proposal of marriage, most probably the only one she would ever be given. Her suitor was Alexander Smagin, a friend of the family. Maria, attracted to Smagin, was strongly tempted. But she felt she needed Anton's approval, for some obvious reasons and some more opaque ones. Years later she described what happened when she told him about the proposal. "He said nothing. Then I realized that this news was unpleasant for him, since he continued to remain silent. . . . I understood he could not confess that it would be hard for him if I left . . . for a family of my own. Yet he never pronounced the word 'No.' "[117]

After much agonizing, Maria turned Smagin down. She remained unmarried for the rest of her very long life, which was spent almost entirely in her brother's service, by his side or within reach during his life and afterwards as curator of the Yalta museum. The story goes that long afterward Smagin wrote and told her that he too had never married, for she had been the love of his life.

Although he didn't expressly disapprove of the proposal, Chekhov can certainly be held responsible for Maria's turning it down. Or can he? Maria, as he wrote to Suvorin a few months later, was "an unusual girl who sincerely does not wish to marry."[118] And maybe that was true. As Ernest Simmons wrote, the brother and sister had a "mysteriously close" bond,[119] and maybe Maria was sustained by her devotion to Anton in a way marriage could not have given her. Or maybe not.

FROM HIS NOTEBOOKS AND VARIOUS LETTERS

If I had not become a writer, I would probably have become a psychiatrist.[120]

It seems to me that if I had not been a writer, then I could have been a gardener.[121]

Help the poor. Take care of Mother. Live peacefully. [To Maria, telling her about his will.][122]

Levitan the painter . . . and I went out to the woodcock mating area yesterday evening. He fired at a woodcock and the latter, wounded in the wing, fell into a puddle. I picked it up. It had a long beak, large black eyes, and a magnificent costume. It looked at us in wonder. What could we do with it? Levitan . . . closed his eyes, and begged me with a tremor in his voice, 'Please smash its head against the butt of the rifle.' I said I couldn't. He kept . . . twitching his head and begging me. And the woodcock kept looking on in wonder. I had to obey Levitan and kill it. And while two idiots went home and sat down to dinner, there was one beautiful, enamored creature less in the world.[123]

There is not a single criterion that can serve as the measure of the non-existent, the non-human.[124]

It seems to me: the sea and myself—and nothing else.[125]

What matters most is to break out of the rut. Everything else is unimportant.

IVANOV
Prologue to a Revolution

"The plot is unprecedented," Chekhov wrote to one of his older brothers, Alexander, in October 1887, soon after finishing the first version of *Ivanov*.[1] It was either his second full-length play or, if rumors of a lost epic written when he was in high school are to be credited, his third. The assertion about his plot was a highly uncharacteristic burst of self-appreciation; much more typically, right up to the final revisions of *The Cherry Orchard* five or six months before his death in 1904, he would groan at his weaknesses as a dramatist, saying such things as, "It seems to me that I was not destined to be a playwright"[2] and, even more emphatically, "Writing plays has demoralized me."[3] But the source of his exhilaration in this instance becomes clear as the letter goes on. "I wanted to be original," he told his brother. "I did not portray a single villain or a single angel . . . did not blame anyone nor exculpate anyone."[4]

"I wanted to be original." This sort of remark is so nearly unprecedented among Chekhov's comments on his own work that we're obliged to give it special attention. His ordinary attitude toward the matter might be summed up in this way: if like any honest artisan you take pains with your craftsmanship, and if you keep your eye out for self-deception, originality will follow or it won't, but you should never strain or pant after it. This instructs us at least to glance at what originality meant to him and how this might have differed from its most prevalent meaning during the long history of theatrical innovation and change that can be said to have begun with Georg Büchner in the early nineteenth century in Germany and continued down to our own times. A most important question is, How does Chekhov's sense of it differ from what originality mostly means to us now?

When we first read *Ivanov* or see it on the stage, it doesn't appear to be at all radical in its form. We're not aware of any revolutionary techniques, nothing on the order, say, of the methods that mark the pantheon plays of the "modern" repertoire: Büchner's *Danton's Death* and *Woyzeck;* Ibsen's *Peer Gynt* and *When We Dead Awaken;* Strindberg's *A Dream Play* and *The Ghost Sonata;* Jarry's *Ubu* plays; Pirandello's *Six Characters in Search of an Author;* Brecht's *Baal;* and Beckett's *Waiting for Godot.* All those plays changed the theater by their aggressive formal means at least as much as by exotic new subjects, if we can ever make such a separation. In contrast, *Ivanov* looks straightforward enough in its structure and procedures, but, as we shall see, this is deceptive.

When we consider the matter of originality in art, several questions propose themselves. To begin with, is there ever "progress" in any of the arts, anything comparable to the forward movement in science whereby a particular discipline is widened and deepened as control is steadily extended over the natural world? Art clearly doesn't go forward in that sense; Etruscan sculpture, the poems of Thomas Wyatt, and Dostoevsky's *Notes from the Underground* are as "modern" as we could wish, while we continue to be surrounded by newly created artifacts that give off an air of stale antiquity. More than that, isn't originality in art a cast of mind, a disposition toward one's materials, rather than the discovery of wholly new things? If anything, artistic originality is a *re*discovery; the avant-garde, Ionesco has said, is always returning to something that has been lost or forgotten.

And beyond that, the "new" in art is always a matter of form indissolubly wed to substance, a word I prefer to the more usual "content," which smacks of packing crates and gallon jars. Form, Etienne Gilson wrote, is "that on account of which a certain thing is the very thing it is," the best and most economical definition of that elusive entity I've ever come upon.

Technical changes, alterations of style, are never exercises in an emotional or spiritual void—that's the nature of *novelty*—but are intimately related to changes having to do with the objects of consciousness. The *methods* of consciousness, the ways in which the mind and imagination work, are changed by differently seen objects or processes, by what it is felt they require for their apprehension and formal rendering, as newcomers to modernity. New styles are always the result of new imaginative tasks, but the principle of aesthetic action—the defeat of habit, the prizing loose of the encrusted—remains constant.

Such new tasks require more or less sharp divergences from traditional methods, and this in turn implies a repudiation of the past, of *its* ways of noting, organizing, and inventing experience. These repudiations may or may not be accompanied by political agendas, and they may be belligerent and highly conscious, as, in the case of drama, was true of Strindberg, Pirandello, and Brecht, or implicit in an art unescorted by any manifesto or call to order, as was true of Beckett, and Chekhov as well.

For the playwrights I've mentioned, some or all of the perennial constituents of drama—plot, character, dialogue, conflict, dénouement, and so on—had through repetition and isolation from life outside the theater grown exhausted or sterile or simply irrelevant. The whole dramatic apparatus was out of coherence with what were seen or intuited by the best creating minds to be the present imaginative tasks of the stage, and the originality of these writers lay in revising or replacing that system of theatrical action. New kinds of dramatic construction arose periodically to challenge the familiar ones: the abandonment of sequential narrative in Büchner; a "cinematic" technique in Ibsen's *Peer Gynt*; the structures of dream in Strindberg; the stage in reciprocity with "reality" in Pirandello; plotlessness in Beckett.

Behind many of these departures from the familiar stands the figure of Shakespeare, to the point where in accordance with my idea of originality as a return we can say that after him innovation in the theater usually owes its provenance, directly or not, to something he did first; he has always been the generous provider of models for the new. Yet for several hundred years Shakespeare's influence had been blunted, ignored, or rejected, until it reasserted itself on Büchner, who wrote that compared to the great Englishman all writers confront "history and nature like schoolboys."[5] Even so, to *use* Shakespeare as a primary teacher was and is impossible, so great are the differences time has imposed. Chekhov was extremely well versed in Shakespeare, thoroughly familiar with a good range of the plays in translation, but never spoke of him as having in any way influenced his own style or, more subtly, his stances of perception; instead we can be sure that from Shakespeare he drew what we can call a kind of creative morale.

In every case the imaginative changes in drama presented themselves immediately, as altered technique, with effects that were startling, disorienting, and opaque. Alone among the great innovators Chekhov seemed to remain almost wholly within a more or less traditional mode of dramatic practice; my *plot* is unprecedented, he said, not my technique. But these things can't be separated. If Chekhov never seems to have pursued technical change as an immediate instrument of revived vision the way other theatrical radicals have done, if originality for him lay more in attitudes than in explicit material actions, he must surely have been aware that he couldn't simply compose a new plot without altering his means. If there is no existing model for your plot, your "story," at least not one within reach, then your techniques must also in some way be new.

And this is precisely true of *Ivanov,* a flawed play, not quite stable, leaning here or there toward excess or obscurity (although not nearly as much as did *Platonov,* Chekhov's earlier full-length play, which we'll look at in a little while), yet fascinating for the dramatic strengths it does have and because new methods of composition do show themselves, modestly, without fanfare, while the originality of plot, which is at the same time necessarily a changed conception of character and action, is allowed to declare itself openly.

Ivanov appears to have had one of its origins in Chekhov's wish to address himself to the question of the "superfluous man," a type of social being much discussed in Russian intellectual and political circles at this point late in the century. Such a person, usually an aristocrat or from the upper classes, with some level of higher education, was characterized as having a feeling of purposelessness, having nothing on which to exercise his talents, not belonging anywhere; in short he (there seems not to have been a comparably superfluous *woman*) was seen to be suffering from what we might now call a vague existential crisis, but a condition with definite sociological roots.

Critics, litterateurs, and amateur cultural analysts found this being's prototype in such fictional creations as Lermontov's Pechorin (in *A Hero of Our Time*), Turgenev's Rudin, and Goncharov's Oblomov, who gave birth to a name for the spiritual affliction of extreme inertia, "Oblomovitis." But the figure was also derived from other imaginative sources, notably Hamlet, a dramatic character for whom the Russian intelligentsia, so powerless in its social role in relation to the *real* powers during the period, felt a special affinity. Hamlet types are everywhere in nineteenth-century Russian literature and the name kept popping up in dinner-party conversations, without, however, anyone showing much understanding of Shakespeare's prince, who was seen mainly in his aspects of indecision, ineffectuality, and dour introspection, in other words as the clichéd Hamlet of conventional misreading. In *Ivanov* we will come upon several references to this sort of inadequately recognized Hamlet.

Far from wanting to add to the literary exploitation of the superfluous man, with his Hamlet variant, Chekhov had quite a different intention, having decided to try to dispose of so artificial a figure once and for all. The project was consistent with the long course of his work, for one of his recurrent themes in both fiction and drama is the way people so often construct their lives and those of others from literary models (today we do it more from movies and television) and so live falsely, within borrowed or invented selves and surrounded by them. These surrogate selves need not reflect us favorably; the point is that at least they make us and others more distinctive. Inept and overblown as *Platonov* mostly was, it had contained elements of this perception, and *Ivanov* contained even more.

The superfluous man was just such a literary invention, but what seems to have made it especially objectionable to Chekhov was that it shifted responsibility for one's behavior onto society: its rationale was that you or I act one way or another because our circumstances force us to. For Chekhov, a brilliant and concerned observer of social reality but a writer for whom personal being could never be wholly, or even substantially, accounted for by objective causes, this was an evasion, and he intended to expose it as one. But as he worked on the play (the first draft took him only a little over two weeks, it appears), he steadily transformed it into something much richer and far less thematically local. (Still, the figure would persist in his work, no longer a target but just another stroke of portraiture. A notable example is a major character in the long story "The Duel," written in 1891, who continually refers to himself, and others to him, as a superfluous man and a Hamlet.)

Ivanov's protagonist is a thirty-five-year-old landowner in an unnamed province of central Russia who for no apparent reason has lost his one-time enthusiasm, his energy, his moral bearings, and his self-esteem. "I used to work hard and think hard," he tells another character. "I never got tired. Now I do nothing and think nothing, but I'm tired body and soul." And again, "I'm quite ill. I'm irritable, bad-tempered and rude these days. . . . I hardly know myself." He is hard pressed financially, but this is a result, not a cause, of his malady, nor does the narrow life of the dull, frivolous, provincial society of which he is a prominent member begin to explain it.

Five years before the play opens he had married a young woman from a wealthy Jewish family (it was a bold, open-hearted act in those days for someone like Nikolai to do this); though we have every reason to believe him when he says he married for love, the charge of being a fortune-hunter pursues him throughout the play. Among the chief symptoms of his present anomie and moral drift is the way he treats his wife. Anna, who gave up her religion for Nikolai and was consequently disinherited by her parents, is suffering from tuberculosis and will die of it before the play ends. Tormented by demons he can neither locate nor name, Nikolai is unable to give her the attention and affection she so desperately needs, and this is the ground of bitter accusations hurled at him by a young doctor named Lvov, who has been staying on the estate and tending, hopelessly, to Anna.

Lvov, an earnest, high-minded, dedicated young man of a type familiar to the agitated social conscience of the time, is also, as we quickly learn, priggish and self-righteous. "Oh, he's virtue incarnate," someone says of him at one point, "can't ask for a glass of water or light a cigarette without displaying his remarkable integrity." Denouncing Ivanov for being "insensitive, selfish, cold and heartless," Lvov goes on to tell him that "someone who loves you is dying . . . she hasn't long to live, while you—you [are] so callous. . . . I do most thoroughly dislike you."

All Nikolai can say after a broadside like this is that he understands Lvov, feels "very much to blame" but simply can't extricate himself from the gloom, amounting more and more to despair, in which he's enveloped: "I feel paralyzed, half dead or something." The two men's exchanges continue, growing increasingly more irritating and painful to Nikolai as the dramatic action moves on.

This action concerns Nikolai's relations with Anna and Lvov, of course, but with some subsidiary characters too, chiefly the family of Pavel Lebedev, an older, kindly, not very bright neighboring landowner who is very much under the dominion of his shrewish wife. Their twenty-year-old daughter, Sasha, is in love with Ivanov, and after Anna's death he reluctantly agrees to marry her. In a final tumultuous scene just before the wedding is to take place, Lvov issues another denunciation of Ivanov, for the first time doing it in public. "Nikolai Ivanov," he calls out, "I want everyone to hear this. *You are the most unmitigated swine!*" Nikolai replies—"coldly," the stage direction advises—"I'm very much

Ivanov

41

obliged to you" and a moment later runs to the side of the stage and shoots himself. (In an earlier draft Chekhov had him dropping dead of a heart attack brought on by Lvov's blast.)

Such is the tale *Ivanov* tells us, its sequence of dramatic events, but the play's true, or truest, action, in Aristotle's sense of "the soul of the tragedy," is very different. This is the time for us to go back to Chekhov's excited assertion that his plot was unprecedented. What was unprecedented about it? What was so original? When he went on in his letter to say that he had not created any villain or any angel, he touched directly on the essence of the matter.

To see what this was, this first of the great shifts in purpose and vision and, indeed, as a consequence of these, changes in dramaturgical means, we have to put *Ivanov* itself aside for a time and go much further back, to the broad history of drama in Russia and elsewhere. We have, too, to look at Chekhov's first play, *Platonov,* the prelude to the prelude to a revolution.

The unheard of nature of *Ivanov*'s plot—unheard of, that's to say, since the demise of the tragic mode in drama several centuries before this time—was that it refused to revolve around the conventional division, or conflict, or tension between heroes and malefactors, more subtly between good and evil, and more subtly still between enlightenment and ignorance; these dualities, narrow and without resonance as they had come to be, had sustained the stage for generations. In all its variations, this Manicheanism had been the motivating principle of bourgeois drama, a theater which at its most serious we might call one of "false tragedy," tragedy in its outward or material form but empty of moral complexity and with all sense of ontological fatality having been removed.

In its other genres it was a theater in which little or no premium was placed on consciousness, which is a property or condition that might best be defined as the relationship between emotion and thought, or between experience and what we make of it. Broadly speaking, such a theater deals in ready-made emotions, experiences whose nature has been determined—labeled, we can almost say—in advance: love, hate, jealousy, contrition, desire, fear—all are presented and manipulated without having been examined and weighed, as the fixed currency of the melodramatic imagination. The other side of reigning nineteenth-century theater was spectacle, the substitution, however innocently contrived, of sensation for art (one can almost add: of sensation for *sense*). In lonely isolation some true dramas would be found to stand out from all this, and indeed such plays constituted the unofficial tradition of the new.

The Russian theater into which Chekhov was now moving could scarcely pretend to any sort of true seriousness or any iconoclastic verve. It lacked masters, an Ibsen, a Strindberg, even a Zola or a Hauptmann, not to mention, further back, a Shakespeare, Racine, Molière, or Calderón. It had no theoreticians, no innovative directors or acting companies with an identifiable aesthetic.

The fact was that theater as a formal enterprise had come into existence quite late in Russia, having begun to metamorphose from its origins in folk and religious ritual only in the second half of the seventeenth century, long after the stage was fully established in England and most of the Continent. When it did arrive in Moscow and St. Petersburg, theater was carried on almost wholly by practitioners from France, Germany, and later Italy. From its beginnings it was closely connected to the state and the tsarist court, a severely restrictive condition, one of whose constituents was a heavy and sometimes merciless censorship.

As something we might call an indigenous theater slowly developed, a few playwrights of talent emerged at long intervals: Denis Fonvizin, often called the "father" of Russian drama, in the 1770s, Alexander Griboyedov in the early 1820s. But it wasn't until 1831, when Pushkin's *Boris Godunov* was published, and, even more noteworthy, 1836, when Gogol's *Inspector General* was produced in Moscow, that Russia could speak of having a dramatist anywhere close in genius to the great European artist-playwrights. But Pushkin wrote only one full-length play and was far more influential as a poet, while Gogol's career was relatively thin and short-lived and he was followed on the stage by no one worth remembering.

A generation later, at the time of Chekhov's youth, the preeminent Russian playwright was Alexander Ostrovsky, whose somber dramas and broad comedies about contemporary life were often disfigured by sentimentality and were seldom revelatory on an imaginative plane; still, they were highly regarded for their "truthfulness" and, a weighty consideration in the self-conscious culture of the period, their "Russianness."

Apart from such scattered works of native provenance, the Russian stage in the 1870s and 1880s presented an occasional foreign classic by the likes of Shakespeare, Molière, or Schiller, but mostly it was filled with melodramas and domestic farces, either translated or adapted from the French or derived from French models, and with light dramatic sketches and vaudevilles. From all accounts acting was on an even lower, which is to say more declamatory, level than elsewhere in Europe, notions of directorial enterprise were nonexistent, and physical staging was usually crude or overblown. Historians of Russian theater like to describe this period as having seen the arrival of a fully mature native practice (how else could you account for Chekhov?), but all indications are that the theater Chekhov began to write for was in almost every one of its sectors a place of banality and contrivance.

Nearly fifty years before Chekhov wrote *Platonov*, Gogol had composed an anguished call to order for the theater. After an invocation to some colossi—"great" Molière, "stern" Lessing, and "noble" Schiller—he went on to denounce the corruption of the stage in Russia by the "monster . . . melodrama." "Where," he wrote, "is our life, ourselves with our own idiosyncracies and traits?" (These are almost the exact words Bernard Shaw would use a half-century later when he praised Ibsen for having given us "ourselves in our own situations.") "The melodrama is lying most impudently," Gogol continued. "Only a great, deep, rare genius can catch what surrounds us daily, what always accompanies us, what is ordinary—while mediocrity grabs with both hands all that is out of rule, what happens but seldom and catches the eye by its ugliness and disharmony. . . . The strange has become the subject matter of our drama. The whole point is to tell a new, strange, unheard-of incident: murder, fire, wild passions . . . poisons, effects, eternal effects!"[6]

It might seem odd for Gogol, whose own works were notable for their grotesque humor and depictions of extreme psychological states, to have invoked an ideal of the normative, the "ordinary." Yet the contradiction disappears when we understand that Gogol was asking for authenticity, fidelity to the truth of things, to existence's fundamental nature.

And what if reality is extreme and grotesque, as it surely was to Gogol? If it is, then those qualities lie in the very texture of ordinary life, "what always accompanies us," and for that reason are universal and aesthetically inevitable. What isn't universal and artistically necessary is the kind of melodramatic imagining which seizes on the exceptional, or sensational, for its purportedly intrinsic drama, its bizarre and incidental flair; to search exclusively for the exotic is to be blind to what inhabits the air around you. A century later Ionesco would voice much the same objection to fancy (in Coleridge's sense) in favor of imaginatively accurate perception when he remarked that formal surrealism was strained, arbitrary, and merely eccentric, because the truly surreal was what we experience every day, what lies at our feet.

Endorsing a dictum first enunciated by Tolstoy, Chekhov once observed that a writer was to be permitted the invention of any sort of reality except one—the psychological—and if we widen the precincts of that word to encompass all realities of the mind and spirit, as we can be sure Chekhov intended, that was what Gogol cared about. The "eternal effects" of which he complained are the perennial curse of the theater as an institution, the result of a failure of, or rather an incapacity for, psychological and spiritual perception.

What was substituted for dramatic visions based on psychological truth were systems of physical activity (including emotions converted into physicality, crude "objective correlatives"): acts of simulated violence, pretended passions, intrigues, material disasters—everything summed up under the rubric of "plot." All these gestures and movements passed themselves off as having been derived from experience, whereas in fact they were mostly appropriated from the history of the stage itself. What had once been true correlatives of human truths were now clichés, arid conventions, and, since the world had kept changing, untruths about its organization and dispositions. Of all the "lies" that the stage had been perpetrating during the long age of melodrama, the most persistent may have been the premise that the best way to apprehend life was to see it as a struggle between good and evil, light and darkness, in theatrical terms heroes and villains, together with the complementary idea that drama is physicality, the more violent the better. To look at *Platonov* is to see the powerful presence of such notions and practices of theater but at the same time to see them beginning to be questioned and overthrown.

Chekhov would turn out to be the "deep, rare genius" of the ordinary whom Gogol had called for, but on the evidence of his first play it would have taken a rather keen eye to predict it.

In 1923 the untitled manuscript of a hitherto unknown play by Chekhov turned up in an old desk in Moscow. It was soon published as *A Play without a Title in Four Acts,* and later a good deal was learned about its provenance. According to Chekhov's brother, Mikhail, who after Anton's death edited a collection of his letters, he had written the play "while a student"[7] in Moscow, which suggests 1881 or 1882 as the year of composition, a time when he had already begun to contribute sketches to humor magazines while he was working toward his medical degree.

Hoping to have it put on by the famous Maly Theater, he showed the play to the celebrated actress Yermolova (with whom he would later become good friends). We don't know her reaction, but in any event the theater rejected the play, upon which Chekhov seems—wisely, we're forced to decide—to have put it aside, or somewhere even more remote. It wasn't until some thirty years after its discovery that it had its first production, when in 1954 a version was done in Stockholm, an English translation of the Swedish title being *Poor Don Juan*. Since then it has appeared in various venues and, drastically shortened and almost always wretchedly "adapted," under a variety of names: *A Provincial Don Juan; Don Juan in the Russian Manner; A Country Scandal; Without Patrimony* (or *Without Fathers*); and *Wild Honey*—and has been published in its entirety in a workmanlike English translation by the indefatigable David Magarshack, who called it *Platonov,* the name of its central character, the Don Juan of all those other titles.

The first inescapable fact about the play is its extraordinary length, something close to the combined lengths of Chekhov's last three plays, *Uncle Vanya, Three Sisters,* and *The Cherry Orchard.* An uncut production—I don't know that there have ever been any—would theoretically last at least six hours. There are twenty characters with names (plus "servants," "guests," and so on), of whom no fewer than sixteen can be considered substantial, and they're involved in all sorts of intrigues and escapades, many of them sexual but also financial and what we might call logistical—people trying to get from one real or symbolic place to another. To try to summarize the action would be to go to work on a small encyclopedia of melodramatic situations, covering everything which Gogol had laid under anathema. Plots, subplots, and sub-subplots; farcical elements and pseudotragic ones; violence and jokes; complication upon complication—throw in enough, Chekhov's thinking seems to have been, and some of it is likely to work.

A character who appears near the end of Gogol's *Dead Souls* is called Platonov, and Chekhov may have borrowed the name. Gogol's man is described as "handsome and well-built," which fits Chekhov's protagonist too, but is also said to be "drowsy . . . a sleepy soul," which doesn't. Chekhov's Platonov is a twenty-seven-year-old former landowner who has fallen on hard times and is now a village schoolmaster but remains a principal figure in the tight, in-grown provincial society. A ferocious womanizer, a soi-disant existential sufferer, he never lets us forget how "weak" and "evil" he is and how "vile" and "filthy" is the world around him. An amoralist of a vaguely Gidean stripe, he has aspirations to Rabelaisian amplitude but is never allowed to escape his neurosis (or his obligations to the workings of melodrama) long enough to take on real size.

The exceedingly young and inexperienced Chekhov can barely hold on to this protagonist's presence and behavior, so the figure keeps slipping in and out of focus, all the time enacting a few understandable gestures and a great many inexplicable ones. Much of what he and others do has an arbitrary quality; events, most of which are physically or verbally violent, seem to occur independently of any pattern, so that dramatic coherence—the play as a possible unity in the mind—becomes mostly a matter of repetition and reminder: if you shout a thing often enough and keep pointing out connections, something of the drama's shape and sonorities might register.

In the end we're forced to conclude that the emotions *Platonov* traffics in and seeks to arouse, and the situations in which these emotions are displayed, stem largely from *ideas about drama,* the things an untaught, amateur, and at this point still heavily literary mind thinks it knows about the stage's purposes and procedures. Very little has been truly dramatized in an originating imagination. Which is another way of saying that the play is in great part derivative, taken from models Chekhov would a few years later, beginning with *Ivanov,* be on the way to repudiating. The crowning artistic indignity is the rankly melodramatic fatal shooting of Platonov at the end by one of the four women (one of them is his wife) with whom he's had or sought to have erotic involvements during the two or three weeks the stage action may be presumed to span.

A set of harsh judgments, to be sure, but having recorded them it remains for me to say that *Platonov* is far from being consistently embarrassing and is considerably more than a simple historical curiosity. Its connections to Chekhov's later work, to *Ivanov* and beyond, may be thin and sporadic, but they exist; its prevailing spirit may be highly "un-Chekhovian," but in scattered places its soul is one we can recognize with pleasure. Traces of the master to come, prehistoric footprints, foreshadowings of material elements, of style, and most subtly of what we might call intellectual dispositions; and one central clumsy first experiment with moral structure—all these are reasons for us to honor *Platonov.*

Some of the anticipations are remarkably specific. Musing about love, Platonov utters the same student's Latin exercise—"amo, amas, amat"—as Masha will in *Three Sisters.* Important characters are named Voynitsev, bringing to mind the Voynitskys of *Uncle Vanya.* A character offers the same quotation from *Hamlet*—"Nymph, in thine orisons . . . "—as Lopakhin will in *The Cherry Orchard.* A woman fends off her hand being kissed in much the same way Carlotta will in that play.

More broadly, there are obvious ties to *Ivanov*—the Hamlet theme and that of unaccountable malaise, the incestuous provincial society; a thematic or at least narrative connection to *The Cherry Orchard* in that in both plays an estate is sold; lines extending to all the later plays in *Platonov*'s sketchy suggestions of the great Chekhovian questions and motifs of work, love, the future.

Anticipations of style are, naturally, more fragmentary and elusive. Chekhov's talent here has very little command of its domain and it often seems that he's nearly unconscious of the way he exercises choice. But we can notice the beginnings of procedures that will begin to consolidate in *Ivanov* and then flower in the later plays. Consider the structure of dialogue in certain sections of *Platonov*. In a greatly tentative way and far from consistently, dramatic utterance departs here from the conventions of the stage by refusing to obey principles of orderly progression, what we might call conversational logic. A speech doesn't necessarily elicit another in a cause-and-effect pattern, bits of talk are left hanging, and seemingly disconnected fragments slide away from one another in the unstable dramatic space.

There is a German term for this kind of speech, *aneinandervorbeisprechen,* which can be translated as "talking past one another," and the phenomenon first appears as a literary practice in the plays of Büchner in the early nineteenth century; Strindberg later practiced something similar in the dialogue of his most important plays. It was without knowing this model and with an untutored genius that Chekhov began to construct stage speech that replaced artificially pat, "reasonable" sequences. This hugely important stylistic mode is in its infancy in *Platonov*, but Chekhov was clearly reaching back to that play when, with *Ivanov,* he began to make it a major way of composition.

Another element of strategy of which *Platonov* makes rudimentary use is the famous Chekhovian pause, so often misunderstood. In Chekhov the pause is something we might call "silent speech." It serves sometimes ironically to contradict what has just been said and sometimes to undermine what is about to be said; it suggests questions, supplies by implication whatever for one reason or another can't be directly acknowledged, provides a fertile space in which characters and audience alike can prepare responses, becoming alert to unexpectedness, to nuance. An example: Platonov tells one of his inamorate, "If I had the strength I should have torn you up . . . from this swamp and myself as well. (Pause.) Life! Why don't we live it as we should?" In that pause we hear his inner turmoil but also a degree of pomposity and a note of impending romantic self-dramatization.

And then there are what I earlier called intellectual dispositions. I'm think-ing of Chekhov's wit, his dark perceptions and lyric moods. Widely scattered in *Platonov,* not issuing from any organic scheme or cohesive tone, they decorate the writing like slivers of the rich textures of the later work. I pluck out a handful:

"A man who's ashamed of his youth is no poet," Platonov says.

"She's the only woman from whom my carnal desires rebound like peas off a wall," a character says.

"Who gave you the right to thrust your cold paws into people's hearts?" someone asks Platonov.

He asks his wife, "Who will you cook dinner for? Whose soup will you put too much salt in?"

Anna, one of his lovers, says to him, "Aren't you ashamed to lie, darling? On such a night and under such a sky—to tell lies? Tell lies in the autumn if you must, when the ground's covered in mud and slush, but not now."

"I'm a polygamist," Platonov says. "A great rogue from the point of view of the family as an institution."

Platonov while delirious: "Little soldiers in chintz uniforms and pointed caps are flashing before my eyes. . . . There's a tiny baby piano crawling along on your bosom, Anna."

Strewn about, isolated, little chunks of disconnected insight, wit, and mu-sic, at times surrealistic before Surrealism, such writing augurs a future when the creating mind will have come into far larger shaping powers, as well as into thematic purpose and clarity such as the Chekhov who wrote this play can only make stabs at.

Whatever he thought of *Platonov* he could never have claimed for it the originality he so rightly saw in his *Ivanov.* The earlier play was too deeply mired in melodramatic situations, which by definition are conventional. Yet at the level of a governing moral idea the two plays do share something. *Ivanov*'s originality lay in its refusal to offer the familiar structure of hero versus villain, and while the earlier play doesn't at all succeed in eliminating that structure, it tinkers with it, knocks it around a bit, and so, perhaps only half consciously, prepares the way for an eventual complete demolition. (In the same way *Platonov* doesn't do very much to challenge the Hamlet figure as a literary stereotype, but it at least introduces a note of scepticism about it. "You all seem to think [Platonov] a second Hamlet," a character says, with an implication that maybe they should all reexamine their ascriptions.)

In *Platonov* heroism and villainy are parceled out among a number of characters, but Platonov himself clearly works the most harm, while there are quite a few faces of innocence. The incipient strain of originality lies in Chekhov's making the moral realities into a question instead of settling them in advance. A character says to Platonov, "You are either an extraordinary sort of person or—a scoundrel, either one or the other." Most of the time it's rather hard for us to decide, for Platonov's undeniable charm exerts an influence, although in the end his rascality does win out. But the point is that we've been seduced by the traditional antithesis—he's either good or bad—because Chekhov hasn't lifted the drama past those moral categories and into a more absorbing dimension of inquiry into the agitations of knowing and its pretensions.

The distance Chekhov has come from *Platonov* can be measured in part by the way he jettisons so much of the legacy of melodrama. In *Ivanov* he refuses to play God, leaves demands for explanations, those expectations of the bourgeois audience, unsatisfied, and while looking at experience with shrewd perceptiveness offers no solutions to its dilemmas and no moralizing summations, such as the banal one Anna pronounces near the end of *Platonov:* "He's not the only one to blame! We're all to blame . . . all of us have passions and none of us has the strength to resist them." Or the even less convincing judgment that another character intones over the dead Platonov: "Why did you sin, you old clown? Killed God's own creatures, drank, swore, condemned people. . . . The Lord couldn't put up with it any more and struck you down."

Chekhov tells a story in *Ivanov,* the one we traced earlier, but the play's true "plot" is a series of moral and aesthetic decisions, the two united in the imagination, which work to sabotage literary and theatrical expectations while establishing an unfamiliar—unprecedented—dramatic proposal in the space that's been cleared away.

In this specific case, as we know from the pattern of responses to *Ivanov,* the chief expectation was clear. Since Nikolai seemed to fit the description of a superfluous man, it was thought that he would behave according to pattern, in coherence with the recognized "type," and that the play itself would offer insights into the social conditions that had spawned him. Nothing like this takes place, for Nikolai can't be labeled. By refusing either to blame or exonerate his protagonist, Chekhov strategically deprives him of any fixed moral status, and by denying social conditions any measurable causal role he strips the play of tendentious theorizing, as we shall see.

When it was first performed at the Korsh Theater in Moscow in December 1887 and soon afterwards published, the response was a jumble: enthusiasm, bewilderment, in some quarters scorn. That the production was badly underrehearsed and, from all accounts, execrably performed made matters worse.

But Chekhov was perhaps more disturbed by some of the praise the play was given, which he felt had been bestowed for the wrong reasons and betrayed a lack of understanding. He rewrote a good deal, including the ending, so that when *Ivanov* was performed again, a little over a year later in St. Petersburg, it was closer to his intentions. Whether or not the public and the intelligentsia grasped things any better, this production was greeted with much acclaim.

Looking closely at the text now, we can see that Chekhov accomplishes his primary artistic objective through several intricately related means. His task is to present his central character neutrally, without authorial judgment, yet at the same time—and this is obviously of great importance—with ample material for a potentially harsh verdict, for if Nikolai were himself a neutral or unprovocative character the dramatist's withholding of judgment would have no weight or point. No, Nikolai is "objectively" guilty of acting in a cruel and perverse manner, but whether he is morally guilty is another matter, while the relation between his present misanthropy and his larger or more enduring self is still another, most suggestive one.

Opinions about Nikolai are therefore all limited, unreliable, and even prejudicial, whether issued by the other characters or by himself. "I'm just a nasty, miserable nobody," he lets us know, alone on stage. "God, how I despise myself. How I loathe my own voice, footsteps, hands—these clothes, my thoughts." The soliloquy is strongly reminiscent of Hamlet's "Oh, what a rogue and peasant slave am I" speech, but something more fundamental than their similarity of tone and rhetoric unites the two discourses. In both cases, as we know from the plays' whole contexts, the speaker isn't offering any absolute view of himself, anything we can take as definitive. This is an *aspect* of my truth, each is in effect saying, it's how I feel at this moment. Their self-loathing is partial and temporary, one element of their complete consciousnesses, their histories and dramatic circumstances. (Platonov is unlike either Ivanov or Hamlet; his self-disgust isn't temporary or situational but permanent and absolute, as well as being coerced by the requirements of melodrama.)

For both Shakespeare and Chekhov, so much the "smaller" dramatist, so much more prosaic and bounded, yet so close to his great predecessor in artistic intuitiveness and imaginative acuity, for these two the "truths" of a work can never reside in discrete elements—particular speeches, especially significant actions, and the like—but are dispersed throughout the whole: a play is an organism, not a piece of machinery. Like Hamlet, to whom several characters foolishly, because romantically, compare him, Nikolai escapes easy understanding; like the prince he moves in and out of shifting lights, presents successive sides of his nature, different eras of his personality, exists in a theatrical context where action and acting are reciprocal, is protean, surprising, and not to be pinned down.

But the butterfly-chasers are after him, nets at the ready, not only Lvov but also Borkin, Nikolai's cheating, unsavory estate manager, who is especially incensed by his employer's neglect of business—"Why, you whining neurotic—if you were a normal man you could be a millionaire in a year"—and Lebedev's wife, whose own grasping temperament induces her to spread the charge that Nikolai married Anna for her money, was violently disappointed, and is now trying the same thing in regard to the Lebedevs' daughter, Sasha.

Lvov's successive screeds are at first met by Nikolai with weary admissions of blame and attempts at explanations, or at least descriptions of his state of mind. "You tell me she'll soon die," he says, " but I don't feel love or pity, just a sort of emptiness and exhaustion." He patiently points out Lvov's youth and consequent inexperience, then, with more than a touch of extremely pertinent irony, tells him, "You may well be right, you can judge so much better, not being involved." But as Lvov presses his indictment, Nikolai grows increasingly exasperated and at last says to the doctor, in words we can think of as constituting the chief experiential rubric under which Chekhov's vision is organized in this play, "You think I'm an open book, don't you . . . man's such a simple, uncomplicated mechanism."

Ivanov is anything but an open book, and his criticism of Lvov for thinking of him that way is in the spirit of Hamlet's warning to Rosencrantz and Guildenstern not to try to "play" him. (Once again Hamlet and Ivanov are linked, but the points of connection are as much points of differentiation; Chekhov is undermining the easy assumptions of cultural identification.) The episode, for that matter the whole play, reflects Chekhov's profound distrust of the knowledge we think we have of others and ourselves. "We all have too many wheels, screws and valves to judge each other" so easily, Nikolai says to Lvov. Theater as an institution designed in its serious modes precisely to arrive at such knowledge is therefore full of the temptation to play seer and mind reader, and Chekhov's own dramatic practice, here beginning to reach maturity, will work as a subversive counterforce to that impulse.

Nikolai has his defenders, too, the upholders of what they see, accurately or not, as his essential self, which his present behavior cannot abolish or replace with a convenient label. Not surprisingly, they include Sasha, who, however, sees Nikolai romantically, through a gaze tempted by literature, as a noble suffering soul. In a scene bright with wit as well as rueful emotion, she says to him: "I understand you, Nikolai, you're unhappy because you're lonely. You need someone near you that you love and who'll appreciate you. Only love can make a new man of you."

To this adolescent notion, as Nikolai regards it (as does Chekhov, who mocks or deflates it in its various forms in a number of his stories, and, more obliquely, in the later plays, as we'll see), he replies: "Now really, Sasha. For a bedraggled old wreck like me to start a new love affair, that would be the last straw. God save me from such a disaster." A little further on when Sasha, "joking, through tears," an unmistakably Chekhovian action, says to him, "Let's run away to America," he answers, "I'm too lazy to go as far as that door and you want me to go to America."

To smile or laugh "through tears" or to cry through an ostensible joke is so revelatory of one of Chekhov's methods—no, it's sometimes inadequate to call it that; one of the ways he apprehends human feeling, then—that we ought to stop for a moment to consider it. (In book 6 of *The Iliad* we find the image "smiling through her tears," but this has few counterparts elsewhere in literature, as far as I know.)

Ordinarily, though we speak of "laughing until we cry" and of "tears of joy" we think of the two actions as separate, and even the exceptions I've cited maintain that separation. To laugh until we cry is a physiological phenomenon, not an emotional one; we're not made sorrowful by the laughter. To weep for happiness is similarly not to have "mixed emotions," as it might appear, but to have a primary one, the joy, which the tears accompany as a secondary act to express not sorrow but relief, a reaction to something we've been spared or surprisingly gained.

Ivanov

53

But in Chekhov when laughter and tears come together they're fused, the experience is simultaneously both pleasurable and melancholy, usually in equal measure. Two aspects of the self are instantaneously brought together; the tears and the laughter *reflect* on each other, so to speak, offering different or opposing forms of awareness. Sasha weeps through her "joke" because she knows it's a hopeless fantasy; she jokes through her tears in an effort momentarily to dispel the sorrow she feels at Nikolai's refusal of her passion.

Later he chides her more directly for her romantic ardor: "My whining fills you with awe and you think you've found a second Hamlet. . . . You should laugh yourself silly at my antics, not sound the alarm-bell." (A memory here of *Platonov*. The difference is that in the earlier play the central figure has no such ironic sense of his own status as a product of community myth making.) And again, "In love, out of love, can't help one's feelings—that talk's so cheap and vulgar." Then, just before the wedding ceremony is to begin he uses her to make it as clear as he can that he has no self-pity and no illusions (another difference from *Platonov*). "Laziness is laziness," he tells Sasha, "weakness is weakness—I can't find other names for them." Yet despite her distorted or inadequate perception of Nikolai, Sasha would be on the side of the angels if Chekhov, as we remember, had not written a play without a single one of them.

In contrast to Sasha, Anna retains a clear sense of Nikolai, of what he was like before his present beleaguerment and in spite of the anguish he is causing her now. In one painful scene which moves between his embarrassment, bewilderment, and shame at the way he's been treating her and her own attempts to understand the situation and to win him back, she calls on lyrical memories of how it once was. The speech beautifully modulates among passion, sorrow, and appeals to homely little actions as the repositories of love, and for this reason it is very much worth quoting in full:

> Look, Nikolai, why not try singing, laughing and losing your temper, as you did in the old days. You stay in. We'll laugh, drink home-made wine and cheer you up in no time. Shall I sing? Or shall we go and sit in the dark as we used to, and you can tell me all about how depressed you are. Your eyes are full of suffering. I'll look into them and cry, and we'll both feel better. (Laughs and cries.) What is it, Nikolai? Flowers come round every spring, but happiness doesn't—is that it? All right, go then.

In another brilliant dramatic moment, all the more effective for being in a minor key, Anna turns on Lvov, her advocate, moving the ever-swaying moral indicator back toward her husband. Again I quote nearly in full:

Ivanov

Never talk to a woman about your good points, let her see those for herself. At your age Nikolai only sang and told stories in women's company, but everyone could see what he was really like . . . he never said things like "I'm honest, this air chokes me, vampires, owl's nest, crocodiles" [epithets Lvov had laid on the ingrown community]. He left out the zoology and all I heard from him when he got annoyed was: "I was so unfair today" or "I'm sorry for that man, Anna." That's how he was, but you—.

If Chekhov has conceived Nikolai in part as a figure to undermine comfortable assumptions about Hamlet-types, superfluous men and the like, he has fashioned Lvov partly as a demystification of another prevailing stereotype, this one more rooted in social actuality, if no better understood. This was the *narodnik,* loosely the sort of person, almost always young and usually well educated, who took a passionate interest in social problems, was committed to abstractions such as the "peasantry" and "reform," and in general went about, like Lvov, with an ardent sense of his or her own virtue, though the stereotype wasn't designed to reveal that. (Among several Chekhov stories in which narodniki figure are "Peasants" and "Good-for-Nothings.")

We have seen Lvov taken down by both Nikolai and Anna for his moralism and for being so full of himself, but perhaps the most incisive revelation of his personality occurs in an extremely off-handed, barely noticeable way. In one of their encounters Lvov says to Nikolai, "What you're doing is killing her. (Pause.) Let me think better of you, Nikolai." In that stage direction, the pause, and in the words that immediately follow it we see expressed, with the economy of which Chekhov was to become such a sovereign, a whole hitherto hidden side of the young doctor. He has in effect accused Nikolai of being a murderer. Now in the space before he speaks again, within the pause, something rushes into his consciousness, the sense he wishes to have of himself. Let *me* think better of you, he says, as if also to say, support *me* in my eagerness to have the world match my ideals, serve *me* for my self-esteem. Characterization could not be swifter or more assured, and this is the sort of economical stroke of perception which Chekhov's later plays will present in such abundance.

Even so, Lvov is not the villain of the piece, as Nikolai certainly isn't its "hero." Predictably, early responses to the play strongly indicated a wish for more decisive characterizations than Chekhov had given. As I've suggested, both popular and critical disappointment and perplexity lay mainly in his not having laid enough blame on Nikolai and not having portrayed Lvov with more sympathy. In other words, stereotypical expectations at first prevented people from seeing what was really there, from seeing what Chekhov had rightly called his originality. Even his younger brother, Mikhail, urged him to rewrite the two main characters so as to bring them more into line with the conventions of drama, most pertinently that of hero versus villain.

Mikhail wanted Anton to have greater popular success and Chekhov of course rejected such well-meaning but naive advice. Then in an immensely interesting exchange of letters he also rejected advice of an opposite kind. Make Lvov broader, more culpable, he was told by Alexei Suvorin, his friend and publisher, who was for the most part one of his most intelligent readers. Chekhov wrote back that for all of Lvov's moralistic zeal and frequent obnox-iousness, he was by no means contemptible. The doctor, he told Suvorin, "is a type of the honest, direct, ardent, narrow and rectilinear man. . . . He will, if need be, throw a bomb under a carriage [a reference to the assassination of Tsar Alexander II by a young radical in 1881], give some inspector one in the snout, won't hesitate to call a man a scoundrel. . . . Such people are needed. . . . To caricature them . . . is dishonest."[8]

The key words are "rectilinear," with its suggestion of conduct strictly defined and undertaken, and "necessary." The closest Chekhov usually comes to the portrayal of outright villainy is to depict narrow lives, ones that unfold like crisply creased paper or stay folded entirely (the short story "Man in a Case" is an especially deft treatment of this sort of person), or are marked by obsession, self-reference, or some dominant appetite. Such lives are necessary, though; without them a scantiness of human variety would exist, a pallor and undifferentiation.

Chekhov even tells Suvorin that Lvov has a likable side, as indeed Ivanov himself allows when he says to his unhappy, witty old uncle, Shabelsky (there's a landowner of that name in a story Chekhov had written not long before, "Bad Weather"), that "I find him terribly trying but I do quite like him—he's so sincere." That Nikolai should speak at all well of his tormentor, granted that it's at an early stage of their connection, can be seen as an example of Chekhov's legendary "fairness," but it's also an element of his design, for simply by suggesting that the doctor may have some redeeming qualities he lends him an ambiguity second only to Nikolai's own.

The movement of balances and shifting perspectives continues. Chekhov has Shabelsky jump on Nikolai's word of praise: "A nice sort of sincerity," he says, ". . . this dull quack would be tickled pink—he'd feel he'd attained his life's ambition—if he got the chance to bash my face in in public or hit me below the belt in the name of principles and humane ideals." Nikolai doesn't reply to this but Lebedev, who's been in on the conversation, does—soothingly and, we should note, as a Chekhovian tactic. "Young men," he says, "always do have some bee in their bonnet . . . my uncle was a follower of Hegel." The dialogue here exemplifies Chekhov's method of a continual deflection of absolutes, offsetting certain weights by others, not allowing linear progressions of theme or characterization to coerce us toward fixed conclusions.

If there isn't any moral dualism in *Ivanov*, neither is there a theme of conflict between the individual and society. Only once does Chekhov even bring up social conditions as a possible factor in Nikolai's psychic distress, and then only to dismiss it out of hand. Late in the play Nikolai asks Lebedev, "Pavel, what's wrong with me?" After replying that he has "no idea," the good-natured, rather simple Lebedev, as though struck by a sudden thought, says ("eagerly," the stage direction has it), "You know what? Your environment's got you down." To which Nikolai curtly replies, "That's silly and it's been said before."

We should notice that this dismissal functions on two levels. No doubt such a diagnosis as Lebedev's has been offered to Nikolai before this (although not in the text), but it has also been pronounced many times in the Russia of the period about people supposedly like him; it's a cliché of cultural and psychological analysis which Chekhov has Nikolai wave away for being tired and irrelevant. This is an early example of another of Chekhov's quietly inventive procedures. The most democratic of playwrights, he lets his characters offer all sorts of opinions on all sorts of subjects but scarcely ever sides with any of them. Beyond that, he very often has one character shoot down another's point of view, the way Ivanov does Lebedev's. The result is that opinions—usually made up of uninformed, derivative "slants" on things, as they are for us too— lie strewn all over the scenes of his plays while the encompassing dramatic visions establish themselves in dominion over all particular perspectives—intellectually shabby as these usually are, but in any case *partial.*

But if the human environment isn't the cause of Nikolai's illness, what about its quality all the same? Chekhov doesn't ignore it; from various characters we learn that the prevailing atmosphere in this provincial place is just what we would have expected: it's boring. "Lord, I'm bored," says a rich widow named Babakin, and Shabelsky is even more emphatic: "I'm bored, bored stiff." Then, in a scene to which I'll return in a moment, Sasha berates a group of guests at her parents' house: "Don't you ever get tired of sitting around like this? The very air's stiff with boredom. . . . If you don't want to dance or laugh or sing, if you're bored with that, then please . . . for once in your lives . . . join forces and think up something brilliantly witty."

Boredom so often figures in Chekhov's plays (in only the second line of *Platonov* a character speaks of things being "a bit boring"), and in his stories too, that we ought to take a closer look at it. Is boredom, ennui, a propensity to yawn, one of Chekhov's subjects? Does he, that is, regard it as one of the determining conditions of his characters' lives? One central strain of Chekhov criticism has always insisted that he does so regard it. The argument is usually nestled in among related propositions: that in all his work, under cover of his characters, he was pointing out, lamenting, or, to put it most strongly—as Maxim Gorky did in a celebrated and thoroughly ill-founded observation— indicting the Russian people's "weakness," their "defeatedness" and, as a sort of anticlimactic defectiveness, their "inability to communicate."

I will take up these fatal misreadings—I don't think the adjective is too strong—in more detail in the chapters on *Uncle Vanya* and *Three Sisters,* where they're most damaging; for the moment it's enough to say that Chekhov's characters are only helpless in certain, almost always inescapable circumstances, that they're defeated only according to suspect criteria, and that they communicate only too well, although only the things their creator wants them to, not what some of his critics think they should.

Boredom is undeniably an element in many of the characters' lives, part of the weather, an aspect of their fates. But it isn't a fate in itself, it doesn't define these invented people, any more than being melancholy does, or frustrated in love, or thwarted in their ambitions. That boredom shows itself in life is on one level a sociological observation on Chekhov's part, one more datum for his imagination to work with; on another plane it provides a backdrop against which other things make themselves known.

Going deeper, though, something else becomes clear. Pirandello once pointed out the enormous difference for a writer between presenting an image of chaos and presenting chaotically. In the same way boredom in Chekhov is never itself boring; if anything, it's usually highly, subtly interesting: as a protest of the soul in its confines, a comment on whatever constitutes *not being bored,* a tiny, oblique revelation of the void.

Even this isn't all, so flexible a notion is boredom, so amenable to tactical deployment. In the story "A Woman's Kingdom," Chekhov several times uses the word "boring" or "bored" to indicate something very different from tedium. A young woman inherits a factory and is made uneasy and guilty by her sudden wealth. Faced with the importunities of scroungers and the flattery of subordinates, she thinks, "How boring and alien all this [is]." In the context "boring" has nothing like its ordinary meaning but serves to block from the woman knowledge of her real mental state: the whole situation is much too unpleasant to think about.

Again, in the story "The Duel" we come upon the following: "Nikodim's hair brushed down over his temples and Katya's red cheeks struck him as such an immense, crushing bore that he was ready to cry out in despair." Whatever lies behind oppressiveness on such a scale as this, we can be sure it isn't ennui!

Something very similar to these maskings of emotion goes on in the scene in *Ivanov* in which Sasha scolds the guests. She has been listening to several people, of whom her own mother is one, accuse Nikolai of being a swindler, and she jumps to his defense. "Oh, that's all nonsense," she says, "nonsense . . . he's been robbed and fleeced right and left—anyone who likes has made a bundle out of Ivanov's idealistic plans." Her father, fondly, it's clear, says, "Shut up, you little spitfire," upon which she asks, "Why must they speak such nonsense?" Then, without anything intervening to explain the shift, she exclaims, "Oh, it's boring, boring, boring. Ivanov, Ivanov, Ivanov—is there nothing else to talk about?" and in the next breath launches into her tirade against the others for finding everything so boring.

What is going on in this agitated little scene? How are we to read it? Sasha surely isn't bored with Ivanov or by the mention of his name. Quite the contrary; she finds him endlessly fascinating. There *is* "nothing else to talk about," as far as she's concerned; in every other scene she's in she literally talks about no one else. But the others don't know him as she thinks she does; they've gone and invented a rascally Nikolai, as gossips will do, so as to have something colorful and diverting to talk about. This doesn't *bore* Sasha, it offends her, but by calling it all "boring" she accomplishes two things: she throws at them an epithet they deserve and she preserves her secret, which she was on the verge of giving away: her passion for Nikolai, which she hasn't yet revealed, even to him. Throughout Chekhov's plays and stories we will come upon scenes like this where something is hidden behind something else, language masking its intentions, and characteristically, as in this episode, he leaves it to us to sort matters out.

Ivanov

But even when boredom is real, a true affliction, Chekhov sees its potentiality for dramatic interest. In his supple use of this "negative" quality or experience he resembles Beckett, with whom he has so many other affinities. Beckett once said that he dealt with a "whole zone of being that has always been set aside by artists as unusable," conditions like "ignorance and impotence," to which we can add failure, weakness, and surely boredom too.[9] Like Chekhov before him, Beckett built his dramas out of the seemingly undramatic.

In *Ivanov* Chekhov is not yet sure enough of his powers to manage this without stumbling back from time to time into a coarser, much more obvious kind of dramaturgy. Earlier I spoke of the play's melodramatic ending, to which I'll come back later, but there are several other events and presences which are likely to embarrass us by their theatrical crudity.

Act Two ends in just such a way. Sasha has maneuvered Nikolai into a corner, overwhelming him with such extravagant declarations of love—"I'll follow you to the ends of the earth"—that he momentarily succumbs, carried away by an uncharacteristic spasm of irresponsibility and groundless hope. He kisses her and then, while still in one another's arms, they "look round" and see Anna watching them from the doorway. "Sarah!" (Anna's Jewish real name) Nikolai cries out "in horror" as the curtain falls.

The scene much resembles the ending of Act One of Ibsens's *Ghosts,* where Mrs. Alving hears Oswald scuffling erotically in the dining room with Regina. And indeed, just as Ibsen (about whom Chekhov seems to have been of two minds, alternately admiring his work—of which he'd read some in translation—and judging it harshly) at this stage of his career still felt the need to finish up all his acts with a suspenseful bang (the orphanage on fire!), so Chekhov, one foot lifted from the theatrical past but the other still slipping and sliding within it, wasn't able to resist the temptation to "grab" his audience in a way he would later have thoroughly scorned. As he wrote to his brother Alexander in October 1887, "I conclude each act as if it were a short story; after having kept the whole act very quiet and peaceful, I suddenly give the spectator a punch in the face."[10]

Other melodramatic lapses or excesses include the prominent presence on Nikolai's desk as Act Three begins of several revolvers, an unsubtle portent of the suicide or at least of some violent action to come. (One of Chekhov's best-known dicta was that if you show a pistol on stage it ought to be used; after *Ivanov* he would obey the precept in *Uncle Vanya,* where, to the relief of the muse of drama, a gun goes off but nothing is hit, and ignore it in *The Cherry Orchard,* where several guns are brandished but not fired.)

Much more serious is a late scene in which Anna accuses Nikolai of never having loved her and of having lied about many things. "I've never lied to you, Anna," he says, truthfully we feel sure, but she persists, giving way at last to an understandable amalgam of anger and desolation. For the only time in the play she forgets his true nature, and now Nikolai, made frantic by the injustice and, at the deepest point, the unreality of her words, turns on her violently: "Stop this . . . or I'll say something I shouldn't . . . something horribly insulting. (Shouts.) Shut up, you Jewish bitch!" (In order to catch the full force of the insult, Ronald Hingley translates in this way what in Russian is literally "Shut up, Jewess!"—something that misleadingly sounds more neutral to our ears; but *Zhidovka* may also legitimately, and pointedly here, be rendered as "kike.") But he's not finished. After she comes at him again he tells her that "you'll soon be dead. The doctor told me you can't last long." The scene and the act end with Nikolai "clutching his head" and saying, "What a thing to do! God. I am a brute. (Sobs.)"

At no other time does Nikolai act anything like so cruelly to Anna, so that the scene comes dangerously close to wiping out our sympathy for him. (I clearly remember the shocked gasps from the audience at Nikolai's words in each of the five different productions of *Ivanov* I've seen.) Yet after wavering for a bit on the edge of a repudiation we step back, conscious of Anna's having provoked him beyond endurance by attacking his integrity, which, after all, has been the basis of our not having condemned him before this.

Still, the risks of bathos in the scene are obviously high, and Chekhov doesn't entirely overcome them. Nikolai's "clutching his head" and calling himself a brute, for example, are not exactly triumphs of the dramatic imagination. Yet something is at work to keep the play in balance, something that would have been impossible for the author of *Platonov;* Chekhov has managed here a very delicate structure of composition whose effects are to curb the scene's tendency to inflate and even somewhat to lessen its horror.

After Nikolai's outrageous epithet, Anna reacts in a way wholly unlike what we would have expected. Instead of responding with "How dare you speak to me like that!" or "You see, that's what you really think of me!" or any other similarly conventional and in the context understandable (yet nevertheless overheated) riposte, she ignores the words, rushing in to say, "I will not shut up." The implication, which we have to seize on the wing, is that she doesn't regard the insult as a decisive blow but rather absorbs it without comment, taking it as a piece of temporality, part of the vocabulary of their present quarrel, not as a proof of her husband's innate and permanent beastliness.

In much the same way, her reaction to his telling her she's going to die soon (she hasn't admitted it to herself yet) isn't anguished or hysterical but greatly understated and therefore all the more poignant. She simply "sits down" and "in a sinking voice" asks, "when did he [Lvov] say that?"

Nikolai doesn't answer her question and during the "pause" that follows, before he expresses his self-loathing, we're left to imagine Anna's thoughts. Whatever they may be—perhaps something along the lines of "So, it's true, then, I'm going to die," or maybe some sorrowful memories of her earlier life— they don't include hatred of Nikolai for having so callously told her about her impending death. If she did feel hatred or any other emotion pertinent to Chekhov's design, we can be sure that he would have had her express it, in words or through some tell-tale gesture. In which case the design would have been different.

One more note on the scene. Immediately after Nikolai's breast-beating, with Anna sitting silently on the bench, the curtain comes down and a stage direction tells us that "About a year passes between Act Three and Act Four." For the reader of the text the direction serves to place at a distance the unsettling business we've just been put through, covering it over with the quietness of unoccupied time. And even in performance once the audience is made aware of the interval, a retroactive muting makes itself felt.

All these are small matters, nuances, but on that account can they not be the stuff of theatrical revolution? Only someone accustomed to thinking of revolution as violent, incendiary, full of upheaval would be likely to regard these nuances as tame. In its root meaning the word "revolution" is simply a "turning" or "turning around," and Chekhov brought this to the theater as surehandedly as any dramatist ever has. As he first began to make it known in *Ivanov*, his own theatrical turning was in the direction of absence: things withheld, the implicit where we would have expected the overt, discontinuities, leaps, gaps, breaks in dramatic logic. Let us look at some other examples of Chekhov's new techniques, so modestly employed in this play that we tend to pass right by them.

The third scene of Act One begins with Nikolai and Borkin on stage. Shabelsky comes out of the house with Lvov, chattering away in a speech about doctors and lawyers to which neither Lvov nor either of the others makes any reply or gives any indication of even having heard. The next scene has Shabelsky walking onto an empty stage and talking to himself, presumably about Borkin: "He's more than a petty crook, honestly—he's a virtuoso, a genius. We should put up a statue to him." The eleventh scene of Act Two consists in its entirety of two guests at the Lebedev house walking across the stage and exchanging a few words about their search for something to eat. Near the end of Act Two a guest named Kosykh crosses the empty stage muttering about a bridge game: "I had the ace, king, queen, and seven small diamonds." He will talk this way again and has almost no other kinds of speech.

Where is the oddness in these things? What could possibly make them worthy of our special attention? The strangeness lies in their lack of narrative context, in their not having been prepared for and not being followed up. They don't contribute directly to the plot but exist discretely, for their own sake or rather for the sake of a governing texture and design, not as links in a chain of cause and effect. For a long time dramatic construction had basically been of this kind: an action logically, that's to say connectedly, giving rise to another, dialogue eliciting responses which in turn incite new dialogue. But Chekhov is moving tentatively in *Ivanov* to create a dramatic *field* rather than a linear progression.

Such stock devices as the soliloquy and the aside might seem to invalidate my claim that these Chekhovian actions are new. But is this so? As conventions, the aside and the soliloquy have been given permission, so to speak, to exist for a time outside the pure narrative flow of the drama, which waits patiently to resume its course. (Or, when the necessary skill is lacking, not so patiently; *Platonov* has a number of awkward and intrusive asides.) In Chekhov, however, the "interruptions" take place *within* the flow, becoming little islands of discontinuity that have the effect, very small and even casual as it may be in *Ivanov*, of opening up the play, loosening the grip of an otherwise inexorable march toward a climax. It should be clear that this is in the service of Chekhov's wish or impulse to write a play along lines other than those that are laid out geometrically, one where not everything is busy setting out the details of a conflict and its eventual resolution.

To the same end he will leave certain important things unsaid or undone, dropping them out of the text, in circumstances where a lesser playwright would have been sure to feature them, and into that subterranean zone we've come to call the "subtext," an often misunderstood notion I intend to examine further at a later point in this book. Or he will have utterances abruptly break off or will eliminate expected connections between them.

Just a few years before Chekhov began to write *Ivanov*, Strindberg in the preface to his *Miss Julie* (which Chekhov was later to read in translation and admire) had spoken of his dislike for the "symmetrical, mathematical constructions of French dialogue," saying that he wanted to let his characters' minds work irregularly, "as they do in real life."[11] Without any pronunciamento Chekhov, beginning as we've seen with great tentativeness in *Platonov*, was to accomplish much the same thing, even more artfully than did Strindberg. As for the matter of "real" life, it goes without saying that neither dramatist intended or created anything like a species of photographic fidelity to actual appearances; their aim was to replace an increasingly artificial, mechanical and therefore unconvincing stage speech with something much fresher. One of the ironies about both Strindberg's and Chekhov's revolutions in dialogue was that their new, far more true speech was at first considered "unnatural," so rudely did it clash with theatrical convention.

It has been said of Dostoevsky that he was a "realist" not because he reproduced the appearances of actual life but because he followed its deep rhythms. The same can be said of Chekhov in regard to both the dialogue he wrote and the larger movements of his mature plays. This, together with his authorial absence or self-effacement, lies behind the common opinion, meant as a high accolade but having the effect of a denigration, that these dramas haven't so much been created as found; Chekhov's plays are not merely like life, this well-meaning but thoroughly false view goes, they *are* life. As though his distinguishing attribute wasn't his formal artistry but a talent for serendipity.

A number of scenes in *Ivanov* are built in part on significant ellipses and disjunctures, such as one between Anna and Lvov, where Strindberg's "irregularity" can be seen both in their conversation and within Anna's longer speeches. Throughout the episode Lvov serves as a sort of straight man for Anna's flights and divagations.

Early in the scene Anna says, "They're playing 'Greenfinch' in the kitchen" and sings a few lines of the song. There's a pause. Then, abruptly, Anna asks, "Are your mother and father alive, Doctor?" After a matter-of-fact exchange she suddenly says, "Flowers come round every spring but happiness doesn't. Who told me that? Now let me see. I think it was Nikolai himself said it." (It was of course *she* who had said those words to Nikolai a few minutes before.)

Then, without transition, she says, "The owl's hooting again." Lvov says, "Let it." Anna, again without transition, says, "I'm beginning to think I've been unlucky." As the scene comes to an end, she asks, apropos of nothing, "Have you any brothers, Doctor?" Lvov says no and a stage direction tells us that "Anna sobs." We have to suppose that the tears come from an inner "story" running parallel to the explicit one.

One more example of dialogue that doesn't always mesh and of thoughts made tacit so as to be enriched. Anna and Shabelsky are together. After denouncing himself at length—"I'm a rotten swine"—he turns right around to complain about the way people treat him: "More often than not they don't hear or notice me." Anna entirely ignores this and says, "He's hooting again." Shabelsky: "Who is?" Anna: "The owl. It hoots every evening." Shabelsky: "Then let it hoot." (As I quoted the doctor above, Lvov later gives a shortened form of this same reply; an important Chekhovian device is to drop particular words or phrases into the dialogue or little ritual gestures into the action, then have them repeated later as textual elements of a musical nature, personal signatures, and even sometimes as minor motifs.) Shabelsky's next words have no connection to his last ones. "Things couldn't be worse," he says. Then he tells Anna that if he won a lot of money in the lottery he would go to Moscow "to hear the gypsies" and then to Paris, where "I'd sit by my wife's grave"—we hadn't known he'd been married—"and think for days on end. I'd just sit there till I died. She's buried in Paris. (Pause.)" Anna, in another instance of boredom being feigned to mask some strong emotion, says, "It's terribly boring. Shall we play [a] duet?"

It's very much worth noting that the characters who chiefly carry out the play's nonlinear movements as these sporadically occur are lesser figures—Sasha, Shabelsky, Anna, the hungry guests, Kosykh—whereas the most important, Ivanov and Lvov, for the most part engage in straightforward dialogue and action, especially in their scenes with each other. As I've pointed out so often, Chekhov isn't yet sufficiently in command of a consistent style, not yet wholly able to trust in his intuitions, and not free enough yet from the duresses of established dramatic practice to be confident in his armaments.

So he keeps Nikolai and Lvov at work fulfilling their duties as bearers of the main "story line." It's as though Chekhov can't yet afford the luxury of letting these characters dance in and out of stage traffic, can't yet dare to have them turn their backs on convention in the pursuit of truths beyond the narrative.

Ivanov

The most conventional, "unoriginal" thing he has Nikolai do is, of course, to commit suicide.

That he shoots himself is certainly a way physically to end the play, the only way Chekhov apparently could decide on, after he'd discarded the even more unconvincing heart attack. But the decision betrays an incompleteness of control as well as a sudden drying up of inventiveness. By his self-inflicted death, which feels arbitrary and hurried into service—let's get this over with!— Nikolai cuts off the stage action, to be sure, yet at the same time he cuts off some of his stature in our imaginations.

He's been distinguished as a character for not resembling the protagonist of any "realistic" play we're familiar with, and here he goes and does the banal, the incontinent thing, as Henry James might have described it. To put it bluntly, the suicide is too easy, too pat, and therefore dramatically undernourishing. Instead of the fruitfully ambiguous air, the deliberately "open" atmosphere with which Chekhov's later plays will increasingly end, this one slams shut on a note of resolution that gives signs of having been derived largely from theater, not from perceived and freshly imagined life. But as is so often the case with Chekhov, the ground is a bit more slippery than that.

I've made much of Chekhov's refusal to explain Nikolai's condition, which seems to me part of a wish to pitch him beyond stereotypes. Still, we can't help wondering about his behavior, its sources if not its clinical causes, and we aren't wrong to do it. Not that we want to "solve" the mystery, far from it; but we're entitled to be shown it in its fullness, instead of having it lopped off before we can begin to place it on our map of humanity under siege.

One cost of Chekhov's protecting his protagonist from vulgar psychologizing and shallow moral verdicts is that he remains shrouded in a partial obscurity that isn't at all the same thing as mystery. Unlike his persecutors or defenders such as Sasha, we don't invent him, but neither do we see him clearly. Yet the mist dissolves a little on two occasions that allow us to see a bit farther into him, at least into the relationship between his present condition of crackup and the person he once was.

Just before he shoots himself, with Sasha having berated Lvov for his latest attack and the whole wedding party in turmoil, Nikolai says: "I'll put an end to all this. . . . I feel like a young man again. It's my old self speaking." He then pulls out a gun. When Sasha screams, "Nikolai, for God's sake!" he answers, "It's time to call a halt. I've outstayed my welcome. . . . Thank you, Sasha." And then the shot.

Everything he says has his usual elegance and crispness, but his weightiest words are of course "young man" and "old self"; to act decisively, as he used to do, to regain for a moment, in however catastrophic a fashion, his old vitality, is a relief . . . and something of a final signature. Although the suicide remains largely melodramatic, making for no real expansion of our consciousness, its arbitrariness is somewhat reduced, it *fits* a little better.

Much more significant is a long speech of Nikolai to Lebedev, almost a soliloquy, just before the suicide scene. As at other times, he says, "[I] won't try to explain myself—whether I'm decent or rotten, sane or mad." But he wants Lebedev, and us, at least to know the background of his breakdown. "I used to be young, eager, sincere, intelligent," he says. "I worked hard . . . had hope." Then, without "taking thought or knowing anything about life, I heaved a load on my back . . . and cracked my spine. . . . I broke under the strain."

The account, which contains a hint that Nikolai had once been partly motivated by a sense of social obligation, is still largely veiled and enigmatic, but it does take the character out of the realm of the uselessly mystifying, where there occur inexplicable disasters without moral or psychic dimension. If we were to describe Ivanov's condition by a contemporary term, the one that comes to mind is "burn-out." The speech introduces a slight crack in our idea of the nonsocietal nature of his disturbance, but it closes over as the suicide draws near; people, we can say on the level of psychological explanation, don't kill themselves over trouble with the neighbors or the corruption of communal spirit.

And so while the speech doesn't tell us very much, it has the virtue of throwing a little light on Nikolai's otherwise baffling behavior. Still, the "point" of the play, which is to say the irreducible experience it affords, isn't Ivanov's behavior in itself but the range of reactions to it and, by extension, the whole question of how much we can know about ourselves and other people. Nikolai is an instigation to this question, its locale as it were, not the problem itself. This is why it's essential that in performance he not be conceived in any way that reduces him to an aberration or a "case"—as an extreme neurotic, or a Byronic figure gone sour, or, needless to say, as a Russian Hamlet. Unfortunately, those are the ways he's still most often played, as Anna is most often played too weepily, Lvov either too nastily or too nobly, Shabelsky too clownishly, and Sasha too much like a scheming, lovesick ingenue.

One thoroughly misguided *Ivanov* I remember was the 1966 production which John Gielgud directed and in which he starred. He did Nikolai as a weary, defeated poet, completely ignoring the character's humor and frequent verve, and directed the play as a languid exercise in provincial malaise. But what could we have expected of a man who so completely misunderstood *Ivanov* as to write these words: "Chekhov must have seen something of himself in both the character of Ivanov and that of Dr. Lvov, the two most intelligent men in the play, whose attempts to understand each other and win each other's confidence result in such violent mutual destruction."[12]

But, then, of all Chekhov's full-length plays this one is by far the least often performed (*Platonov* is never performed in its entirety) and perhaps the one most likely to be wrongly perceived; its very unfamiliarity causes you to slide off its slippery surfaces. As I've tried to show, this is due in part to its uncertainty of technique and vision, shuttling as it does between old destinations and new departures. But it's also because *Ivanov*, unlike the dramas that will follow, has a dominant figure whose fate overshadows everyone else's. The risk this brings is that we can lose sight of the pattern, fragmentary and delicate as it is, the dramaturgical work of dispersing what "happens" horizontally over a broad field, instead of from top to bottom. With Nikolai as the magnetic "top" in such a dispensation, the play threatens to become skewed, turning into the character's personal story, the account of an ill-fated fellow in the provinces in whose downfall lies something hazily instructive or at any rate sobering.

But the chief "story" of *Ivanov* is much less obvious: that of a problematic man at the center of a battle of interpretations, of attempts to fix and appropriate so elusive a presence. Chekhov hasn't written a melodrama with patches of new consciousness but something very near the reverse: new dramatic awareness disfigured here and there by melodramatic lapses and concessions.

There isn't anything one can do about the suicide or Anna's discovery of Nikolai and Sasha in one another's arms except to play these scenes as unstridently as possible, without histrionics, in a natural manner, and without embarrassment either. For the rest, any production ought to rely more than most do on Nikolai's frequent periods of "health," the many moments when his wittiness and intelligence shine through, and on the delights scattered throughout the work in the conversation of lesser characters such as Shabelsky. On seeing the Lebedev and Babakin women: "Two money boxes on one sofa. What a lovely sight." Or in connection with a bit of drinking: "Wise men have cogitated since the dawn of history without hitting on anything better than salted cucumber."

Ivanov stands as something more than an apprentice work (that slot is filled by *Platonov*). The play is a preliminary to Chekhov's mature manner, in some ways a rehearsal for it, but its forcefulness and "original" plot, its little incidental triumphs of shrewd imagination, give it more than just historical interest. After one false start (*The Wood Demon*), Chekhov a few years later would write a play in which many of the energies and modes of composition that had their first sustained stage-life in *Ivanov* would come of age: *The Seagull.*

THE SEAGULL
Art and Love, Love and Art

Some preliminary notes, ideas, observations, questions, and reminders for an essay on the play.

Its title is the most nearly symbolic of those for any Chekhov play but, like its closest rival, *The Cherry Orchard*'s trees, the bird isn't symbolic in any pseudo-poetic or culturally anxious way.

The Russian word for the title, *chaika*, is used for both "gull," the genus, and the particular species "seagull."

The play's chief subjects are art and love, never far from each other thematically. Or perhaps a better way of putting this is in the form of questions: What does it mean to be in love? What does it mean to be an artist? And to be both in love and an artist?

This is Chekhov's first play that doesn't have a dominant figure, a protagonist whose fate, and our interest in it, dwarfs all others, and so his first thoroughly to disperse action and sentience among a considerable number of people of whom, in this instance, four can be thought of as major characters, dramatically equal; four protagonists then.

Though it ends with the suicide of one of the main characters, Chekhov made a point of calling the play a "comedy."

Its architectonics or musical structure is easily discernible, more surehandedly laid out than in *Ivanov* yet not so finely balanced as this quality of composition will become in the three plays that will follow. Another artistic advance over *Ivanov* (I will leave out the intervening *Wood Demon* and discuss it in the chapter on *Uncle Vanya*) is that the earlier play's melodramatic disfigurations are mostly gone.

The Seagull stands in relation to its successors in an even more nourishing position than its predecessor does to it. How does this show itself? Obviously that will have to wait until we come to the later plays, but a few ropes into the future can be thrown out in this section.

Some commentators on the play, including Vladimir Nabokov, have chosen to dwell on the things they think faulty. Ronald Hingley, the Chekhov translator and biographer, perversely considers *The Seagull* inferior to *Ivanov*.

In his pioneering but now somewhat out-of-date study, David Magarshack accounted for Chekhov's arrival at artistic maturity in *The Seagull* by drawing a distinction between his earlier "scientific" approach to writing and a new spirit of humanistic concern, and saw an even more important differentiation between his old method of "direct" action and a new "indirect" mode of composition. How useful are these distinctions now? Do they go far enough, or too far?

My favorite critical observation about the play is from an originally unsigned review by H. de W. Fuller in the *Nation* in 1916: "If the boy [Konstantin] had had the advantage of some athletic sport, he would doubtless have worked off most of the vague feelings which he mistook for the stirrings of genius."[1]

I think the reigning spirit of *The Seagull* is that of antiromanticism.

To write about any Chekhov play, or story for that matter, is to risk going off on digressions, the homeopathic reason for this, or the imitative fallacy involved, being his own digressive procedures, his continual deviations from an expected narrative line. Is the temptation to wander off on side-trips especially strong when writing about *The Seagull*? One reason it may be is just that relationship to the previous and ensuing plays I've mentioned. This one is so full of ripening method, archetypal situation, that one wants to seize those things for light on the whole of Chekhov's theater. Not that *The Seagull* doesn't have its own substantiality, independence, and artistic specificity; but as a storehouse of things to come it continually presses you to think ahead.

Another reason for the mind's being led afield by Chekhov is the way his writing so often suggests so much more than it directly says. All good writing does this, of course, but in his case the unstated has an especially rich life. You want to hunt down his implications, gathering them as fuel and instigation, his very reticence setting in motion the loosening of your own tongue.

I'll save the question of the title until near the end of this chapter, since by then the text, explored and meditated upon, should have something to say about its own name, and I'll look now at the words Chekhov used to describe the play, "A Comedy in Four Acts." We can assume that he knew exactly what he was doing, for he most likely chose the subtitle with the same care he exercised on those for all his other plays. *Ivanov* is a "drama," *Uncle Vanya* is "Scenes from Country Life," *Three Sisters* is another "drama," and *The Cherry Orchard* is another "comedy."

All these terms or descriptive phrases are to one degree or another tactical alerts to audiences and readers. In effect they tell us not to bring to these works preconceptions about types of drama, they ask us to be supple in the way we wield artistic categories and to be open in our anticipations. The extreme flatness and neutrality of "Scenes from Country Life," for example, have an ironical quality in the light of the text, which is scarcely a pastoral idyll, but they also warn us not to expect or look for a "high" theatrical experience, one that will induce in us what we think of as pity and terror in the classical sense. On another level the subtitles would seem to indicate the relationship of the plays to each other in Chekhov's mind: lighter, graver, more subject to misinterpretation, less so, and the like.

The most notorious instance of his gentle advice being ignored was Stanislavsky's staging of *The Cherry Orchard* for its première at the Moscow Art Theater in January 1904. We will take this up again, but for now it should be noted that Stanislavsky was a most serious man; his own writings and the accounts of others tell us that wit and humor weren't his strong points. And so it isn't surprising that he directed Chekhov's last play as something of a tragedy, with a wide strain of melancholy the text does not support. Like a number of directors after him, and performers and critics for that matter, Stanislavsky wasn't able to see that for all the losses some of its characters sustain, others are given accessions, so that *The Cherry Orchard* is far from being a heavy or in any way depressing play. For its mood of recognition and reconciliation, it can even be thought of as making up something like Chekhov's *Tempest*.

In much the same way *The Seagull* is also a comedy, not in spite of the suicide and other painful events but in part because of them, in a quietly original way that at the same time has classical precedents. To discuss that now would be to run far ahead of myself, but to talk more generally about "comedy" as a designation for a work it might not seem to fit wouldn't be inappropriate. And so a digression.

The two towering examples that come immediately to mind are of course *La divina commedia* and *La comédie humaine.* In both cases the word clearly isn't being used to denote a conventional genre or to describe the main substance of the works; both, after all, enclose more than enough suffering, evil, and death, everything grievous, somber, and cruel. Instead it points to or controls a final, governing response. The word "comedy" suggests the answers to the following questions: What is our state of mind or spirit supposed to be after we finish these works? How are we to understand them, to "take" them, as we like to say?

With Dante the matter is comparatively clear. Because the movement of his great poem is from suffering to rejoicing, hell to heaven, it ends happily, that much is obvious. Not so obvious, we might think, is why this outcome should earn for the entire work the description of comedy. After a little reflection we can see that it does so because such is the state of morale, the lasting attitude, wrung from the whole arduous yet ultimately successful journey "upwards," that Dante has toward his creation and that we are meant to share.

For beyond its ordinary function of making us laugh or smile, comedy has a wider and deeper action, as formal comedies like Shakespeare's have always made evident: to restore, to heal, to embolden. Just as there are "thoughts that lie too deep for tears," so there are those that lie beyond the relative simplicity of laughter. In Dante's universe, comedy is a lightness retroactively at work for those who qualify, the potentially saved (and, by analogy, for nonbelievers of goodwill, as T. S. Eliot pointed out); it's a relief from spiritual anxiety, a reminder of redemption, a restoration and a new existence of hope; it's God's difficult yet loving "joke."

Balzac uses the word in a different, much more problematic sense, deliberately and more than half-mockingly adapting his title from Dante yet in the end retaining some portion of the poet's meaning. The new title suggests a God-like perspective, with the novelist's eye replacing the divinity's omniscience. In this secular world life is comic in a negative sense because it lacks the dignity of tragedy as well as the metaphysical structure to sustain a tragic view, and in a positive one, which is to say one it does deserve, because it contains its own principle of redemption.

Forever defeating itself, like a haplessly suffering circus clown, it roughly resembles what we call a "comedy of errors," rather more grave and consequential than is customary in such a genre, no doubt, but still full of endless deviations from or betrayals of the ideal, perpetual failures of understanding, slip-ups, workings at cross-purposes, and gaffes—some of them, to be sure, with fatal outcomes. But though it may be a black farce at times, a comedy we sigh over, whose humor is often of the gallows variety, it isn't in the end conducive to despair.

This is because the imaginative act has intervened. Simply to see this roiling series of mistakes, miscalculations, and failings, this burlesque of the ideal, to observe its inexhaustible variety—comedy is always much more multifarious than tragedy—and to organize all that in the creating mind as a sort of failed *Divine Comedy,* is paradoxically enough to bring some of the relief Dante gives us. It's to offer hope through privileged perception, a "cure" through a well-wrought description of the disease. Even the darkest moments in Balzac, the particular novels or sequences within them that recoil most strongly from being called comic, take their places in the general easing of anxiety which occurs whenever experience is recovered from shapelessness and made less inexplicable.

Chekhov, it goes without saying, is much closer to Balzac than to Dante. Like the French writer, he hasn't any religious convictions that can make for comedy in a sublime sense, he isn't dealing in salvation. Like Balzac, he gives us nothing that resembles a conventional "happy ending" either. But Chekhov has an even more wry and rueful appreciation of human folly and frailty than Balzac, and he is far less disposed to draw moral conclusions—he isn't disposed that way at all—or to impose his own views. He doesn't try to substitute for God, as Balzac often seems to be doing, nor does he claim knowledge of *everything* or wish to extend his artistic dominion over it all. His comedies aren't part of any broad "canvas" but the products of alternations in his moods or in particular visions.

When Chekhov is engaged in writing a comedy the situations he invents receive their identifying energy and shape from his decision to keep them open, not yet determined; something can be done about what otherwise would be taken as inescapable fate. Clearly the comedic aspect of *The Seagull* (and of *The Cherry Orchard* too) lies in its attitude or point of view, not in its literal series of events or despite any of them. This is so obviously true that I hesitate to make anything of it. Yet misunderstandings abound of how these things work, especially in regard to Chekhov, whose subject matter is so often seen to dictate his manner, instead of the other way round.

Attitude shows itself, of course, not declaratively but in structure, design, and tone. One thing we will see in *The Seagull* is that Chekhov constantly deflects matters away from being taken too seriously, which in this context means either tragically or in too absolute a way. This is true even in the plays he didn't call comedies, as we saw with *Ivanov* and will see again. In the more "serious" works there is still an openness to the idea that destiny may not be fatal, though physical ways out of disaster or dilemma have been closed off.

The resulting "lightness" in the noncomedies is nothing like a diminution of seriousness, and in the comedies it's nothing like frivolity. In their different ways both kinds of play offer us something like breathing room, space in which we can maneuver, take emotional or intellectual steps of our own, set matters in order, compare, *recognize*. All this is an act of freedom from what deconstructionists would call a programed response. As a corollary of this, or as its executive means, Chekhov's tone in *The Seagull* is bantering, excited, matter-of-fact, or affectionate, but never somber and never cold. He'd enjoyed writing the play, he let it be known, something rather rare for him, and the pleasure permeates the text.

In a much quoted letter of October 21, 1895, Chekhov wrote to Alexei Suvorin that he was at work on a new long play, his first since *The Wood Demon* of five or six years earlier.[2] During that interval he had several times expressed his disgust with the condition of the theater in Russia; a representative, if rather elaborate, comment was this: "We must strive with all our power to see to it that the stage passes out of the hands of the grocers and into literary hands, otherwise the theater is doomed."[3] Yet he had also given voice to those by now familiar doubts as to his own talent for writing plays; "as far as my dramaturgy is concerned, it seems to me that I was not destined to be a playwright"[4] is a comparatively mild expression of those misgivings. But now he told his friend and publisher, "I can't say I'm not enjoying writing it, though [it would have been more accurate for him to have said "because"] I'm flagrantly disregarding the basic tenets of the stage. The comedy has three female roles, six male roles, four acts, a landscape (a view of a lake), much conversation about literature, little action and five tons of love."[5] (The Russian text actually reads five "poods" of love; a *pood* is a unit of approximately thirty-six pounds.)

Chekhov had some way to go before he finished writing it, but *The Seagull* would turn out to be almost exactly as he had described it, with the addition of a fourth, minor female character and rather more action than he had suggested. Later on I'll take up the supremely important nature of this action.

Chekhov wasn't exaggerating the weight of love in his play. It announces itself almost immediately and by the end of the first act a character will remark, "What a state they're in and what a lot of loving." As we'll see, what a cross-hatching too of amorous relationships and would-be liaisons! He wasn't over-stating, either, the prominence of what he had called "conversation about literature." Actually, the conversation—and not just that but also monologues, interjections, spoken thoughts, and private murmurings—is about fiction and writing it, plays and writing them, the state of the theater in Russia, the nature and profession of acting and, most widely and pertinently, the life of both art and the artist.

The Seagull, then, is a play, a comedy, largely "about" art and love, creativity and the erotic. I put "about" in quotation marks so as to make what I think is an important point, the one Beckett was making when he said of Joyce that "his writing is not *about* something; *it is that something itself.*"[6] This is to say that the subjects of imaginative literature—in which for my present purposes and while recognizing the difference I include plays both as texts and in performance—don't exist independently of the writing itself. They're not like prey waiting to be pounced upon by a verbally gifted hunter or seedy rooms needing to be refurbished by a painter in words. In turn writing isn't the expression or treatment of a preexisting reality but an act that discovers and gives life to a "subject" within itself.

Ibsen once said that "I have never written because I had, as they say, a 'good subject'" but out of what he called "lived-through" experience.[7] And Picasso, to turn to another art to which Beckett's observation is every bit as pertinent, said once, "Je ne cherche pas, je trouve." By which he certainly didn't mean that he found promising things to paint—just imagine him coming upon a woman with three noses or legs like giant sausages and crying "Aha!"—but that he found aesthetic reality of a visual order in the making of the painting.

Following on this *The Seagull* is about art and love not so much in the sense that they are its topics but in the sense that the entire play quite literally surrounds them, providing those abstractions with the dramatic context or field in which they can come to life, working themselves out as motifs; or rather it might be more useful to think of them as something like "notional presences," ideas attached to bodies and impregnating them. Chekhov takes art and love *into* his writing, turning them from their disembodied state into dramatic energies. These are then deployed throughout the play, and in the process art and love necessarily assume new identities, since they are being written, not being written *about*. This is what happens whenever we encounter something in an imaginative work and say, I never saw it that way before; you couldn't have, because it wasn't that way before.

But this isn't all of it. What his characters say or think about love or art has to be revelatory of what they are, of their natures, not discrete attitudes or a series of opinions (although having more opinions than passions is itself a revelation of character). Which is only to say that themes have to be active, incarnate, endowed with physiognomies we might almost say, or else they plague us as inert, gaseous thought.

Who are these characters in so many of whom love and art have lodged or taken over like an infection? An anatomy of the dramatis personae seems in order at this point.

Irina Arkadina is a famous or at least a well-known actor. (In accordance with current tendencies and common sense, I intend from now on to use "actor" when I refer to a performer of either sex; "actress" has become silly and demeaning and ought to be buried along with "authoress" and "aviatrix." Of course Chekhov was committed to the usage of his own day, so that we'll find "actress" in the text and I'm not about to tamper with that.) Vain, voluble, a "foolish, mendacious, self-admiring egoist," Chekhov said about Arkadina, which on the play's balance might be just a bit strong; she's concerned about her son Konstantin Treplev, yet constantly forgetful of him or actively hostile, and she's in love with her companion, Boris Trigorin. Treplev is in his early twenties when the play begins, at the outset of a career as a playwright and writer of fiction; he's self-absorbed and self-pitying, with, one suspects, something of an oedipal fixation on his mother, and he's romantically in love with Nina Zarechnaya.

Trigorin is a famous writer, possibly modeled on someone Chekhov knew and containing elements of his own self (by which I mean something more specific than the usual generalities playwrights take from their own biographies for their characterizations). He's absorbed in his craft but indifferent to his celebrity. An essentially selfish man, he'll leave Arkadina for a while when he falls in love with Nina. She's an aspiring actor, sensitive, impulsive, someone we might in today's debased vocabulary call "vulnerable." She's in love with Treplev at first, then falls violently for Trigorin.

These are the four principals. It's more than interesting to note that all are actively in love and all are practicing artists in one way or another.

A few degrees below them in significant presence are Pyotr Sorin and Evgenii Dorn. Sorin is Arkadina's brother, a retired civil servant, self-deprecating, genial, yet also fussily melancholy over the imminent prospect of old age; he's rather reminiscent of Shabelsky in *Ivanov* and somewhat of a characterological ancestor of Gayev in *The Cherry Orchard*. Dorn is one of the five doctors in Chekhov's full-length plays (only *The Cherry Orchard* lacks one); an intelligent, wryly sceptical man with an impulse toward lyricism and a mild philosophical bent, he might be thought of as the only "balanced" person in the play.

The other four characters occupy with varying bulk the remainder of the dramatic space. We can think of them as participants in subplots or as secondary agencies for the working out of perception, but they are never simply functional, never purely instrumental figures like the servants, guards, and messengers of classical drama.

Ilya Shamrayev, Sorin's estate manager, is a brusque, officious, somewhat despotic man and the only character apart from Sorin who isn't either in love or the object of someone else's carnal, or at least amorous, desire. His daughter Masha is an intelligent, self-dramatizing young woman hopelessly in love with Treplev (in an early draft she turns out to be Dorn's daughter), and her mother, Polina, is an efficient, loyal family retainer lifted from a merely functional status by being unrequitedly in love with Dorn. And Simon Medvedenko, a schoolmaster both long-suffering and pedantic, pathetically desires Masha, who treats him contemptuously for his pains, though she'll later with unchanged contempt agree to marry him; he's a direct forerunner of Kulygin in *Three Sisters*, though he lacks the latter's redeeming kindness.

The setting for the comedy they enact, Sorin's estate in the country, is similar to those for all of Chekhov's major plays with the apparent exception of *Three Sisters*, which has an urban milieu; still, that play is linked to the other mises en scène by the extreme provincial dullness and isolation of the town. These settings provide Chekhov with dramatic conditions, or conditions for a drama, that wholly suit his artistic intentions; and thinking about that irresistibly compels a digression at this point.

The places are isolated, at a considerable distance from the hurly-burly and multiple distractions of big cities, from "culture," careers, formal amusements, professional entanglements, politics, ideas, the sway and clutch of complicated, often abstract associations. In his long story "The Duel," written in 1891, Chekhov has a character "stuck" in the Caucasus and ardently (if a bit journalistically!) longing for the pleasures of Moscow and St. Petersburg. People in those places, he says to himself, "discuss trade, new singers, Franco-Prussian accord. Everywhere life is vigorous, cultured, intelligent, brimming with energy." And in a story written as early as 1886, "Difficult People," someone is "reminded . . . of . . . Moscow, where street-lamps were burning and carriages were rattling in the streets, where lectures were being given." And then of course we will hear the Prozorov sisters' repeated "Moscow! To Moscow!" in *Three Sisters*.

In the settings Chekhov chooses, the characters, deprived of the stimulation the metropolis affords, are pressed back on themselves and on each other. Some of them—Arkadina, Trigorin, and, at the end, Nina of *The Seagull*, Ranevskaya and some of her extended family of *The Cherry Orchard*, and the Prozorovs and army officers of *Three Sisters*—have known or will come to know what the larger world, the great world, is like. In his two comedies Chekhov offers that kind of relief from the narrowness of provincial or rural life—this is one reason they're comedies—but even so the alternative is given to us indirectly, talked about, offered as a possibility but not lived visibly on the stage.

On these isolated estates people gaze, speak, gesture, kiss, think, and weep in a severely limited atmosphere. They're enclosed in an enclave, tiny, burdensomely self-sufficient, stifling at times yet also, for the purposes of Chekhov's art, in a very special way "pure," reduced to essentials. They are far from the vast sprawling human country whose distant voices they hear, speaking of another, richer life. And they're there because Chekhov has put them there, as part of a design, so as to exist in one kind of play rather than another, not, as those who see him fundamentally as a concerned social observer think, because he looked around and there they were, leading "deprived" lives and so making up fitting objects for his famous brooding, pitying, humane, and mournful glance.

In the way he *chooses* to circumscribe the situations his characters inhabit, he is closer to Beckett than to any of his contemporaries, or to any other Russian writer for that matter; Gorky put many of his people into a romanticized poverty, Tolstoy put some of his in a romanticized asceticism. The restricted circumstances Beckett and Chekhov fashion for their plays are of another order; beneath their enormous physical differences they greatly resemble each other, for the artistic purpose of the confinement is very much the same for both.

In their plays—so much straitening, so much absence! In *Endgame* as in *Uncle Vanya*, in *Waiting for Godot* as in *Three Sisters,* the inescapable fact is that there's nothing much to do. Beckett's plays are of course far more radically denuded than Chekhov's, though they're certainly not better on that account, but the surprisingly dramatic result of the scarcity and want in the lives both playwrights invent, so unpropitious for drama, one would think, is nearly the same.

For what *is* done is closer to fundamental life than the seductions toward activity, toward choice and mobility as the very essence of meaningful existence, ever allow us to come in the conventional theater or to see in our own lives. Deprived of distractions or having to rely on their own primitive, sadly provincial, or solipsistic ones—all that keeping "the ball rolling" or fussing with the bag in Beckett, all those card or lotto games or musical evenings in Chekhov—bereft of the consolations of staying busy, on the road neither to "fulfillment," that fictive aim or shibboleth, nor to wisdom, nor even in most cases to understanding, all of Beckett's characters and nearly all of Chekhov's are reduced to the essential tasks of getting through the days and nights, making their way, with what is left to them, through time. Once again, we remember that in Chekhov's comedies more is left to them, but even so such a residue is on hold, so to speak, reserved for the future, which in both dramatists, for highly significant reasons (which in Chekhov's case we'll take up later), has no status, is simply a fiction.

And then, or rather along with this, they go off in that quintessential human way of holding back the darkness, they talk; they tell their lives, they ad lib their hopes, joys and sorrows, creating their fates in language as they go, more precisely our recognition of their fates. These outwardly minimal existences come to us with all the freshness, peculiar as the word may sound in this context, of the root, of the way it is at bottom, Beckett's *comme c'est ça.* "Oh what a curse, mobility," Winnie cries out in *Happy Days.* The artistic undoing of the curse, the blessing, makes itself felt in the characters having to stay still; this is the condition in which we can see "how it is."

And so the characters of *The Seagull* talk. Naturally, there are physical events too, but nearly all of the decisive ones take place off stage. This is one of the things Chekhov meant when he spoke of consciously ignoring the fundamental tenets of the stage, and it is at the center of David Magarshack's argument about Chekhov's emergent mastery. The subject is so dense and important that I'm tempted to go off in full pursuit right now, but I'll content myself with simply saying here that among the theatrical principles, pieties we might better call them, he was challenging was the notion that off stage is only for actions which for reasons of propriety or mechanical impossibility can't be shown directly. In Greek and Roman drama, of course, important events took place off stage, as they did in Shakespeare and other classical writers, but for the most part these were events inconvenient or impossible to show, and in any case for a long time off stage had been chiefly where the stagehands waited.

ART

As he does in every one of his full-length plays after *Ivanov*, Chekhov quickly brings on all the persons of the drama. From *The Seagull* on no play will fail to introduce well before the end of the first act everyone of any significance— which is to say nearly everyone, since almost no Chekhov character, however "minor," lacks dramatic weight. The strategic point of this is that it can work against the linear or accumulating movement of the usual play. Nobody will come on stage later, bringing important news or actively furthering developments and so extending a line of more or less strictly unfolding narrative. The quietly revolutionary effect of this is that characters take their places almost like players in a game such as basketball or soccer, occupying a field and ready for whatever will happen.

The very first stage direction informs us that art, in the form of the theater itself, is going to figure in *The Seagull*. Setting the scene, Chekhov writes of a stage "hastily put together for an amateur performance" and of "workmen . . . coughing and hammering . . . behind the lowered curtain." Then in the first lines of dialogue "love" also makes its first appearance, in intimate if a little ludicrous connection to art.

Medvedenko and Masha are on and, glancing at the crude stage, she says, "The Play will start soon." "Yes," Medvedenko says, "Konstantin Gavrilovich wrote it, and Nina Zarechnaya will act in it. They're in love, and tonight their souls will merge in the creation of a single artistic symbol." After this banality he goes on to complain that unlike Nina and Konstantin "my soul and yours don't share a common ground." Masha has a moment earlier indicated her own lovesickness in the play's wonderful second line, the dourly cryptic "I'm in

The Seagull

81

mourning for my life," after Medvedenko's opening "How come you always wear black?"

After a few more exchanges they're soon joined by all the other characters, who lay out for us, offhandedly and in some respects unconsciously, most of their ruling qualities and idiosyncracies, as well as what binds them factually and emotionally to one another. Little signatures show themselves—Sorin's self-deprecating laugh and his habit of finishing his remarks with "and that sort of thing" or "and so on," Dorn's bemused singing of snatches of songs—the kind of thing that so unaccountably irritated Nabokov. And we hear the first mention of a seagull when Nina says that she feels drawn to the lake as though she were one of those birds.

They've gathered for the performance of Konstantin's play. They're mostly in an amiable mood, except for Masha, who's almost never amiable, Treplev, who's nervous, and Arkadina, who's clearly disgruntled by her son's having dared to step onto her territory. "When is this thing ever going to start?" she asks and then breaks out in a pointed, only partially accurate quote from Shakespeare—"My son! Thou turn'st mine eyes into my very soul . . . ," to which Konstantin replies with another (paraphrased) speech from *Hamlet* that in the most literary way reveals his oedipal rivalry with Trigorin (he's already revealed his envy of him as a writer): "Nay, but to yield to wickedness, to seek [out] love in the depths of sin."

The inner play begins with a prologue by Konstantin, who "loudly" orates: "Oh, you venerable old shadows that linger above this lake at night. . . ." The curtain parts to reveal Nina, in white, sitting on a large rock. "People, lions, eagles and partridges, horned deer, geese, spiders, silent fish dwelling in the water," she begins, launching into a long futuristic monologue that speaks of a time when everything in the world is dead except for some vague spirit that will do battle with the Devil and, victorious, will bring "matter and spirit . . . together in perfect harmony."

The "decadent gibberish," as Arkadina so cruelly yet not without reason will call it, suggests the worst of German expressionist drama of a generation later, in its whole tone and in specific lines like "I am that great World Spirit." Still, it does give some evidence of anarchic talent and urgent ambition and this, rather than any reasoned scornfulness, lies behind Arkadina's jibes, so jealous is she of what she considers her own fiefdom. After she's interrupted Nina several times, Konstantin abruptly stops the performance, saying bitterly, "I'm sorry. I forgot that writing plays and acting in them was only for the chosen few. I intruded on your domain!" Everyone is left buzzing.

In a generally most perceptive essay on *The Seagull*, Robert Louis Jackson makes an ingenious case for Konstantin's play as being highly significant in its own right.[8] He offers a detailed reading of it in terms of a creation myth, a metaphor for the artist's journey and a disguised oedipal confession, and then extends his findings beyond their source and into the main text. I owe a great deal to Jackson's other ideas and will make grateful use of them in this section, but I think he makes too much of this one.

Whatever the literary motifs of Konstantin's little play, they seem to me less important in themselves than what, among other things, they tell us about Konstantin himself, which, to be sure, Jackson partly acknowledges. Yet he pushes his interpretation a little too far, somewhat overloading with abstract ideas a relatively uncomplicated if subtle comedy, and in the process losing sight of a very concrete function of the inner play, which, as I see it, is to set going talk about art and the artist. We can be sure that Chekhov didn't provide Konstantin with any old overblown piece of writing in an effort to discredit him, but he didn't give him such an arcane and ponderously philosophic one as Jackson thinks either. (I don't want to leave this point without stressing how enormously useful Jackson's insights are in general; his ideas about *The Seagull* as a play about what being an artist means are some of the main sources of my own thinking.)

The talk set in motion by the inner play, Chekhov's "conversation about literature," which as I said earlier is about other things as well, begins even before the aborted performance. "It's hard to act in your play," Nina tells Konstantin as they wait for the others to take their places, "it has no living characters." "Living characters!" Konstantin explodes. "We must represent life not as it is, and not as it should be, but as it appears in our dreams." Nina calmly ignores this, going on to say, "There's so little action, it's just one long monologue. And I think every play really ought to have some love interest."

The exchange tells us a good deal about where they are in relation to their art at this point and obliquely suggests their eventual destinations in the comedy. Treplev's ideas are vague, soft, *inexperienced*, making up a young man's aesthetic, and they're peculiarly belligerent. He'll drop the programmatic aspect later on, but for tactical reasons, not out of conviction, when he turns into a technician in the fiction he comes to write. But he won't overcome the absence of life from his work, and by continually trying to justify his writing on one basis or another, most often by attacking other people's, he reveals something dangerously defensive, polemical, and theoretical in his approach to art.

As for Nina, she's basically right in her criticism but she too betrays a weakness, provisional in her case, as it happens; her remark about a play needing "love interest" indicates that she's not yet a serious actor, or artist, but is in the preliminary phase of being stage-struck. We should notice that in a delicious piece of irony Chekhov has written her into a play with an abundance of what might be called love interest, only of a kind whose weight and dramatic implications are as far as they can be from what she means here.

Treplev's play provokes other responses besides Nina's and Arkadina's and each provides a little revelation of character. Trigorin is neutral, evasive in his "Every person writes what he wants to and can" and Medvedenko adds to his reputation for boring pedantry with "No one has the right to separate spirit from matter, since perhaps spirit itself is the sum total of material atoms." Dorn's surprising approval—"I liked the play. There's something to it"—can be ascribed to his usual kindness but is better explained by his confession to Konstantin after praising him that if "I could have experienced the lift of the spirit that artists feel when they create something, it seems to me . . . I'd have flown away from earth and into the sky." And the play also inspires Sorin to confess to having in his youth had aspirations to being a writer.

Understandably, the talk about art and the artist has as its chief participants Treplev, Trigorin, Arkadina, and, with especially great consequence at the end, Nina. They are the artists and each has something to elucidate, press for, or defend. In everything they say we can feel Chekhov's presence, in more than the obvious sense of his having written the dialogue; the points of view and attitudes he presents touch, often intimately, on his own concerns as a writer. He doesn't necessarily endorse any of them, he clearly disapproves of some, but he anchors the "debate" in animate personalities who have a stake in its outcome, and so keeps it from becoming abstract.

As we would expect, Treplev is most vociferous. Besides the conversation with Nina before his play begins he also talks to Sorin about his mother and the theater, the two "topics" merging into one argument. "She loves the theater," he says of Arkadina, "she thinks she's serving humanity, the sacred art, but in my opinion the contemporary theater is stuck in a rut. . . . These great talents, high priests of . . . art . . . they try to dig up a moral from banal pictures and phrases . . . a thousand variations [of] the same old thing."

To this point his views would certainly have been echoed by Chekhov (except for the note of envy they contain), as would his remark about needing a new kind of theater. But when he adds, "We need new forms . . . and if we can't have them, we're better off with nothing," an alarm ought to go off.

As we know, Chekhov never spoke of "new forms." He wanted changed morale, a theater of truthfulness and resiliency instead of dead mechanics, but he never consciously or avowedly aspired to technical change or pursued it as an end in itself, as Konstantin seems to do. When Trigorin says of him that "he grumbles, snorts and preaches about new forms," the verbs suggest that Konstantin's quest for originality has something inorganic and inauthentic about it, in large part because it's a mission too conscious by far.

At the end of the play, after he's achieved an empty success as a writer of fiction, Konstantin will partly recognize his own condition. "I've talked so much about new forms," he tells himself, "and now I feel that I'm gradually falling into a rut." He unhappily ponders Trigorin's "easy" methods for a while, quoting some images from one of Trigorin's stories (actually they're from a Chekhov story, "Wolf"), comparing them to his own stressful, slick, and brittle style (qualities we identify from his own and others' comments), and then says, "This is agony. (Pause.) Yes, I'm coming to believe more and more that what's important isn't old and new forms at all, but the fact that one writes without thinking of any forms. A person writes because it flows freely from his soul."

Chekhov isn't advocating, through Treplev, any naive or primitive aesthetic; he's not saying anything so simpleminded as "The hell with how you write, it's what you write that counts." But for him technique was always in the service of vision and experience, not the other way round, just as originality was a possible outcome and never a goal. Konstantin's "agony" is spiritual, not the result of wrong methods. Dorn, who admires him, says near the end, "It's a pity . . . that he doesn't have any particular mission." (This is an observation Chekhov had made in his preliminary notes on the Treplev character; for "mission" or, another possible translation, "aims" we can read "intentions beyond the ego.") "He conveys an impression and nothing more. And impressions alone won't get you . . . far." Trigorin sums it up: "There's something strange and vague about his work. . . . He doesn't have a single living character." A most subtle point Chekhov is making about Konstantin is that in the dominion of art, ideas, no matter how "correct," don't guarantee anything.

The Seagull

Trigorin talks even more about writing than does Konstantin, but never aggressively and never as a matter of theory. Quite the contrary: in the play's longest speeches he tells Nina about the writer's, or artist's, life, countering with prosaic, deflating comments her breathlessly romantic notions of what it must be like. When she speaks of "fascinating, brilliant lives full of meaning," he replies, "All these nice words—forgive me—remind me of . . . candy, which I never eat." When she insists that his "life must be wonderful," he says, "What's so good about it?" and goes on to tell her that writing for him is compulsive, not a matter of inspiration. "I write without a break, like a runaway train. . . . I can't help it. What's so wonderful and brilliant about that?"

In her infatuation with him or at least as much with the life he seems to inhabit, Nina continues to press him. When he keeps denying that his vocation is glamorous, she tells him, "You're simply spoiled by success." Trigorin's reply is crucial to an understanding of Chekhov's idea of the artist in *The Seagull*, as are also some balancing things Nina will say at the end. "What success?" he asks. "I've never pleased myself. I don't like myself as a writer. Worst of all, I'm in a kind of stupor and often don't understand what I write."

The words may not precisely represent Chekhov's feelings and attitude in every respect, but the self-critical position does. He once wrote in his notebook that "dissatisfaction with oneself is one of the fundamental qualities of every true talent," and this, among other things, is what distinguishes Trigorin from Treplev, whose later self-depreciation is a matter of injured ego, not creative modesty. Moreover, Trigorin's scoffing at Nina's immature idea of success— acclaim by the world—echoes Chekhov's often expressed and passionately held opinion that success defined in that way is more than contemptible. Though he wasn't without a reasonable interest in his own reputation, he hated the sort of celebrity which produced followers, a cult. In 1898 he wrote to Lydia Avilova, an erstwhile fiction writer who was in love with him, that "writing itself is not what repels me but this literary entourage, from which one has no escape."[9]

There are other connections between Trigorin and Chekhov, including, on a minor note, their both being avid fishermen. When, for example, Trigorin tells Nina that early in his career, when he was a playwright, he was afraid of the public, he says, "When I had to stage a new play, it always seemed to me that the dark-haired people in the audience were hostile and the light-haired people were cool and indifferent."[10] This is an immediate reminder of a well-known letter of Chekhov's to Suvorin in which he says that before performances of *Ivanov* he was sure that "the dark-haired men" among the onlookers would be "hostile." None of this is to say that Trigorin is anything like Chekhov's alter ego; there are extremely important differences between them, which I'll take up later. But the connections are clear.

If Trigorin isn't an egotist about his work, he's not free from one occupational disease of the writer, which is to exploit others for the sake of one's art. "I try," he tells Nina, "to catch you and myself in every sentence—every word—and I rush off . . . to lock up all those sentences and words in my literary storehouse on the off-chance they might come in handy." And indeed we see him at this work of plucking what he calls the living "flowers" for imaginative use. Into his ever-present notebook go jottings about Masha—"Takes snuff and drinks vodka. . . . Always wears black. Loved by the school teacher"—and Nina too: "A plot for a short story," a story about her and a seagull, he says of one note she sees him making.

Dangerous as it is to interpolate from a writer's life to the work, it seems justified at times and this is one of those cases. On several occasions, most notably concerning a short story of 1891, "The Butterfly," Chekhov was accused of having exploited for literary purposes some embarrassing facts about friends of his. He denied any conscious intention of doing it and there is no reason not to believe him, but the matter must have remained vaguely oppressive to him. We're put in mind of how Ibsen tried to expiate in his last plays his guilt for having "sacrificed" to his art the people closest to him, his wife and son. While Chekhov is nowhere near such moral anguish, he does, I think, render Trigorin in part as a cautionary figure and a delegate from his own conscience.

Arkadina doesn't talk so much about art as about the artist—herself, as it happens. Chekhov called her an "egoist" and many touches contribute to a portrait of the actor as Narcissus. We've seen Arkadina attack her son for his own artistic ambitions; later she'll announce that she's never read his published stories, "I just don't have the time." In their famous quarrel as she bandages his self-inflicted head wound, she tells him that he has "no talent—just pretensions" and he in turn calls her a "hack." Though it's not quite fair, Konstantin's epithet is rather more accurate. Fame, éclat, position are what his mother wants. When she does speak about acting, it's to call attention to her successes: "They gave me the warmest reception in Kharkov, my dears. My head is still spinning! . . . I wore a gorgeous gown."

There's fine irony and splendidly deft characterization in her reaction to a Maupassant story they've been reading aloud at the beginning of Act Two. Arkadina reads from "On the Water": "When a woman has chosen a writer whom she wishes to captivate, she bombards him with compliments, kindnesses and favors." She breaks off reading to say, "Well, that may be true for the French, but we're not like that at all" and then reads some more lines to herself and tells Nina that "the rest isn't interesting or . . . accurate."

She speaks highly of Trigorin's stories, but we suspect that, as was true of her son's work, she hasn't read them, having instead captured him and his name. She's a miser who gives three servants a ruble to split among themselves; she's a prima donna in almost every respect. But though she clearly incarnates Chekhov's deep dislike for the artist or practitioner consumed by self, something a little more positive about her, a few bases for redemption, escapes his authorial vigilance. She does love her brother and in a beleaguered way her son, and is generous enough to encourage Nina to go on the stage.

Whether or not she is a really bad actor, a fake in other words, as some commentators think she is, seems to me not to be the point. We've only Treplev's assertion that she's a "hack" (or "drone," as the Russian word *rutinyor* can also be translated); in his screed against her, Chekhov never even hints that she's untalented. No, her presence in the play is as a specimen of existence and behavior in whom self-absorption is a deep coloration. She should never be played on a single strident note, for she isn't a villain but the occupant of one end of a spectrum covering the variations of selves as they engage with love and art, the way Nina stands at the other end.

Nina. I wrote earlier of how she begins as stage-struck and of her infatuation with some presumedly thrilling elements of artistic life; as an aspect of that phase we see her also as "star-struck." When Shamrayev rudely tells Arkadina that no horses are available to take her to the station, Nina says to Polina, "To refuse . . . a famous actress! Surely her slightest wish, her merest whim, is more important than your farm? Simply incredible!" The evolution, or education, that carries her far past these immature conditions of mind and spirit lies behind Chekhov's having written, "To me, Nina's part is everything in the play."[11] But I have to defer my consideration of how this "everything" accumulates and decisively asserts itself, until we have the rest of *The Seagull*'s substance in our grasp.

LOVE

If we were to imagine a piece of music inspired by some aspect of *The Seagull*, a likely one might be called "The Love Variations" or maybe, borrowing from

Bach, "Chaconne for Violin Solo on an Amorous Theme." "Five tons of love," Chekhov had jestingly said the play contained, but of course the real point isn't such undifferentiated heft but the diversity on display, and the intermeshings. In that last regard there are moments when we're reminded of Arthur Schnitzler's play *Reigen* or, as it's better known to us, *La ronde,* written five years later out of a very different, far narrower sensibility and idea but somewhat resembling Chekhov's play in the way its characters link up in a chain of carnality or carnal aspiration, as well as in a skein of romantic longing.

I'll begin with the lesser characters' desires, all of them, as it happens, unsatisfied. I say "as it happens," but Chekhov never lets things simply happen, for he's always and wholly the deliberate artist. Not to have your cravings fulfilled is as instructive and dramatic as to attain satisfaction, especially in light of the fact that for the major characters satisfaction is always partial, temporary, or fugitive. What love *doesn't* do or bring is a central "action" of *The Seagull,* and how it affects other aspects of life, most pointedly the morale of artistic practice, is another and even more important one.

Medvedenko loves Masha, Masha loves Konstantin, Polina loves Dorn. None of these lovers is, in the old-fashioned term, requited, and much of the play's lower level or integumentary buzz and hum of conversation and musings is made up of their sense of injury or deprivation. Medvedenko is the first to declare his emotion, to which Masha's response is, "I'm touched by your love but I can't love you back and that's that." Then, in a fine example of how Chekhov, beginning with *The Seagull,* will often have his characters change the subject whenever it threatens to become too ponderous—or, at times, too disturbing—she adds, "Have some [snuff]." Later, in despair over Konstantin's indifference to her, she consents to marry Medvedenko, rationalizing her decision to Trigorin: "To love without hope, to wait whole years for something . . . . But when I get married I won't have time for love."

She's lying or deceiving herself. When she does marry Medvedenko she continues to treat him with brutal scorn and keeps the torch burning for Treplev, to the point where her mother Polina embarrassingly pleads with him on her behalf: "All a woman needs, Kostya, is to be looked on kindly. I know for myself." For her part Polina "imploringly" says to Dorn, "Evgenii, my dear, my beloved, let me come and live with you." Dorn, who earlier had made the remark about the "lot of loving" going on, tells her, "I'm fifty-five . . . it's too late for me to change my life." The most sceptical of all the characters, as well as the most detached, Dorn moves to deflect and disarm the passions swirling

The Seagull

around him with bits of balladry, half-mocking commentary on the love-charged atmosphere: "Tell me not your young life's ruined" and "Oh, speak to her, you flowers."

These three minor characters in love aspire to an "other" as an agency of deliverance: Medvedenko from his material and emotional impoverishment and the lack of self-esteem his sententiousness masks; Polina from her unhappy marriage to the cold-spirited Shamrayev; Masha from the emptiness of a life without any man she thinks equal to the high estimate she's made of her own worth—Medvedenko clearly doesn't fill the bill. And motivations or dispositions like these are present in the major characters too, only with greater complication and weightier consequences.

Arkadina needs Trigorin for her own amour propre and as a shield against the loneliness or, more deeply, the solipsism her selfish, brittle life creates. In turn Trigorin stays placidly with her, out of what he calls his "flabby, spineless" nature (one way he doesn't resemble Chekhov!), until his writer's quest for new material and his need for emotional replenishment, or rejuvenation, encounter Nina. She begins by being in love with Konstantin, mildly, as a kind of early habit, we suspect, then falls for Trigorin, who seems to beckon with the promise of a glamorous new life. And Konstantin needs Nina for reasons of ego as well as for a muse, a reliable source of inspiration.

And so for all the characters-in-love the common condition is need. This sometimes displays itself directly, but more often it makes its way to everyone's consciousness through speech whose excessiveness and rhetorical zeal betray a disjunction between feeling and fact, emotion and its object. I said at the beginning that I think the prevailing spirit of *The Seagull* is one of "antiromanticism." This negative quality is grounded precisely on repeated expressions of romantic desire itself, flowery outbursts about the wonders of the other and dirges on love's absence. The characters lay bare their hearts and in so doing reveal their dreamy or febrile overvaluation of love.

Listen to the twittering eloquence of the love birds, along with some harsher notes:

Konstantin on Nina: "I can't live without her. . . . Even the sound of her footsteps is wonderful. . . . My enchantress, my dream. . . ."

Masha (talking to Dorn) on Konstantin: "I'm suffering. No one, no one knows how I suffer! (Puts her head on his breast, quietly.) I love Konstantin."

Trigorin on Nina: "Young love . . . delightful and poetic—that carries you off to a world of daydreams—only such love can give one happiness on this earth."

And to her: "You're so wonderful . . . your marvelous eyes . . . your indescribably . . . tender smile . . . that expression of angelic purity. . . ."

Nina to Trigorin: "If you should ever need my life, then come and take it," a line from a short story, ostensibly by him but actually from Chekhov's "The Neighbors," which Nina has had engraved on a medallion. And to herself: "It's a dream."

Arkadina to Trigorin: "My wonderful, marvelous man. . . . My happiness, my pride, my joy. . . . If you leave me, even for one hour, I won't survive. I'll go out of my mind."

A few notes on these urgencies and avowals. One of Chekhov's purposes throughout his writing is to expose or, if that's too harsh, to bring out the ways we fashion our feelings out of culture, articulating them along literary—that is to say borrowed—lines. Konstantin's "I can't live without her" is just such an appropriation; the point is we do live without "her" or "him," or ought to be able to if it becomes necessary and, in the way *The Seagull* unfolds, Konstantin's incapacity to do this, his making an almost literal condition out of a stock phrase will become part of a cautionary tale.

The line on the medallion Nina gives to Trigorin, from Chekhov's story "The Neighbors," was actually engraved on a medallion by Lydia Avilova; on the back were the words "Short Stories by Anton Chekhov." Avilova evidently hoped to stir his passion, but Chekhov wasn't to be moved by such a literary solicitation, not even of his own authorship.

ART AND LOVE

Those two themes or motifs or subjects—better to go back to a term I coined earlier, "notional presences"—begin to converge as the play moves toward its close. In a brilliant stroke of the dramatic imagination, which I'll discuss more fully a little later on, Chekhov prepares the way for the final fusion of these presences—the confrontation at the end between Konstantin and Nina—by having some of the narrative's central pieces of action occur off stage.

At the end of Act Three, which closes on a "prolonged" kiss between Nina and Trigorin, a stage direction reads, "Two years pass between the third and fourth acts." The events of this period include Masha's marriage to Medvedenko, Treplev's unexpected literary success and, most important, Nina's affair with Trigorin and the subsequent start of her career on the stage. All this news reaches us almost entirely through apparently casual conversations; one

The Seagull

in particular, concerning Nina, is between Dorn and Konstantin, who has kept up with her life, even "follow[ing] her" secretly for a time.

The facts, as he knows them, are these: Nina had a baby, who died, Trigorin "fell out of love with her" and went back to Arkadina, and the "disaster" of Nina's life, as Konstantin sees it, extended to her acting stints in provincial theaters. He saw some of her performances and tells Dorn that her acting was "crude . . . with a good deal of ranting and raving," though with a few high histrionic notes too—"she screamed . . . and died brilliantly." Later he'd had some letters from her, "intelligent . . . warm and interesting" ones, but he had "felt that she was deeply unhappy." She'd seemed to him "slightly unhinged" and had strangely signed the letters "Seagull."

Chekhov drew most of his material for Nina's life away from our gaze from a longish piece of fiction of his own called "A Boring Story," written in 1889. In the story a stage-struck young woman runs away with an actor, has a child who dies in infancy, is jilted by her lover, and then goes on the stage, although she has severe doubts about her talent. To this point her story is almost exactly Nina's, but the moral and intellectual consequences of these material details are wholly different for Katya of the fiction and Nina, as we'll see in a moment.

The Seagull's climactic actions, some of the most passionately unfolding and swiftly revelatory in all of Chekhov, begin with Konstantin in his room, meditating on writing, technique, his own feeling of sterility. The others are playing lotto in an adjoining room. Nina knocks on the French window and when Konstantin brings her in she "puts her head on his breast and sobs quietly," reminding us of Masha's having done the same thing earlier with Dorn.

But once again, as so often in Chekhov, material actions that resemble each other have entirely different aftermaths. From this point on, in Konstantin's and Nina's agitated, discordant, and ultimately "failed" conversation, everything having to do with art and love, talent and the ego, is brought together and we witness what can best be described as the exposure and testing of the two characters' deepest—or rather, since Chekhov isn't interested in depth psychology, their most dramatically representative—selves.

For Konstantin, Nina's reappearance seems to be a miracle; she's come back to save him, he thinks. Earlier he had told his mother, "She doesn't love me and I can't write any more," but now his hope springs up. Nina is at first bewildered, almost incoherent at times, struggling to express the hard wisdom her recent life has taught her and about which Konstantin knows nothing, despite his possession of the "facts."

"I'm a seagull," she says several times, identifying herself with the bird as victim and with her youth at the lake, and then, "No, that's not right," quickly taking on a real description, not a fictive one—"I'm an actress." And she says to him, still partly under the sway of their easy youthful romance and shared ambitions, "So, you've become a writer. You're a writer, and I'm an actress." Then, in a prologue to the rapid, violent change in attitude she will soon have to him, a movement away from the waywardness of memory and the pull of early desire, she tells him, "I loved you and dreamed of being famous. But now—." The "now" indicates that neither of these things is any longer true and the break leads her to recite a few details of her physical life as an actor. She thus unwittingly baits a trap into which Konstantin will immediately fall.

Ignoring her words and so revealing that his interest in her is selfish and instrumental, a function of his need, Konstantin pours out his misery and persisting desire, telling her that since she left him "life's been unbearable" for him. Then, in the most fateful line in the play, he says to her, "I call out to you, kiss the ground you walked on." To which Nina, "taken aback," responds, "Why does he talk this way?" emphasizing the crisis by saying it again, "Why does he talk this way?"

Nina's use of the impersonal "he" instead of "you" beautifully indicates her sudden understanding of Konstantin's character, so that her "why"s aren't really questions but a recognition and an expression of regret. He has in effect hanged himself by the romanticism that coats her in such sentimental language and by his having pinned his sense of himself as a writer, his vocational ego, to her erstwhile and potential love for him. Early in the play he had engaged in the "she loves me, she loves me not" game with the petals of a flower (in relation to his mother), and this seemingly innocuous activity can be seen in retrospect as a foreshadowing of his fatal lack of emotional maturity.

What Nina regrets or fleetingly mourns is, I think, her loss of innocence in regard to Konstantin, the death of their shared values and beliefs. She has already lost her larger, more comprehensive innocence. In several long, beautifully modulated speeches she traces the course of her spiritual growth. Because of "the worries of love, jealousy" and his "always laugh[ing] at my dreams," her life with Trigorin had made her "petty and small-minded" and her acting had "lost all meaning" and suffered "terribly." But now, she says, "I'm not like I was." Through a process of maturation that Chekhov doesn't describe, and doesn't have to, she has learned to esteem herself and "delight in" her work. Most significant for *The Seagull*'s pervasive themes, she has learned what it means to be an artist.

"I know now, I understand," she tells Konstantin, "that in our work—it doesn't matter whether we act for the stage or write—the most important thing isn't fame or glory, or anything I had dreamed about, but the ability to endure. To know how to bear your cross and have faith . . . when I think about my vocation, I'm not afraid of life."

For all their differences, Nina has come to share with Trigorin an attitude towards what it means to be an artist, or rather towards what it ought not mean. It isn't "fame or glory" that one should be after, it's not narrow egoistic satisfaction but something strangely "impersonal," worked at with a kind of detached love or at least a freedom from self-importance. Nina is more "advanced" than Trigorin, we might say, more "positive"; but both are better equipped to go on, to survive, than Konstantin, whose sick ego is lost in conflicting realms of types of satisfaction.

We'll remember that Nina's education began with Trigorin's deflation of her romantic view of the artist's life, in those speeches of his about how unglamorous it really is. And now her speech to Konstantin completes the process of maturation, or is its sign. In various ways Nina's idea of "enduring," spiritual stamina, will be active in every Chekhov play to come; the great difference between Katya of "A Boring Story" and Nina is that the girl of the story gives up in the face of adversity.

In profound contrast to Treplev's having allowed his romantic hunger for Nina to ruin his self-possession, she neither denounces Trigorin nor pines for him, as a lesser dramatist would certainly have made her do; instead she confesses to still loving him, "passionately, desperately," yet without allowing this to at all weaken her resolve to forge her own life as an artist or in any way diminish her determination to endure. She has been able to separate the realms of love and work, the *Lieben und Arbeit* of Freud's prescription for a happy life, those two central components, of which most often it's only given us to possess one.

When she leaves she allows herself a moment of fond remembrance, quoting from Konstantin's little play, something from their mutual past. Along the way she has exorcised the image of the seagull with which both Trigorin, for whom she and the bird had been material for a story, and Konstantin, stuck in barren literary imaginings, continue to identify her.

Left to himself, Konstantin offers one last revelation of his weakness and immaturity. If his mother were to learn of Nina's visit, he thinks, "It might upset her." A few minutes later, from behind his closed door, we hear the shot.

THE ART OF *THE SEAGULL*

"I'm flagrantly disregarding the basic tenets of the stage."[12] In that famous high-spirited letter I quoted from earlier, Chekhov, for one of the few times we know about, spoke of, or at least alluded to, matters of technique in his work, the methods he was choosing to make his plays take the shapes he wanted them to have. Uncharacteristically, he had claimed originality for *Ivanov*, but that was in regard to its plot, which, we'll remember, he had called "unprecedented" because it had broken with the long tradition of plays as moral struggles, pitched between heroes and villains. And though *Ivanov* had exhibited a number of innovative dramaturgical steps, they were uncertain or incomplete and were surrounded by elements of a not yet fully superseded practice; nor, in any case, did Chekhov make mention of any of them.

The most basic theatrical "tenet" he was ignoring in the composition of *The Seagull* was that of the nature of *action,* as this was conceived by the largely melodramatic or farcical imagination out of which at the time proceeded nearly all the plays of the reigning French style and its Russian imitations. But this principle he was spurning or sidling around had energized most classical drama too, though much more subtly.

A play has to be materially active, it was thought, full of incidents or built around one or two really big ones, and what physically happens on the stage is of a different order from, and almost always more decisive than, what is said. Chekhov's implicit reply to this was that speech can be a good part, perhaps even most, of what "happens" in a play, as much an action as any sword thrust or discovery of a lover in a closet or arrival of a letter with fateful news.

Eugène Scribe, the high priest of *les drames des boulevardes,* those well-made plays of French popular theater, once wrote that "when my story is right, when I have the events of my play firmly in hand, I could have my janitor write it." How can you not be impressed by the magnificent shamelessness of this assertion, which stands as the polar opposite of Chekhov's method, indeed of his entire sense of drama as an art?

For him events don't dictate the writing but very nearly the other way round. Speech is action, something taking place. Dialogue can therefore be much more than comment on physical activity, or an environment for it, an instigation toward it, or its verbal counterpart. Beginning with *The Seagull* things *said* in Chekhov's theater constitute most of the drama. Material occurrences have their own necessity and integrity, but in a shift with enormous consequences for the future of the stage, they mainly serve now to spring speech—the executive instrument of thought—into life, behaving as language's outcomes more than its causes. Or events accompany language as a sort of ballast, preventing words from flying off like balloons, the way they do in the sort of sterile dramas we disconsolately call "talky," of which Konstantin's little play at the beginning of *The Seagull* is an example.

That the play's chief physical eventfulness—Nina's flight with Trigorin, her baby's birth and death and her early career as an actor; Masha's marriage to Medvedenko; the shooting of the gull; and Konstantin's suicide—that all this takes place off stage, out of view, with most of the events not even made known until time has passed, has several powerful effects. It deeply undercuts if it doesn't entirely eliminate the possibility of melodramatic excess; it "cools" the play down and so allows reflectiveness to control sensation; and it therefore enables us to experience the play more as a pattern of animate consciousness, a set of moral and psychic rhythms and discoveries, than as a narrow, emotionally overwrought tale.

This shift from the explicit to the implied or reported on, from activity before our eyes to that which reaches us through language, is the movement David Magarshack so usefully if incompletely and programatically described as being from "direct" action to "indirect." For all its basic accuracy the formulation is too neat; it tends to blur the relationship between physicality and speech and gives insufficient weight to language's own directness, the way it can exist as action in its own right. In his effort to account for the radical change in Chekhov's dramaturgy, Magarshack saw the process in too formulaic a way, but his fundamental argument—that at some point Chekhov stopped building his plays around large physical scenes in favor of a dispersal of action and the replacement of statement by suggestion—was a greatly original perception at the time and remains essentially sound.

Whatever its nature, the "indirect" has the great and mysterious virtue of freeing us from the tyranny of a priori assumptions, the ones on which sentimental drama, or any heavily plotted kind, is based. Melodrama, I once wrote, "may be defined as physical or emotional action for its own sake, action without moral or spiritual consequences or whose consequences of those kinds have atrophied and turned into cliché precisely by having been the staples of previous 'high' drama." Theater—this is as good a time as any to say it—is the most cannibalistic of the arts, forever chewing on its own history.

The a priori assumptions—amorous passion can be fatal, murder is detestable, a cuckold is ridiculous, and the like—move us in the direction of the already known; they create a stasis of imagination, its defeat, really, by sensation, habit, cliché. On the most trivial level physicality tends to carry its own fixed meanings; to scratch one's head is to indicate bewilderment, to shake one's fist, anger. In regard to the theater, where the connections between inner and outer reality are of course paramount, these correspondences have always been present and were more than once codified, perhaps most notably by Goethe, who composed a manual for actors in which a great range of emotions and states of being were given their "correct" physical equivalents or objective correlatives.

We may be more sophisticated than that, yet so strong is our compulsion to read things this way, so thorough has been our indoctrination in it, that one secret of good acting, *pace* Goethe, is to make gestures that are unexpected, unpredictable, yet that feel exactly right in the *aesthetic* context—to scratch one's head in anger, it might be, for the purposes of this argument, or to shake one's fist in bewilderment.

The larger point about this in relation to *The Seagull* is that had we witnessed any crucial parts of Nina's life between the acts (to take one large part of what Chekhov moved "off"), had it been given to us unmediated, we would have been swayed toward emotions too inelastic and circumscribed for the play's amplitude, too small, paradoxical as that might sound in light of the broad material scope, because fixed and conventional. Pity for the infant's death, sympathy for the abandoned lover, perhaps contempt for Trigorin: such "natural" feelings would have flattened out the subtleties of Chekhov's scheme and converted the truest action—Nina's movement into spiritual and psychological maturity against a frieze of other characters more or less arrested within their situations and personalities—into the story of an ill-treated, doggedly ambitious young woman who somehow manages to survive.

As the play is constructed, Nina's inner change takes place away from our awareness; what we do see are the crystallization and articulation of her new self. We get the "facts" about her interim life first from Konstantin, who wholly misinterprets them because he sees them conventionally, and then the truth from her own lips. The contrast, which is at the same time the difference in their natures, is superbly dramatic, unfolding as a *coup de théâtre* in the realm of consciousness such as an ordinary drama of highlighted physical events could not have given us.

Except for Anna's death *Ivanov* had offered its chief physical particularities to our direct gaze. And surely the most instructive demonstration of Chekhov's growth from that play to *The Seagull* is in the suicides with which both dramas end. Nikolai shoots himself before our eyes, Konstantin away from them. The obvious difference is that the latter suicide is at a distance, reaching us obliquely—the sound of the shot, Dorn's whispered words to Sorin—and that this greatly diminishes the emotional impact of the event. But this is an accession to the imagination, not a loss, for the assault on the senses of the suicide on stage, no matter how discreetly done, leaves no space for reflection, specifically about the significance of the act, in itself and, more important, in relation to other things. No space for reflection and not much material for it.

Ivanov's shooting himself is essentially solipsistic, isolated from the rest of the drama, or, more pertinently, from any large pattern of consciousness, the way such melodramatic actions tend to be. We've interpreted the suicide, relying on the character's own words, as in part an attempt to recapture his "old self," through a last catastrophic but at least decisive act. It's also of course simply a way out of his untenable situation and a device by which Chekhov can end the play. Missing from it is any significant connection to other lives.

Suicide is always carried out in the moral and psychic neighborhood of other people, directed toward them ("See what you've made me do!") or implying something about them, so that taking one's own life invariably poses questions about those who don't take theirs, those who continue to live. Camus called suicide "the one serious philosophical problem,"[13] and this dimension of thoughtfulness, of ontological query, is just what's lacking in Ivanov's shooting himself. By contrast, it's abundantly present in the circumstances and aftermath of Konstantin's self-destruction.

His suicide exists at the imaginative center of *The Seagull*'s concerns, which are chiefly the different ways people confront themselves in situations of love and vocation or, if they lack a calling, like Sorin and Masha, in whatever niches they do occupy. Especially being tested is the relationship between love and talent, with Nina and Konstantin as the exemplary figures, while most of the other characters circle at various distances from this thematic center.

When Konstantin kills himself, it's squarely in the light of Nina's stamina, her *going on*. Her strength has revealed to him his own weakness in two connected ways. She has taught him in an instant how pallidly romantic and compensatory is his desire for her, and he has learned (we sense rather than are told this) that he lacks the courage—a clear-headed capacity to continue on through vicissitudes and setbacks, on the most profound level through *complexity*—that she incarnates. Her visit and its words hover in the air of the final scene, as the lotto game so casually goes on and behind the closed door Konstantin, brooding about what she has shown him, "defeated" by her example, prepares his pathetic counterstatement. (A remarkably shrewd analysis of the play and especially of the ending was made by a famous contemporary jurist and friend of the arts, Anatoly Koni. "How good the ending is," he wrote to Chekhov. "It is not . . . she, the seagull, [who] commits suicide (which a run-of-the-mill playwright, out for his audience's tears, would be sure to have done) but the young man who lives in an abstract future and has no idea of . . . what goes on around him."[14]

This is why the play is a comedy, in one of the ways I defined the genre earlier, why the suicide is neither tragic nor bathetic. For Konstantin's death is the result neither of some fatal crack in existence nor of an attempt to pass beyond limits; its "reality" is brilliantly seen against a contrasting one, a choice of life that will be lived bravely and with honor. Something essential has been saved out of the entire human substance of the play, the principle of relief from fatality that governs all comedy is now in place, so that the imaginative balance is toward what remains, not what has been lost. Konstantin is the cautionary figure in this dramatic positioning of selves and self-questioning, as Nina is its force of redemptive acceptance.

The mainsprings of its plot having been moved off stage, *The Seagull* presents a surface without any visible peaks, the landscape of a remarkably flat terrain. But this flatness is of a physical order, not an aesthetic or intellectual one. On those levels ceaseless activity goes on, usually small, often casual seeming, an intricate meshing of gesture, speech, and idea. And something else becomes apparent when we have adjusted our sights to the newness of the dramaturgy.

For the first time in Chekhov we see the drama proceeding as though its language and actions are gradually filling in a field, not moving in any sort of conventional straight line, the usual unfolding of exposition, development, and dénouement. The energy thus released, the force of locomotion turned into presence, is exactly the principle of "newness" in Chekhov's theater, Magarshack's idea of the "indirect" but more accurately formulated this way, I think.

The Seagull

Ivanov had begun this transformation, but stumblingly and, as I wrote earlier, with an incompleteness that came from Chekhov's inability at that point fully to shake off the past, the seductions toward melodrama, the mechanical deference given to physical sensation. Resisting these, Chekhov could greatly extend, by freeing them from their surrounding narrative pressures, all those kinds of scene without preamble or immediate aftermath, without *plotted logic,* that had constituted the rough technical originality of the earlier play.

In *The Seagull* characters move in and out of our sight and of each other's, in a constant traffic of direct encounters, glancing meetings, conferences, interruptions, breakings up, and reassemblings, all of it governed sometimes by mutual understanding and sometimes by its lack. A seemingly structureless drama, it's really all structure, if by that we mean, as we should, something inseparable from texture and pattern. The play isn't an edifice laid horizontally yet rearing its "meanings" skyward, but a meshing of revelations, withholdings, recognitions, everything serving as clues to the whole.

The entire substance is somewhat thinner than it will become in Chekhov's next plays; its characters' destinies, Nina's most saliently, are a little too *predicted* beyond the play instead of being fates wholly within it; but the ground for the full flourishing of Chekhov's imagination has been prepared. His vision will darken in *Uncle Vanya* and even more in *Three Sisters,* to lighten again in *The Cherry Orchard,* but here in *The Seagull* for the first time vision and method have largely fused.

UNCLE VANYA
or How It Is

In all but the last of Chekhov's seven full-length plays, pistol shots figure more or less decisively in the action. So conscious was he of this history of detonations that while he was working on *The Cherry Orchard* in September 1903 he saw fit to write to his wife, the actress Olga Knipper, that "incidentally, there's not one shot in the entire play."[1] The ones that had resounded in the other six plays had resulted in three suicides—two of them carried out off stage—a murder, a man killed in a duel, and two "bang"s that didn't hurt anybody.

Those two, which we hear in *Uncle Vanya*, are aesthetically the most interesting of the whole series, but all of them taken together make up a prime lode for students of Chekhov's methods. In their particular circumstances, the differing artistic intentions behind their use, what we might call their contextual positions, they tell us as concisely as anything else about his development as a dramatist.

I've written earlier in this book about three of those guns going off. Platonov, in the play of that name, is killed by one of his lovers; the protagonist of *Ivanov* shoots himself before our eyes; Konstantin, in *The Seagull*, commits suicide off stage. The shots call decreasing attention to themselves (though the later ones are not necessarily of lesser importance), and this is a function of Chekhov's continual, though for a time unsteady, movement away from the theatrically obvious. The placement behind closed doors of Konstantin's suicide is a special accession to the imagination because by lowering the histrionic temperature, it deflects the immediate violence of the action and so gives us a chance to think about its meanings. This is one more element in Chekhov's putting theatrical conventions behind him in order to release a new kind of dramaturgical subtlety, a new system of implication and suggestion, although it never proceeded according to any sort of formula.

The fourth shot (about which I'll have more to say a little later on) occurs as another off-stage suicide, in *The Wood Demon*, the fifth and sixth are the ones that go wild in *Uncle Vanya*, and the seventh is in *Three Sisters*; that one will reach us from a great distance, "muffled," as the text says, on the remote painful edge of consciousness. With this fusillade on hold in our hearing, let us turn for a moment to *The Wood Demon*, about which the first thing to say is that along with *Platonov* it's the least impressive of Chekhov's major dramas and in most respects an artistic regression from *Ivanov*.

Chekhov wrote it in 1889, a year or two after *Ivanov* (he seems to have started the new play in collaboration with his friend and editor Alexei Suvorin, who soon dropped out of the project); was shaky about its quality from the start, though he kept telling himself and other people that he was excited; saw it turned down by the Maly Theater for its "absence of action"[2] (an exceedingly strange criticism, as we'll see), then produced elsewhere to mostly dismal notices; and finally put it away, in the lowest drawer of his desk, we may suppose. About six years later he wrote *The Seagull* and a year or so after that *Uncle Vanya*, an apparent reworking of *The Wood Demon* yet with everything essential having been changed from the earlier play.

Most strangely—or, as we will see, perhaps not so strangely after all—Chekhov always denied that *Uncle Vanya* was in any way related to *The Wood Demon*, which he claimed was an entirely independent work and one, moreover, about which he didn't want to talk. (In 1899 he did tell a correspondent, "I detest this play and am trying to forget it."[3]) Yet the relationship between the two works is absolutely clear. The central characters are outwardly the same, even to most of their names, and a number of scenes are carried over almost in their entirety to the later play, as are some separate incidents and large swatches of dialogue, as well as many stray observations, comments, and quips.

The material changes Chekhov did make were to eliminate four of the original eleven substantial characters (while adding a minor yet not insignificant personage), set the play in one location instead of three, transfer some speeches from several characters to others, and pare down both dialogue and physical events to the point where *Uncle Vanya* is only about two-thirds as long as *The Wood Demon*.

Yet these objective changes don't begin to explain what makes the two plays so distinct from each other. Chekhov may have been oddly and uncharacteristically naive in protesting against their being linked, since nobody was going to fail to make the connection, but at bottom he was right. *Uncle Vanya* is a universe away from *The Wood Demon* in spirit and tone, something Chekhov was implicitly insisting on when he crankily denied even their superficial resemblances.

The new imaginative purpose, the altered sense of life, are as different as they can be from the artistic program and morale of *The Wood Demon*. Chekhov called that play a "comedy," one of three full-scale works for the theater he described that way, the others being *The Seagull* and *The Cherry Orchard*; in contrast *Uncle Vanya* is subtitled, with extreme flatness, "Scenes from Country Life." The immediate suggestion is of an altered, darker mood and a consequent change in categorization. The new title reflects a related shift, in this case from the centrality—if by no means a full status as chief protagonist—of one character, an optimistic, "positive" one, to that of a troubled, even anguished figure.

This brings us back to the highly instructive and fascinating matter of the pistol shots. In *The Wood Demon* Yegor Voynitsky, who will become Vanya Voynitsky (the closest English equivalent of the Russian "Yegor" would be "George"; similarly, if we wanted to convert "Vanya," a less serious, or sober, name, it would be "Jack"), kills himself off stage; in *Uncle Vanya* his new incarnation fires twice at another character and misses both times, ludicrously. There are some rich implications in the difference between the two events. Most broadly, if not least subtly, the suicide, for all its having been removed from our direct observation, is a melodramatic action, whereas the failed shots are if anything farcical, although with a deep underlying gravity. Something crucial follows from this.

After Vanya's inept onslaught, Dr. Astrov, the successor to Khrushchov, the title-figure of *The Wood Demon*, tells him: "You felt like shooting somebody, you should have put a bullet in your own head." But this is just the point. Chekhov has replaced the conventional suicide of the earlier play by something much more original, subtle, and powerfully ambiguous. It's important for us to notice that both suicide and murder, Vanya's most likely choices once he's sought out the revolver, are conclusive actions, finalities to put it mildly, whereas to refuse to perform one and then to fail at the other leaves an inconclusiveness, an indefiniteness, such as everything tells us Chekhov wanted for the play as a whole.

Like Yegor Voynitsky's suicide, *The Wood Demon* itself is nothing but conclusive, sealed tight in its structural aspects as comedy. In an obedience to formula that was certain to have dismayed Chekhov when he came later fully to recognize that he'd been guilty of it, the play ends with several sets of lovers united, a married couple at least technically restored to one another, and a celebratory mood reigning over everything. This is of course a classic comedic ending, which is again precisely to the point. With *Ivanov*, Chekhov had already begun to move past a reliance on traditional theatrical models, which means that *The Wood Demon* is in this major respect a step backwards.

In the chapter on *The Seagull* I wrote at length about the meaning of "comedy" as a designation Chekhov used for some of his plays. Here it's enough to mention that just as Konstantin's suicide doesn't disturb the basically comic nature of the play (comic in Chekhov's special sense), so Yegor Voynitsky's killing himself doesn't prevent *The Wood Demon* from being a comedy, however unoriginal, labored, and "un-Chekhovian" it may be. His shooting himself is almost incidental to the plot and suggests, one is tempted to say, that he's simply going to miss out on all the fun. In much the same way the farcical aspect of Vanya's wild shots doesn't dictate the tone of the play but adds a complex, darkly comic note to an otherwise mostly sober drama. All this is partly what I meant earlier by "contextual positions," the meanings an action has not in itself but in relation to everything that surrounds it.

How can we account for Chekhov's having slipped back in certain ways from *Ivanov*? Is there any need to account for it? For those who want lines of artistic development to be clear and unimpeded or, in case of a detour or obstruction, to be given a reasonable explanation, I can offer only a speculation or a guess.

After his first two heavy, gloomy, "negative" plays, *Platonov* and *Ivanov*, Chekhov may have decided to write a light one. Was he looking for a change of pace, or soliciting his artist's soul to go easy for a time? Did he think that with a "friendlier" play he might have a bigger public success and so some much needed additional income? (Chekhov was never the kind of artist who scorns money, if any such people really exist; quite rightly he wanted to be paid for his literary work, not the least reason being that he was so often not paid for his medical services. So he quarreled with editors and publishers over their out-rageously low payments for his stories and was pleased to make more money than he'd expected from his short plays like *The Bear*.) Was that why he had recourse to some of the spirit and methods of his very early humorous sketches and stories? Whatever the reason was, he wrote to a friend during the composi-tion of *The Wood Demon* that he was writing a "long romantic comedy" with "good, healthy people who are half likeable; there is a happy ending."[4]

But though he could of course write with marvelous lightness at any time and some of the best of *The Wood Demon's* occasional wit is brought over to *Uncle Vanya*, he wasn't yet able to shape an entire comedy without having to reach for what lay at hand in the theatrical past. Later he would fashion a true comedy and in the process would change the definition of the comic in drama, with *The Seagull*, and that play would in turn, through its technical discoveries and growth in suppleness, make possible the more assured, graver intricacies of so very different a work as *Uncle Vanya*.

"Scenes from Country Life." It may be that this flawlessly neutral, thoroughly uninformative subtitle has acted as a deterrent to understanding—it very likely was intended by Chekhov to be a barrier to *easy* understanding—but whatever the case, none of his acknowledged masterpieces has given rise to both so wide and so peculiarly narrow a range of interpretation, about none has there been so much disputation and uncertainty or, again, such peculiar reductiveness as to its "subject" or central ideas, most relevantly about its author's attitude toward his characters.

Vladimir Yermilov, a mid-century Soviet critic and an intelligent if greatly sentimental and ideology-ridden writer on Chekhov, thought that "the main theme of the play [is] beauty and its destruction."[5] In his extremely useful 1946 essay "Craftsmanship in *Uncle Vanya*," Eric Bentley wrote that in the play "the Might-have-been is Chekhov's *idée fixe*" and went on to list an extraordinary and, in the end I think, self-defeating number of "antitheses" of which the text is said to be thematically composed: "Love and hate, feeling and apathy, hero-ism and lethargy, innocence and sophistication, reality and illusion, freedom and captivity, use and waste, culture and nature, youth and age, life and death."[6] And David Magarshack, along with Bentley a most productive analyst of the differences between *The Wood Demon* and *Uncle Vanya*, said about the later play that its "principal theme . . . is not frustration, but courage and hope."[7]

Magarshack may have been a long way off the mark, but he was completely right in opposing the most prevalent reading of *Uncle Vanya* as a study in failure, wasted or ruined lives, a portrait of disappointment, anomie, and despair. With variations this view is the one most critics—even, or especially, admiring ones—have taken of *Ivanov, Three Sisters* and, in some respects, *The Cherry Orchard* too, but *Uncle Vanya* provides the most ample presumptive evidence for it.

After all, as I wrote in *The Making of Modern Drama*, "the main characters fail in their ambitions, are disappointed in marriage or love. . . . They drink too much, live idly . . . they make fools of themselves or, if not, their dignity is desperate, tenuous, held to as to an almost forgotten injunction." What else are we to think, before going deeper into the text, but that "almost all the lives *Uncle Vanya* exhibits are incomplete, unrealized, and to some degree morally culpable."

Incomplete and unrealized, yes, though we will have to look carefully into what that means; morally culpable, no. If we're tempted to think of the characters that way (however much sympathy for them we may also have), we should be aware that Chekhov surely doesn't. Neither does he exonerate (whatever that might mean) these creatures of his imagination, but then he isn't in the business of ascribing blame and dispensing absolution; he isn't a priest or a judge in dramatist's clothing, the way some commentators like to think of him, although, naturally, they have nothing formally religious or juridical in mind.

Among those chiefly responsible for establishing the idea of Chekhov as confessor or jurist was Maxim Gorky, his somewhat younger contemporary and friend. In a greatly influential passage of his *Reminiscences of Tolstoy, Chekhov, and Andreyev*, Gorky wrote: "In front of that dreary, gray crowd of helpless people there passed a great, wise and observant man; he looked at all those dreary inhabitants of his country and, with a sad smile, with a tone of gentle but deep reproach, in a beautiful and sincere voice, he said to them: 'you live badly, my friends, it is shameful to live like that.'"[8]

By "dreary inhabitants of his country," Gorky obviously meant both "real" Russians and their reflections in Chekhov's stories and plays, and in both cases his high-toned, fawning rhetoric, which I once naively saw as well-intentioned praise—it's seductive stuff when you first come upon it—now sets my teeth on edge, and his view of Chekhov as a sort of literary Saint Francis or King Solomon is thoroughly absurd. Compounding his foolishness (which Chekhov in his vast tolerance, or perhaps out of a little pocket of vanity that Gorky played to, wasn't disposed to see), Gorky wrote in a letter to the author: "*Uncle Vanya* is a completely new species of dramatic art. It is a hammer with which you pound on the public's empty heads."[9] (Gorky wasn't usually quite so insensitive as this to Chekhov's art and its uses, but it's the sort of thing he kept on saying.)

But judgments, moral attitudes, or, at least as often, attitudinizing are as pervasive in our own thinking as they were in that of Chekhov's contemporaries, many of whom blamed him for not being hard enough on his "dreary" characters. Tolstoy, for instance, more and more a banal moralist as his old age advanced, absurdly denounced the actors playing Yelena and Astrov for what he considered the characters' disgusting erotic antics.

And we ourselves find it nearly impossible to get rid of the habit of judgment even in the face of the exquisite neutrality Chekhov maintains throughout *Uncle Vanya* and the two plays that follow. Indeed, he had set this neutrality in place some years earlier, crudely yet with a justified feeling of elation at his "unprecedented" dramaturgy, when in *Ivanov,* as he wrote to his brother Alexander, he had not portrayed "a single angel nor a single villain."

This neutrality has nothing to do with indifference or a refusal to make moral discriminations but is simply—and the world of Chekhov's art turns and catches hold and arranges itself around that word concealing everything . . . *simply!*—a promise to his characters that he will let them live on the stage without the distortions and biases that imposed moral verdicts always create.

Talent, Jean Genet once wrote, means being courteous to matter. It consists in "giving song to what was dumb," and the ceremonious action these wonderful lines describe has had no more consistent a practitioner than Chekhov. His courtesy toward his characters—the "matter" of his imagination—shows itself best perhaps in his famous authorial absence. Seen often as a deprivation of form—Chekhov the artless, the mere transcriber or camera-eye—his unwillingness to intervene on behalf of or against this or that personage or position makes possible the truest shaping of invented beings. Neither liberated nor enslaved, they take the steps they have to take, according to their coiled and waiting destinies, away from classification, beyond judgment, deputies for all our own lives at their roots.

In Chekhov, then, the view isn't of "what it should be" or even of "what it might have been" but of *how it is.*

Anyone who has opened this book at the present chapter or is reading these pages as a separate essay will have noticed my possibly annoying habit of digressing. I won't apologize for it, but I do lay the responsibility at Chekhov's feet. As I wrote earlier, his own digressive style is infectious and makes up a model for wandering. But the movement, the straying and hopping, is purposeful, not random. Anybody who writes on Chekhov is tempted by the reflections his plays and stories continually give rise to, wants to pursue them, dropping for a time one's own intellectual "narrative" or continuity of analysis for the sake of becoming better equipped to grasp the whole of the work.

And so the seduction is toward what I earlier called "side-trips," excursions into themes, ideas, practices, even discrete images that can't be contained inside particular plays and stories but keep on reappearing in one or another form within the larger Chekhovian world. And it's just his renowned "economy" that doesn't let you settle for the texts themselves in their docile order; there's too much pressure of thought, insight, perception, and intuition behind the explicit dialogue and the stage directions for you to be content with ordinary, straightforward attentiveness bound by the order of events. Hence digression: the work of going "outside" so as to return better equipped.

In a short story of 1887, "The Enemies," Chekhov wrote of "the subtle elusive beauty of human grief, a beauty which would not be understood or properly described for a long time to come, and which, it seems, only music can render. . . . Kirilov and his wife were silent, they were not crying [their small son has just died]; it was as if they were conscious of the lyricism, as well as the burden, of their loss."

Chekhov would never have been so immodest as to claim that he had himself understood the beauty that inheres in grief and found the means "properly" to describe it. Yet this is one of the central modes of vision in *Uncle Vanya* and *Three Sisters*, as well as in *The Cherry Orchard*, though there it is more muted and so to speak incidental because it's a Chekhovian sort of comedy. When in "The Enemies" he writes that music alone can "render" the elusiveness of the beauty of grief and loss, he lets us in on the secret.

Yet what kind of music is this? Obviously it appears in its familiar guise in *Uncle Vanya* when Yelena talks about playing the piano and when Telegin does strum his guitar. But this is only part of music's presence, and a minor, superficial part at that. *Uncle Vanya* and its successors or, for that matter, *The Seagull* as it roughly begins the process, aren't "musical" because of any large function granted to the formal art or through any direct imitation of it, but because

Chekhov has found music's verbal and gestural equivalents, its dramaturgical counterpart. The distinction is similar to the one Jean Cocteau once drew between what he called poetry "in the theater" and "of the theater,"[10] between, that is to say, verse drama and the theater's innate, informal poetry. In this usage "poetry," like "music" in relation to Chekhov's plays, functions as both a quasitechnical designation and, more expansively, as a generic term for aesthetic richness, nuance, and grace.

The music of *Uncle Vanya,* then, as of *Three Sisters,* in particular their lyricism of mourning and loss, is a matter of the relationships among all their parts, the subtleties of connectedness, the alternations of rhythms and cadences, the way words and physical movements, language and gesture, build up in reciprocity states of the soul, its existence as form and its inhabitation by forms. It's also very much a matter of spaces, rests, things left unsaid or undone but implicit, tacit, like hovering notes unsounded, and of climaxes deferred or never, though they constantly beckon, taking place. Summing it all up, among the more acute observations of Vladimir Yermilov was this: "In Chekhov's plays music is born in the depths of the text itself and the [characters'] experiences."[11]

The result is an emotional and intellectual leitmotif, if it helps to think of it that way, but never simply a "mood" or an "atmosphere." The so-called moody or atmospheric quality of a Chekhov play, its "poignancy," say, or its "bittersweet" air, something that, for example, Bernard Shaw thought he saw along with a haphazardness of structure and tried to emulate in a play like *Heartbreak House*—this quality is most often taken as Chekhov's ingenious (or, to detractors, hapless) way of compensating for a lack of action. I wrote about Chekhov's revolutionary new mode of dramatic action in the chapters on *Ivanov* and *The Seagull.* Here I want only to offer a reminder that to think a play like *Uncle Vanya* lacking in action is to have experienced it—for better or worse—as deficient in conventional plot. Which it most surely is.

Now we might define such plotting, with peremptory succinctness, as a sequence of occurrences in thematic connection. This usually follows a familiar progression—exposition, development, dénouement—and this in turn composes an eventful narrative that may be coherently extrapolated and reported on as though it were a piece of fiction. It's the paring away of much of the apparatus by which the sequence is kept going that allows precisely for the creation of what I've been calling "lyricism," a musical exhalation, as it were, an essentiality of perception. "The more elaborate the plot of a given [Chekhov] story is," Hingley writes—and to "story" we can add "play"—"the less effective it tends to be as a work of art."[12]

I think this is true of much fiction and drama beyond Chekhov. There are several reasons for this, but the pertinent one here is that physical events or dialogue about such events—responses to them, say, or speculation about them —which are ordinary plot's main components, are almost never subtle or elusive enough, to borrow Chekhov's own words; the more dramatic space they take up, the less room there is for the creation of conditions of the self, its awarenesses, beneath appearances. Appearances, to be sure, have their own integrity and worthy dramas are made from them, but Chekhov, without ever beginning to set it out explicitly, much less codify it, was after something else. If we think of this, in regard to *Uncle Vanya,* as the music of grief and loss, we are in a position to start to question the idea that the play is wholly or even primarily about failed lives or in any useful sense at all about hopeless ones.

I have one more step to take before we can at last turn directly to the text. It seems to me that at the heart of Chekhov's mature manner and of his creative intelligence at its most flourishing was something intimately related to his ideas or, to put it better, his intuitions about the relationship between music and writing. I've decided to call it his amorousness toward the invisible.

This is very likely to be misleading. It smacks of mysticism or, worse, pseudomysticism; it suggests an overrefined, attenuated sensibility in search of that empty objective with its empty word, the "ineffable." And so before we go further with this idea of Chekhov in love with the not-to-be-expressed, it may help just to mention that he was engaged in something with a rough connection to (as well as basic differences from) a particular enterprise in European aesthetic history toward the end of the nineteenth century.

Dissatisfied with the limitations of theatrical realism or, in the case of poetry, which was the governing art of the movement, with the boundedness of ordinary language, certain writers (painters make up a complementary but, for technical reasons, different story) preached and sought for a presumably liberating abstraction, a realm of meaning beyond immediate reality and therefore at a distance from the "known." A cult of essences, as we might call it, a hunger for occult quiddities, the movement or impulse rests with some discomfort under the name "symbolism," whose chief theorist and practitioner in poetry was of course Stéphane Mallarmé and in drama the Belgian playwright Maurice Maeterlinck.

Chekhov several times expressed a qualified admiration for Maeterlinck's work, but it seems clear that he had no desire at all to emulate him. Though they shared some fundamental dissatisfactions with the conventional theater and Chekhov was sympathetic to aspects of Maeterlinck's artistic ambition, we can assume that the Belgian's work, for all its incidental beauty, was too dreamy, too immobile, too abstract, indeed precisely too symbolic for Chekhov's taste. In an essay of 1896 called "Le tragique quotidian" (Everyday tragedy), Maeterlinck had spoken of the writer's task as that of revealing the mysteries of infinity, the invisible world behind reality. But this aesthetic program had resulted in plays with bloodless characters, nearly disembodied ones who spoke a repetitive dialogue of extreme allusiveness punctuated with lengthy, portentous silences.

Maeterlinck's plays are best known to us today for the music some eminent composers wrote for them. Fauré, Schoenberg, and especially Debussy for *Pelléas and Mélisande,* an otherwise vague metaphysical tragedy, redeemed through their music Maeterlinck's own greatly obscure "musicality." The music of Chekhov's plays is of so different an order from this, so inimitably does it move to its own promptings, that to write operas based on the dramas would be a peculiar act of supererogation, which is no doubt why no such operas have been composed (although a silly operetta has been made from his story "The Wedding"). It is the matter of bodies, physical presences on the stage with complex lives that look real and stand for nothing beyond themselves—not for any "values" or essences or higher truths or deeper ones—that so radically separates Chekhov's plays from theatrical symbolism or takes them so far beyond the dramatically symbolic.

A play like *Uncle Vanya* has the appearance of actuality; its situations are recognizable, familiar, not fantastic like Maeterlinck's; it has nothing to do with allegory, fable, or parable; no "poetic myth" is being elaborated; the air that's breathed isn't rarefied. The scenes are from life in the country, a true place, imagined, not from some compensatory "country" of the mind.

If the symbolists were in quest of a reality behind the easily available, the commonplace, Chekhov can be said to have involved himself with the reality of the commonplace itself. He once wrote that "people sit down to their dinner, do nothing but eat their dinner, and in the meantime their happiness may be [being made] or their lives are being wrecked."[13] To look into this meant nothing so straightforward and highly conscious as what we think of as naturalism. It meant that he would both have to go beyond appearances and to work within their interstices, those spaces in the forms of things and phenomena where meanings gather. As they wait to be recognized, they continue to be the not-yet-visible; his art will give them a habitation and a name. In a sense this is the artist's perennial action: bringing to light what we haven't seen or known before. But Chekhov's great originality, like that of a painter of the "domestic" such as Vermeer, lay in making the most ordinary objects and situations give up their secrets, which, as it beautifully turns out, are the secrets also of larger, stranger things. The romance of *things*.

I think of a remark of Hegel's: "The known, because it is the known, is the unknown." Familiarity breeds not contempt but mystery. And everything visible, the richness of banality or the blankness of the functional, spawns mystery, too, incites, or ought to, inquisitiveness about the unseen and desire for it or, it may on occasion be, fear. Think of this remark about "cultured people" from one of Chekhov's letters: "Their heart aches for things they don't see with the naked eye."[14]

Once again, this is subject to misinterpretation unless we look closely at the meaning the word "cultured" had for Chekhov. It was one of his highest encomia and, like another of his favorite words of praise, "talented," he sometimes used it within its usual span of meanings and associations and sometimes apart from them. He once wrote that the French and Russians led more "talented" lives than the Germans,[15] meaning not that they were more gifted at watercolors or had greener thumbs but that they had less tastelessness, by which he in turn meant that they were more percipient, less sentimental. In the same way, to be cultured, in his vocabulary, wasn't necessarily to be refined or educated in the arts or "sensitive" to beauty, as in our own meanings that have turned somewhat effete; it was to be humane (another of his terms of high praise,) to care about the spirit and aspire beyond the practical. He was extremely unlikely to have known about it, but I'm sure he would have taken pleasure in Baudelaire's definition of materialists: "Fanatics of utensils, enemies of perfume."

Here is another quotation in this area, from the painter Max Beckmann: "What I want to show in my work is the idea which hides itself behind so-called reality. I am seeking for the bridge which leads from the visible to the invisible."

One more, from the French Catholic writer Charles Péguy: "The bourgeoisie always and inevitably prefer the visible to the invisible."

And still another, from Jonathan Swift: "Vision is the art of seeing things invisible."

Every Chekhov play works itself out under the influence of some particular event or circumstance that has occurred or come into being before the drama actually starts, and that sets it in motion. In *Ivanov* it's Anna's fatal illness and Nikolai's concurrent psychological crisis; in *The Seagull*, the arrival on Sorin's estate of Trigorin and Arkadina, whose coming provokes postures and pronouncements about art and love; in *Three Sisters*, another arrival, that of the regiment in the Prozorovs' town, with its reminders of the "great world," of Moscow; and in *The Cherry Orchard*, the return home of Liubov Ranevskaya and her extended family to news of the impending auction of their beloved estate. In each case the event releases thoughts and emotions that have been unacknowledged up to then or have not yet found their voices.

The instigating occurrence in *Uncle Vanya* is still another arrival. Professor Serebryakov and his much younger wife, Yelena, have come to stay at an estate legally owned (the point will turn out to be important) by Sonya, his daughter by his late first wife. Together with her uncle, Vanya, her dead mother's brother, Sonya runs the place, which includes a small farm and on which are also living Vanya's mother; Telegin, a long-time friend; and the old family retainer, Marina. Dr. Astrov, a neighboring landowner who spends much time here, completes the tight little circle.

(Serebryakov, Yelena, Sonya, and Voynitskaya have been taken over from *The Wood Demon* with their names intact, but, except for Vanya's mother, they've undergone major changes; as for the other characters, Vanya was Yegor in the earlier play, Astrov was Khrushchov, Telegin, his place now reduced, was Dyadin, and Marina is new.)

And so on the same type of small estate in the Russian countryside where all of Chekhov's full-length plays except *Three Sisters* are set, these characters move through their sometimes eerily placid, occasionally droll, more often agitated scenes from country life. We can group them in the approximate order of their importance to the play's overt activity as well as to its thematic substance. Most prominent are Astrov, Vanya, and Sonya; a shade below them is Yelena, followed by Serebryakov; and filling out the company, although with considerably more status than as supernumeraries, are Voynitskaya, Telegin, and Marina.

Four men, four women: no other Chekhov play is so evenly balanced in this way. And though considerations beyond gender enter into these numbers, the sexual demographics are salient enough. "What a lot of loving," Dorn had said about the actual and would-be liaisons in *The Seagull,* and some observer a step or two away from the center of the action in *Uncle Vanya*—Telegin, perhaps— might pertinently have said it here.

If there isn't so complicated a pattern of amorous desire or its rejection as in the earlier play, this is because the cast of *Uncle Vanya* is smaller and the three lesser characters have other dramaturgical tasks to perform. Waffles (Telegin), Marina, and Vanya's mother are anyway unlikely candidates for erotic escapades.

But among the major players love, marriage, and the romance of the "other" consume a great deal of energy. Yelena is unhappily married to Serebryakov, who alternately takes her for granted and harasses her; she has an abrupt and quickly suppressed impulse toward Astrov, who makes no secret of his attraction to her. Vanya is also in love with Yelena but has no hope of her reciprocating, while Sonya longs for Astrov, who shows her affection but not a flicker of desire. (In *The Wood Demon* the doctor and Sonya end up madly in love, Yelena and Serebryakov arrive at a reasonable understanding, and only Yegor [Vanya] comes up empty-handed.)

To know both plays is to see at once that the big difference between the presence of love in *The Seagull* and in *Uncle Vanya* is that in the later play nobody's passion is satisfied, everyone is left bereft or, if in one or two cases that's too strong a word, at least disconsolate.

That in *The Seagull* a couple of characters do get some sort of sensual satisfaction is one very minor reason for the play's being a comedy, but to have a good many people going around feeling erotically and romantically successful is of the essence of *The Wood Demon's* comic structure. We can, then, trace a movement in Chekhov's imagination from that play to *The Seagull* and *Uncle Vanya,* continuing on into *Three Sisters,* a movement in the direction of hopelessness concerning love, if you see it that way, or, as I think, toward a sober realism about it.

From either perspective, love among Chekhov's characters steadily loses its power to triumph over circumstances—a central action of much traditional comedy—along with its power as myth. I say among his "characters" because he himself never subscribed to any belief in love's redemptive or transforming power; to act as if he did, in *The Wood Demon,* is one reason the play is so artificial and unpersuasive. For himself, he seems to have had only one period when carnal love was important, the few years of connection and marriage to Olga at the end of his life. Yet even this union was prevented from becoming a site of irrational overvaluation by the wry banter, the imaginative slyness, with which both of them surrounded it; love as deliverance couldn't stand up to their wit.

If in *Uncle Vanya* love is still pursued as an agency of salvation, the way Vanya chases it almost to the end (and both Masha and Konstantin do in *The Seagull*), if love in some manner goes on being thought of as the springs of elation or as succor or consolation, the reality is that the loss of love or its absence or its defeat, the silence in the unaccepted or powerless heart, has now become one strand of the burden and lyricism of grief.

Still, for all its importance, being or not being in love, suffering from it, is not the only or even the central condition in the play but takes its place as one constituent of a beleaguered existence. If art can be said to be the thematic equal of love in *The Seagull*, work is its complement in *Uncle Vanya*. What does work mean to these people? What is it for? Above all how does it affect their sense of self?

In perhaps no other modern culture has the question of work been so violent and melancholy an issue as it was in the Russia of the later nineteenth century and up to the Revolution, with its extremes of a depressed peasantry and a growing lumpen proletariat, and a class of idle, often parasitic rich. Though *Ivanov* touches on it, *Uncle Vanya* is Chekhov's first play fully to engage the question of work (*Three Sisters* will take it even further), through characters who see it variously as arduous necessity, justification, or source of identity and who, whether they admit it or not, experience it largely as illusory satisfaction, if satisfaction at all. ("Utility," Nietzsche wrote, "is a figment like any other and may be the one by which we will some day perish.")

Love and work. In both realms the self is urged toward, given vitality or sent into depression by, one's idea of the future. How does time to come, in our heads, affect what we do and feel in the present? To put it another way: we live in such and such a manner now, but what might be different for us later? What might be different for our successors on earth? And is there a reciprocal influence, from us to them, from them to us?

I spoke of the idea of the future, a sovereign subject in Chekhov's last three plays; we will see *Uncle Vanya*, *Three Sisters*, and *The Cherry Orchard* composing a sort of trilogy of the human tenses, of which the future is the most treacherous. To summarize it here before coming to it in the text, Chekhov's imaginative point is that time to come is always unreal or, what amounts to the same thing, not yet real, but that we habitually ignore or suppress this obvious truth, hypostatizing futurity and so allowing it to live illegitimately, and most often destructively, in the present. In rather the same way we reify love and work.

The impasse or permanent stasis with which both *Uncle Vanya* and *Three Sisters* end, and which is surely the chief reason these plays are so often thought of as chronicles of helplessness and defeat, isn't the outcome of some social or psychological defect, something remediable by, and for, stronger people, but the result of a recognition, if seldom a full acquiescence in it, on the part of characters who with one intensity or another have passed beyond illusion: love will not save me, work will not ennoble me, the future won't rescue the present.

It should be evident that I have reversed one usual order of literary or drama criticism: going through a text to adduce its large issues and motifs, determining the evidence for this perspective or that, investigating the way structure determines meaning. If this were a detective story, I'd have already given away the murderer. But I think it more useful to look at the text in the light of the ideas and subjects it immediately throws out, to see how, once identified, they live as drama.

In the chapter on *The Seagull* I wrote about themes and motifs as being nothing in themselves, gaseous abstractions, inert thought, unless they're made to exist as what I called "notional presences," ideas inseparable from bodies. Let's look now at the bodies of *Uncle Vanya*, those characters in whom "love," "work," and the "future" live, and through whom the invisible, the not yet heard music, will come.

The disturbance, later amounting to turmoil, into which the arrival of Professor Serebryakov and Yelena has thrown the household involves every one of the central characters and the others more marginally. Clashes of personality, hitherto repressed resentments, awakenings of desire, confessions, little intrigues, credos and programs all emerge, are articulated or rendered indirectly, and gradually fill in the dramatic space. Even before the curtain has gone up, the professor and his wife provide the play with its principle of propulsion, keeping this purportedly "plotless" drama from jumping about chaotically or circling tediously round a still center. Toward the end the professor's plan to sell the estate, together with that plan's reception and aftermath, will become the narrative climax of the dramatic enterprise, if not of the aesthetic one.

As he is about to begin this new play we can imagine Chekhov at his desk, pausing, taking a breath, then starting it all off the way he has done before and will do again. The strategy of these beginnings is the same in all the plays, as, in most cases, is the tone. With apparent offhandedness, in conversations off to the side of any "plot line" (Nikolai and Borkin in *Ivanov*; Masha and Medvedenko in *The Seagull*; Olga and Irina in *Three Sisters*; Dunyasha and Lopakhin in *The Cherry Orchard*; and Astrov and Marina in *Uncle Vanya*), we are given hints, seeds, forecasts. By the end of the first scenes these will have expanded into motifs, full weights, the plays' essences.

I said the first "scenes," but they are actually the whole first acts, since after *Ivanov* Chekhov never indicates any formal scene divisions but treats each of the four acts in each play as an extended "take," a cinemalike method I'll look into more closely later on. In all the plays, by the end of the first "take" every character will have imparted some ruling element of his or her nature, some part of the music he or she will be responsible for, and ideas and dramatic materials will have been sent into circulation. It will all have been done through the patient building up of patterns, discontinuous fragments of expression adhering to each other like molecules in a magnetic field, rather than through any ordinary logic of "development."

Astrov and Marina are on the lawn as *Uncle Vanya* opens. She offers him tea, then vodka, reminding him of how he likes his "little drink." He turns it down now, in a tic of sobriety, but will accept it from her when he leaves just before the play ends. Framed this way, Astrov, who's close to alcoholism if he isn't already there and so likes more than an occasional drop, is seen at beginning and end to be associated with one of the classical remedies for despair. This first mention of vodka, of drinking, with the drama barely underway, is revelatory of another aspect of Chekhov's method: something is announced, dropped, taken up again, put through thematic variations.

Vanya is even more avidly, or glumly, in pursuit of the "remedy" than Astrov. Early in the second act Yelena asks him why he's drinking, to which he replies in a line—"So I can feel for a few minutes like I have a real life"—that brings to mind "the illusion that we exist" from *Waiting for Godot*. A little later Sonya scolds Vanya—"Uncle . . . why did you and the doctor have to get drunk again? You're behaving like a pair of teenagers!" and berates Astrov for encouraging him.

In remonstrating with the doctor, Sonya for the first time fully reveals her admiration for him, which at this point covers up her deeper passion. To his question why he should stop drinking, she says, "It's so wrong for you! You're a sensitive person, you have a gentle voice, and more than that, you're—you're beautiful, more than anybody I know." The sequence splendidly illustrates Chekhov's method of combining several thematic elements in dialogue that doesn't directly touch on any of them. And when Sonya goes on to entreat the doctor to give it up—"Why are you destroying yourself? Why?"—and he vows to stop ("I'll stay [sober] for the rest of my life"), another Chekhovian "effect" will be made ready.

Astrov's pledge prepares the way for a most delicately painful moment, his acceptance of the glass of vodka from Marina at the end. By breaking his vow, with Sonya silently looking on, Astrov adds to the composition one final note of sorrow, the subtlest indication that, after all, things haven't changed, and won't. (Even more subtle is his not taking the piece of bread—which would serve to cut the effects of the alcohol—that Marina also offers him; he has no more interest in total sobriety.)

Astrov and Marina move into a conversation one of whose implicit subjects is time, the alterations it's brought and may or may not still bring. I said a "conversation," but in fact Marina's talk mainly serves to set Astrov's going, as it will do for other characters later on; in another of her functions she will comment, choruslike, on the often exacerbated goings-on and at times insert into these events little islands of shrewd recognition.

"You used to be young and good-looking, now you're not," she bluntly tells Astrov after remarking that he's been coming to the estate for more than eleven years. Whereupon Astrov launches into the sort of speech, part complaint and part disquisition, he will several times deliver later on. He works too hard, life is "boring" and "stupid," "people are freaks," he's grown a "stupid" moustache, he doesn't "have any feelings anymore" (which recalls Nikolai Ivanov), he doesn't "love anybody" except Marina, by which, we gather, he means there isn't anyone he's in love with.

Most consequentially, he introduces the subject of the future, that tense whose absence of contents never prevents Chekhov's characters from making raids on it. "What are people going to say . . . a hundred years from now?" he asks Marina. "We're supposed to be paving the way for them . . . you think they'll admire us for the way we live now, Nanny? They will not!" To which

Marina, a *coeur simple,* if an occasionally sharp-tongued one, responds with matter-of-fact piety: "Maybe they won't, but God will."

Toward the end of the play Astrov will revise his prediction, to deliver an even heavier blow against the present age. "Maybe a couple of hundred years from now people will realize how stupid we were, what a mess we made of our lives . . . maybe by then they'll even know how to be happy," he tells Vanya. "But you and me . . . the only thing we have to look forward to is a little peace and quiet when we're finally in our graves."

Something deeply problematic resides in this little outburst. Astrov's invective, his surly critique of the present time, of his surroundings and the lives they all lead, is with variations echoed again and again throughout the play—everyone is "bored," everyone's "stupid" and "petty." It's the sort of diatribe we heard in *Ivanov* (and in *Platonov* too, for that matter) and will hear again more mutedly in *Three Sisters* and even in *The Cherry Orchard.* It's food for Gorky's notion of Chekhov's dreary, hopeless characters and for all sociological-moralistic interpretations of *Uncle Vanya.* But they don't hold up.

To begin with, why should we take at face value the denunciations by Astrov and others? Are these people really so unattractive, so unintelligent? Is life here so fatally boring? In the chapter on *Ivanov* I wrote about how in Chekhov, in the plays and fiction alike, to say that one is bored more often than not masks another condition, one more painful or dangerous to announce: distress, embarrassment, anger, grief, or fear. I want to add to that now some words from a letter by Chekhov of June 1889. "Poor Nikolai [his brother] is dead. I have turned stupid and dull. I'm bored to death. . . . I have no desires, etc., etc."[16] What could be clearer than that boredom here, apathy, is a defense against sorrow, a psychic emptying out designed to keep away the unbearable? Chekhov's very use of those "etc."'s is a giveaway: they reveal the formula involved, the conditions, conventionally arranged and conventionally understood, by which we try to disarm grief.

In the same way Yelena, so frequently sighing about being bored, is, we can be sure, covering over what would be riskier, more difficult, or more intractable to reveal: her sense of estrangement in this place, the strains of her marriage, her flash of attraction toward Astrov.

Not that the characters of *Uncle Vanya* don't experience stretches of tedium; the point is that we don't *see* them experiencing it, for this tedium is less circumstantial than broadly existential. On the immediate level these people are no more truly bored than we, watching them, are. They've too much to do:

work on their plans for love, rail at Serebryakov, protect the forests, run the farm, read pamphlets that promise new life, write on art. Boredom isn't a governing condition of their day-to-day lives; it certainly isn't a condition of their lives *on stage,* as everything in this compact, animated, often taut play tells us.

In the same way, nearly all the characters are far from unattractive and very far from stupid, however much some of them try to convince us and each other that they are. Astrov himself, Vanya, and Yelena, despite their various moral or psychic afflictions—dilemmas is a better word—are appealing, sometimes wise; most of all they're substantial. Sonya is full of a rough sort of charm, innocent at first and then marked by sorrow. Telegin, for all his timidity and seemingly irrelevant stories (perhaps because of them), touches us. Marina is the old mothering nurse we'd all like to have had. Even Serebryakov, pompous and hypochondriacal as he may be, is far from contemptible. Only Vanya's mother, forever scribbling in the margins, can be said to be wearisome, which is why Chekhov strategically keeps her off at the dramatic edges, having her stick her nose in only once in a great while, a note of tiresomeness and banal rectitude.

Why then do so many of the characters complain about being "stuck" with each other and in this place? To answer this we have to take up some other questions first. Why do so many Chekhov characters reverse the myth of a Golden Age, installing it in the future? (The very old ones, like Marina of *Uncle Vanya,* Anfisa of *Three Sisters,* and Firs of *The Cherry Orchard,* those for whom any future has all but disappeared, are sustained by the past, whether truly seen or mythologized; that all three are servants enters into their quietism too and is something I'll speak of again.) And why do so many younger figures manage their lives in a constant draining fever of expectations, hopes, reveries about "tomorrow," next year, next year in Moscow? From "A Visit": "White, wan, slender and very beautiful in the moonlight, she was expecting tenderness; her constant dreams of happiness and love had exhausted her."

How often in Chekhov do people imagine the future, near or far, as splendid, full of wishes granted? "A new life will dawn one day," says a character in the remarkable long story "Ward Six," "and justice will triumph. . . . I may not live to see it . . . but someone's grandchildren will." And from "A Visit": "She was making plans for the future . . . and this life, when she was working and helping others, seemed wonderful and poetic to her." Time to come: imminent or remote, but either way transfigured, a promise kept. But by whom, to whom?

Chekhov once wrote in a letter a most disturbing line, enigmatic at first but quickly opening up its meaning: "I call peering into the future by no other name but cowardice."[17] How are we to take this? Chekhov wasn't absurdly saying that we ought never to plan, or look ahead when necessary or even when not; he wasn't advocating immobility or that we avert our eyes from everything but the moment. The key words in the sentence are "peering into," with their suggestion of eavesdropping, looking through a transom, craning over the top of the actual world to gaze on a presumably different reality. The itch to know about time to come in "ordinary" people, that's to say those without professional or scientific interest in the future, without formal status as prophets, is a mark of restlessness, disgruntlement, or sterile dreaming.

Chekhov's "cowards," his people who so ineffectually, if understandably, try to occupy the future, who practice, charmingly sometimes, or earnestly or windily, this barren farsightedness, in that way displace their discontents, projecting them onto time to come, for absolution, transfiguration, or simply relief. They wish to know, to find out (Olga's "If we could only know" why we suffer) or to be elsewhere (Moscow as the future) or to become someone else ("If I were to be born two hundred years [from now], I'd be a different [better] man," from "Ward Six"); or they anticipate, like Astrov, that time to come will chastise present delinquencies, or, like Vershinin in *Three Sisters*, that it will supplant present sorrow.

And then they are forced back from their temporary and forgivable pusillanimity by the way the plays work. They are stuck, though not in remediable circumstances; they're where they are, not elsewhere, they're who they are, not other beings, and they have to live through this life. Like Beckett's characters in urns, in a heap of sand, on a lonely road at evening, or like the Unnamable inching through the ooze, they're within time where, because of the secret pact among the tenses, it's always too early or too late. Later in this book we'll see that the Prozorov sisters don't get to Moscow because *Three Sisters* is *about* their not getting there. In the same way, through painfully arrived at recognitions the characters of *Uncle Vanya* will know themselves to be in a drama about how it is, now.

One more point. Everything I've been saying about Chekhov and the future is true for the darker plays. In the "comedies," *The Seagull* and *The Cherry Orchard*, time to come offers a loophole. But it looks out on an open, undefined space, not yet exploited or in service, and is reachable only through some sort of sacrifice, some letting go—of the orchard for Ranevskaya, of her ego for Nina. The future isn't compensation or redemption, but whatever they will make of it.

It's true that the complaint against the way things are is, in Chekhov's work, directed against circumstances, material ones; the despoliation of the forests and countryside in *Uncle Vanya* is real enough, the constrictions of provincial life are not to be denied. But, we have to think, what would prosperity do for these people? What would it mean for them to be part of a scintillating society, or to have "satisfying" careers? How would a transformation of their local world redeem them? We should remember how, in *Ivanov*, Nikolai curtly dismisses Lebedev's well-meant suggestion that "your environment's got you down" with "That's silly, and it's been said before." It's a cliché of social and situational analysis. Nikolai's true anguish, like that of all Chekhov sufferers, is ontological, mysterious, a matter of the structures of existence out of the reach of therapy or civic planning. Sociological interpreters of Chekhov will always reject this, and ideologues will deny it too, as from a different perspective deconstructionists scorn the notion of any permanence in human nature, any perennial condition of the self.

In a profound irony the Soviets chiefly celebrated Chekhov as a literary fore-runner, seeing him, the way Gorky did, as an accurate portraitist of the gray-ness and misery of life, the injustice of it, but stressing that this was the way it was under the *tsarist* system; they regarded expressions of yearning for the future by Chekhov characters as a yearning toward the Soviet state. "Surely we can feel in 'The Steppe,'" Yermilov writes, "the breath of the fresh wind of the heroic life which was one day to triumph in our country!"[18] And this biographer-critic mourns Chekhov's ignorance of the Marxist movement that was starting to assert itself in the nineties.

Chekhov wasn't ignorant of Marxists. He despised them as he did all nar-row, future-crazed fanatics; in a letter from Nice in the winter of 1896–97 he said that one pleasure in being away from Russia was that he didn't have to see "Marxists with their arrogant physiognomies."[19] With the steadiest of eyes on the present, he stayed with what he saw and could imagine, offering no solu-tions and giving his contemporaries their own lives, gray and miserable or not, simply theirs, at the same time as he gives us, as Shaw said of Ibsen, "ourselves in our own situations."[20] One of those situations is perpetual loss, the grief of the actual.

The swift thematic exposition continues in *Uncle Vanya*'s first act, and is accompanied by—is indistinguishable from—an equally rapid laying out of facts, impregnated, as always in Chekhov, with emotions. With Astrov and Marina already there, Vanya comes on stage, yawning from a nap; then Serebryakov, Yelena, Sonya, and Telegin pass through, chatting after a walk; and then Vanya's mother enters, "with a book" which she immediately starts reading. The entire company has been presented to us in the most casual way and the ground laid for their antics and sorrows—all in no more than a few minutes of stage-time, and all rendered without the slightest pressure on us to get ready for a "formal" drama.

Astrov has had his aria and now Vanya has his. The function of these early speeches, some of them lengthy, is the same for both: to reveal the respective starting points of these important characters within an atmosphere for which they provide preliminary descriptions. Vanya's self-exposure is especially ample and, as so often in Chekhov, is at the same time a view of others, partial, even biased, to be sure.

Without preamble he announces his infatuation with Yelena. "Those eyes," he says to Astrov. "What a wonderful woman!" He lashes out at Serebryakov, that "mouldy mackerel with a college degree," someone "who for the last twenty-five years has been lecturing and writing about art, and . . . knows nothing whatsoever about it!" He describes his "dear old" mother as a "magpie" who with "one foot in the grave and the other on a stack of pretentious little pamphlets" is "still on the lookout for the millennium."

Most significantly, he apostrophizes his own bitterness and frustration, speaking of being "depressed . . . angry, all that time wasted when I could have been doing everything I can't do now because I'm too old!" He's forty-seven. (People begin to feel themselves "too old" in Chekhov at almost any age, from the early twenties, Irina, to thirty-five, Ivanov, to fifty, Dorn. Is this a sociological phenomenon having to do with contemporary life expectancy? Hardly. The "data" are inward, as possibilities for growth or change are sensed as closing off.)

At a moment of crisis later Vanya will wail that "I might have been another Schopenhauer, another Dostoevsky," a remark that Chekhov carried over from

The Wood Demon; that Vanya should have chosen two such gloomy giants shouldn't be lost on us.

What has aborted his gifts? From the beginning Vanya carries around a map of injustice, a chart of perceived unfairness whose agency isn't some sort of existential incivility, the rudeness of fate, but quite specifically a person, Sere-bryakov. Vanya, who confesses to once having greatly admired the professor, now envies him his superficial success, feels himself the victim of his selfish-ness, his freeloading (for years Vanya and Sonya have lived frugally while sending the farm's small profits to help support Serebryakov), and is driven to despair by his possession of so beautiful a young wife. Like Konstantin in *The Seagull* and, more darkly, Solyony in *Three Sisters*, Vanya tends to locate the source of his anguish outside himself. But then, to lesser degrees, so at times does almost everyone else.

I spoke before of Astrov's and Vanya's "arias," which may be misleading. Their large speeches, and others like them throughout all the plays, do have some-thing of an operatic flavor, but it's important to see that Chekhov never gives privileged status to such oratory, never allows anyone's philosophy or opinions or personal agenda to dominate the proceedings. He slips Astrov discoursing on future generations or on the shrinking forests and Vanya ranting about Serebryakov into an intricate pattern of general conversation, talk coming from everywhere, which has the effect of cooling off any feverishness or of lowering, sometimes through mockery, the intensity of any entreaty.

Or in still another tactic Chekhov will have other characters react with deflating incomprehension or indifference to someone's impassioned plea or tirade. In *Uncle Vanya*, for example, when Yelena doesn't respond to Astrov's ardent account of the destruction of the countryside, the play's longest speech, he shows his annoyance and she lets him know she's been thinking of some-thing else: "I'll be honest with you, I haven't . . . been concentrating." This is often used as evidence for Yelena's emptiness, but I think such arguments miss the point, miss Chekhov's whole technique in fact. Astrov has no doubt been saying "important" things, but Yelena at just this time is tuned in to another script, her own thoughts about private matters, about love, Sonya, and herself. Her failure to respond to Astrov's lecture or sermon doesn't prove anything about her, certainly not some putative shallowness, but exists side by side with his eloquence: he talks, she has something else to "listen to."

Placing a speech like this one of Astrov's in a dramatic environment without distinctive highs of meaning, one in which almost anything said is as important or unimportant as anything else, means that these "turns" will add to the textures but never become reigning points of view. There are no spokesmen in Chekhov plays, a pity for those critics who, for example, read the cutting down of the forests as the play's governing motif, Yermilov's "destruction of beauty." That the woods are dying is indeed a loss of beauty, but the erosion *Uncle Vanya* depicts is broader than that. (In rather the same way a Chekhov short story of 1894, "Rothschild's Fiddle," also talks about the spoliation of the forests but in fact has a wider theme.)

Another point. As we saw with Ivanov's soliloquies on his damaged psyche and Konstantin's screed against the Russian theater, characters who seize the podium usually offer only narrow, ad hoc disclosures of their personalities or obsessions, so that any oratorical flight has to be taken in context, with more than ordinary caution. Nikolai's libretto of malaise is accompanied by his honesty and humor, Konstantin's justified attack on the theater by his self-pity. So it is with Astrov, whose forcefulness and normal good sense balance his cynicism, and with Vanya, who is as fundamentally good-hearted as he is self-lacerating and consumed with rage.

The other characters make themselves known with varying expansiveness. In the first act, next to Astrov and Vanya, Sonya has the most to say, Serebryakov the least. Yet one of his few bits of dialogue reveals something of the professor's nature, as Vanya, anyway, sees it. When the assemblage is about to have tea, Serebryakov asks to have it "sent into the study. . . . I have some more work to do today." Naturally this irritates Vanya, who, however, doesn't say what we can guess he's thinking—"The unsocial genius! The pretentious loner!"—but points out that despite the heat "the great sage is complete with overcoat, galoshes . . . and gloves," thus converting for tactical purposes a large moral condemnation into a smaller but more biting physical one.

During this first act Sonya is seen almost entirely in her aspects of kindliness and concern for others. She praises Telegin when he feels slighted, steps between Vanya and his mother when they quarrel (Voynitskaya has coldly accused him of not having "done something" with his life; she will take Serebryakov's side against her son throughout), and speaks warmly and at length about Astrov's crusade to save the trees.

Along with its ardor and generosity, this speech, which comes directly from *The Wood Demon*—where, however, it was delivered with satiric intent by a different character, her uncle—reveals a noticeable fervor of romanticism in

Sonya, which will gradually be dampened and finally extinguished by the events to come. She speaks of the way "forests help to temper a severe climate" and of how in mild climates "people . . . are kinder and gentler . . . better-looking and taller and more at ease with their emotions . . . the arts and sciences flourish among them." A romantic and a naif too; Sonya is another *coeur simple,* her innocence about to be tested.

Apart from a few perfunctory remarks, Yelena is barely present until the end of the act. But then in a lively exchange with Vanya she defends her husband as "no worse than you," takes up an earlier remark of Astrov's comparing the ruin of the forests to the thoughtless cruelty people inflict on each other (the occasion here is Vanya's pressure on her to acknowledge her misalliance), complains of being bored, and fends off Vanya's embarrassing amorousness ("You're my life, my happiness, my youth! . . . let me tell you how much I love you") with an icy "This is really too much."

As we've noticed, for all that they find her so alluring, both Astrov and Vanya speak of Yelena as "indolent" and idle, with a suggestion of emptiness, and their view is endorsed by many critics, including Bentley, for whom she's "artificial, sterile, useless."[21] What's behind this serious misjudgment, as I think it, at least what's behind her fellow characters' obtuseness? (In regard to the critics, to see her this way gives support to their various Manichaean readings—Bentley's sets of antitheses, for example.)

After *Uncle Vanya* appeared, an amateur provincial actress named Marianna Pobedimskaya wrote to Chekhov asking if "Yelena Andreyevna . . . [is] an . . . intelligent woman . . . a thinking and decent person, or is she an apathetic, idle woman, incapable of thinking or even of loving? I cannot reconcile myself to this second interpretation. . . . [I see her] as a reasoning, thinking person . . . made unhappy . . . by dissatisfaction with her present life." Chekhov wrote back: "Your opinion of Yelena . . . is completely justified. . . . [She] may produce the impression of being incapable of thinking or even loving, but while I was writing *Uncle Vanya* I had something completely different in mind."[22]

But of course Yelena produces no such negative impression on us if we see beneath certain surfaces, unless, as unfortunately often happens, the actor playing her, or the director, wrongly conceives the role. Though she indeed speaks of her own idleness and boredom and at times seems to float through the proceedings, these are largely protective devices; more often she exhibits a sharp wit, a fine sensitivity to others' situations, and a generosity of spirit.

It's Vanya and Astrov who misread her, unable, or unwilling, to relinquish their first impression, using her to reinforce their own pessimism. "See what we're like here!" it's as though they're saying. "Such a beautiful woman and not a thought or an ounce of energy!" So throughout Chekhov's work do characters misconstrue each other, as we've already seen Sasha and Lvov do with Nikolai Ivanov, Masha with Konstantin Treplev, and Konstantin with Nina, and will see again in the last two plays. We have always to be alert to such biases.

Apart from Vanya's egregious declarations, love is initially announced in the most indirect ways, hidden within commonplace remarks. When Astrov prepares to leave near the end of Act One, he casually invites Yelena to visit his estate, then adds, "you and Sonya here," using Sonya as his cover. When he does leave she asks him when he'll be back, then says, "Will we have to wait another month?" And Yelena muses to Vanya about Astrov: "He has an interesting face, that doctor. . . . Sonya['s] in love with him. I can understand why."

Each of the principals is positioned now for the unfolding of his or her destiny in regard to love. Act Two opens with a temporary drop in erotic pressure, really a counterstatement to desire, after which the pulsations of longing will pick up again. Yelena and Serebryakov are in the dining room at night. Irritable, full of complaints, the professor plagues her to exhaustion. When he speaks of his fear and hatred of death and of how the others are repelled by him for being old, she replies in one of the play's saddest lines: "Just be patient. Five or six years and I'll be old too."

We might notice in this scene a fine example of the small rhythms of Chekhov's dramaturgy, those which flow or coalesce into the broader movements. The professor has plaintively asked: "Don't I have the right to a little selfishness in my old age . . . don't I have the right to a little peace and quiet, and a little respect?" Yelena, worn out, replies: "Nobody's denying you your rights." At this point "a shutter bangs in the breeze." "The wind's come up," Yelena says, "I'd better shut the window. (closes the window) It's going to rain. No one is trying to deny you your rights." The stage directions read: "Pause. Outside the watchman makes his rounds; he taps his stick and sings a song."

It's easy to pass over the suppleness of composition here: the reciprocity of objects and words; the way Yelena's two tired assurances that no one is denying Serebryakov his rights are separated by a zone of neutral words and matter-of-fact physicality, so that the repetition comes with painful, weary force, as though she's reminded herself in the interval; the watchman providing a coda and, going on to the next speech, the way Serebryakov will resume his self-centered behavior without the slightest response to Yelena—"I have devoted my entire life to scholarship . . ."—as the scene moves on.

Though we fully sympathize with Yelena, moved by her predicament, the professor isn't quite the monster he's most often taken to be; I'll come back to this later on. For now we ought to see that he too is caught, he too has a "case": Vanya's envy genuinely bewilders him, he *is* getting old.

Later Yelena will tell Sonya that she married the professor out of love, an amorous "fantasy," she calls it, based on her having seen him as a glamorous intellectual, but her feeling was sincere as far as it went. Now, despite her unhappiness, she intends to honor the commitment. An interesting, subtle difference from *The Wood Demon* shows itself here. In the earlier play Yelena explains her inability to leave her husband, or to have an affair, by her "coward-ice" and, most significantly, her fear that for her to act that way would encour-age "other wives" to do the same. In *Uncle Vanya* there is none of this moraliz-ing and fake sociology. We're left to intuit her reasons—abstract fidelity or an "I made my bed" fatalism. This is just what Vanya and Astrov can't grasp or accept, and so Vanya keeps vainly pursuing her and the doctor prepares to make his move.

To another of Vanya's songs of despair, with its text about a loveless life and an implicit plea that she rescue him from it, Yelena replies, "Whenever you talk to me about love, I simply freeze up, I don't know what to say." Astrov's suit is much less desperate, although serious enough, and, already attracted to him as she is, she is open to it the way she has never been to Vanya's campaign. But by the time the doctor finally makes his sortie the intricacies of the amorous sentiments among all of them have become so complex, have spun out such lines of interconnectedness, that every nuance of thought and emotion, every eventful moment between any two of them, mercilessly affects the others.

Before Astrov makes known his desire for her, Yelena has agreed to speak to him on Sonya's behalf, suppressing her own interest in the matter. (The devil theory of Yelena has persuaded at least one critic that she does this out of a secret scheme to eliminate Sonya from the picture or, worse, out of a sort of motiveless malignity. Nothing in the text supports this foolish notion.) It will then happen that, after Astrov tells her that while he's "very fond" of the girl he isn't attracted to her "as a woman," Yelena will endure even more pain, compounded now of her own regret and, by empathy, Sonya's loss, when he makes his assault.

She turns aside his ill-chosen, insulting rhetoric—"You're a real little weasel, aren't you, you've got sharp claws under your soft fur"—language issuing from his misreading of her that I spoke of before, struggles against his embrace, can't prevent him from kissing her, succumbs momentarily, laying "her head on Astrov's chest," recovers, cries "No!" and tries again to pull free. And all this time neither she nor Astrov is aware that Vanya has been watching the whole incident from the doorway (very much like Anna seeing Sasha and Nikolai embracing in *Ivanov*), "carrying a big bouquet of roses."

A bunch of roses: love's emblem. The irony and pathos of this are intensified by Vanya's having previously told Yelena he was going to get them for her as a "peace offering. . . . Autumn roses . . . so beautiful, and so sad." When he leaves in that earlier scene, Sonya and Yelena stand looking out the window; Sonya repeats Vanya's words about the roses—"so beautiful, and so sad"—and Yelena says, "It's September already. How will we ever make it through the winter." The scene, in which nothing is directly stated, invisibility making itself known, is of course a pre-vision, anticipating and preparing for the losses to follow. It hovers musically in the mind, like Anna's remark in *Ivanov* that "flowers come round every spring but love doesn't."

As the failure of love becomes more evident, the suffering this brings becomes less demonstrative, a matter now for internal attentiveness. (Notice the symmetry between love's oblique beginnings and the way it turns tacit after its defeat.) After the scene he's witnessed Vanya has no spirit left to importune Yelena. Astrov will make one more gesture, dry and formal, and she will again respond for a moment, embracing him "violently" and saying, "At least once in my life. . . . Why not?" after which "they both move away from one another."

Stanislavsky, never able wholly to shake off his background in conventional drama (and conventional psychology), completely misunderstood this scene. He saw Astrov as still madly in love with Yelena but pretending not to be. Chekhov had to chastise this sentimental notion in a letter. The truth is that both Astrov and Yelena have passed well beyond their earlier desire, into a fragile stoicism. Their embrace now is a sort of memorial, quickening nothing, simply a testament to what had once so briefly and agitatedly formed between them.

It is for Sonya that the denial of love is most desolating and, not coincidentally, in her that the "burden" and "lyricism" of grief are most finely rendered.

Like the heroine of "A Visit," she has been waiting for "tenderness," dreaming of joy ("I look at the darkened window and I think I see his face," she tells Yelena), so that Astrov's rejection leaves her heartbroken if not unprepared. The whole text facilitates our intuiting all this in the face of her silence. Everything leading up to the fateful news and the manner in which she learns it makes for a special triumph of Chekhov's art of concealment, understatement, and indirection; at each step of the way a little more of Sonya's internal "story" is revealed—her self-appraisal, her undoctrinaire modesty and equally undoctrinaire strength. Note by note she makes known her portion of the music.

Slowly, trailing her innocence, Sonya has moved toward Astrov. Taking a step past her shyness, she asks him how he would "react" if he were told that "a friend or a younger sister" of hers were in love with him. Later, pondering his reply—he wouldn't have a reaction, he says to her, he "couldn't love" such a person—she tells herself that "he didn't understand." But she knows he did. Immediately after this attempt to delude herself she laments not being beautiful, remembering hearing a woman say of her recently, "She's such a good girl, such a sweet disposition, it's too bad she's so plain." "Plain," Sonya repeats, and the word, that calm acknowledgment of fact, must crack the stoniest heart.

The matter will come up again when for the first time she confesses her love for Astrov to Yelena, the scene where Yelena agrees to speak for her. "I'm ugly," Sonya says, and when Yelena tells her, "You have beautiful hair," she looks in the mirror and says, "No. . . . That's what people always say to an ugly woman, they say: 'Oh, you have beautiful eyes, oh, you have beautiful hair.'" Such rueful knowledge: in Chekhov, characters so often voice the little unexpected perceptions which their meticulously observant creator has picked up, so to say, on his own.

But Sonya agrees to let Yelena be her Miles Standish, and when she leaves to fetch Astrov she at first asks to be told "the truth" about his response, then stops and says, "No, not knowing is better. At least then there's still some hope." A few minutes later, as everyone is gathering for an announcement by Serebryakov, she "looks . . . intently" at Yelena's face and says, "I understand. He said he wouldn't be coming here any more. Didn't he?" Yelena nods.

From that moment, with about a quarter of the play still to come, Sonya will never again speak of the matter. In another of Chekhov's remarkably delicate dispositions of dramatic consciousness, a deftness of technique by which something not said fills the air more efficaciously than if it had been, he has Sonya's forever unassuageable grief move to a place in her spirit where it won't get in the way of what she knows she has to do, or be, next.

According to the stage directions, the heat and sultriness of the first act are followed by lightning and rain throughout much of Act Two, before it clears. In rather the same way the dramatic storm gathers, broods, and finally breaks near the end of the third act, with Act Four making up a whole new weather. Serebryakov's plan to sell the estate, which causes the heavens to open, is more like unconscious rain making, though, than a natural event; it breaks the intolerable heat spell, but in a way nobody has wanted or imagined. But before a melancholy calm descends on the household, Vanya has cracked, Sonya has been driven frantic with fear, dismay, and pity, and Yelena has become convinced that she has to leave "this madhouse" at once.

The scene is more than a hectic physical turning point in the narrative. The passions let loose, the inflammations uncovered, the agitation of souls pressing toward the materialization of so much that has up to now been hidden—all this afterwards resolves itself into the more or less permanent condition of the beings in this play. When the atmosphere clears they will all have understood, consciously or not, what remains for them to live out. Astrov, Vanya, and Sonya are of course at the center of this movement toward stasis, the unbroken extension of the present, but the others too will be carried along into a future without change.

Astrov, the only one of the characters not at the meeting, is spared its tumult. But he has already laid out for himself his relatively arid time to come. In *The Wood Demon* he had been an optimistic figure who says things like "I may not be much of a hero, but I'll be one some day, I'll grow an eagle's wings and I shan't fear . . . the devil himself." In *Uncle Vanya* the fire in him is going out. He suffers less than Vanya, Sonya, and Yelena, but he does suffer. He still has bursts of passion about his ecological projects and can still denounce human destructiveness, but his cynicism is gaining, a gap is opening between his public concerns and the way he lives.

A Soviet reading, absurdly anachronistic and politically self-serving, sees him as "a man who despises half-measures and philistinism, and yet [unfortunately] was far from the revolutionary movement of the working class developing more and more in the nineties."[23] If only Astrov, otherwise so well read, could have found a pamphlet by the young Lenin!

The point about Astrov is that he isn't an exemplary figure, as Khrushchov so unsubtly was in *The Wood Demon*; he isn't Chekhov's surrogate conscience or "progressive" voice but only one voice among many. He's a more than ordinarily gifted and energetic man whose talents and vigor don't, in the end, solve anything. Nor do they at bottom satisfy him. (In that regard at least he's rather like Chekhov.) *Uncle Vanya* isn't the story of this paragon's defeat by an inimical society, by people unworthy of him. Who is worthy? Astrov too has blindnesses, zones of shallowness; like the rest of them, he's caught in the way things are. He's likely to step up his drinking. He won't save the trees, he may even gradually lose interest in them and, rejected by Yelena and unable to appreciate Sonya's virtues beneath her plainness, he won't have love.

Telegin will continue to tremble and tell stories whose apparent pointlessness sometimes masks an outsider's useful perspective. Vanya's mother, impervious as ever, will go on scolding her son and reading her tracts. Yelena will carry out, elsewhere, her joyless vow to stay faithful to her husband. And the professor, truly astonished at the furor he's caused, will, without having understood anything, go on writing, but, again, somewhere else, since he finds this country place, on which he's unwittingly visited such chaos, very much "another planet."

If I talk so much about Serebryakov, who after all is physically a rather peripheral character, it's because he's one key to the dispute about the play's "meaning" I spoke of before. Against the dominant critical reading of him as malicious and a source of corruption, I would point to his unconscious or radical blindness, which makes for one sort of culpability rather than another. The professor lacks self-knowledge and won't gain any in the play; like nearly all of Chekhov's "negative" characters, he also lacks sensitivity to others, wrapped as he is in a solipsism which is less an agency of evil than a gathering place for it.

Evil in Chekhov is seldom a matter of specific sins and crimes issuing from diseased moral being; it's more often a deficiency: spiritual blindness, dead spots on the soul. It's the absence of imagination, too. The most "villainous" character in all the plays, Natasha of *Three Sisters,* is wholly unable to conceive of feelings or values different from her own.

So it is with Serebryakov, though less flagrantly. He is not so much the cause of Vanya's torment, or of Yelena's for that matter, as its occasion. When Vanya accuses him of having kept Sonya and himself in poverty all those years, we have no reason not to believe his protest that he didn't know about it and that

Vanya could have taken what he needed. And in regard to Vanya's related but far deeper anguish, "the best years of [his] life . . . destroyed" by a man he once deeply admired but now thinks a fraud, how is the professor to be held responsible for that? The point is crucial to an understanding of one large dimension of *Uncle Vanya*.

Nothing in the text remotely suggests that Serebryakov worked on Vanya, seduced him into thinking he was devoting himself to a genius. No, the professor may be untalented (though we've really only Vanya's assertions to go on; in *The Wood Demon* Khrushchov speaks warmly of his reputation), he may be an empty vessel, but it was Vanya himself who poured into that available container his own imperiled or simply inadequate sense of self, his own afflicted ego. Serebryakov is Vanya's mode of self-deception, not his traducer. (No declaration by Stanislavsky is more damagingly wrong that what he says about *Uncle Vanya* in this regard in *My Life in Art*: "In the end Serebryakov is shown up as a fraud . . . while talented people like Uncle Vanya and his friend Astrov are forced to rot in the darkest corners of the provinces."[24] The professor is most certainly not "shown up," and while Vanya may be on occasion clever and is fundamentally good-hearted, nothing indicates that he is in any way "talented." *Uncle Vanya* is the furthest thing from the morality play Stanislavsky seems to have seen.)

There's a larger point to be made. No character in Chekhov is ever the sole, deliberate cause of another's suffering (not even, as we shall see later on, Natasha or Solyony, who kills Tuzenbach in the duel in *Three Sisters*). Indeed, people don't so much cause each other pain as participate in a mutual incapacity to prevent it. In such a scheme or pattern there are degrees of responsibility, shadings of innocence and guilt; but Chekhov's devils have at least the rudiments of wings and his angels the beginnings of horns.

But what ideologue or conventional mind will this satisfy? We all feel the need for sharply defined culprits and cleanly traced victims. A Soviet theory holds that the professor represents the ineffectual intellectuals of the pre-Revolutionary era, the false prophets who seduced and betrayed idealistic but weak people like Vanya. How much "evidence" had to be concocted to support this idiotic and contemptible conversion of *Uncle Vanya* into a clumsy political fable?

And so poor Vanya, poor sweet Vanya, accomplice in his own victimization, its perpetrator really, wakes one day to find he's backed the wrong horse, then switches metaphorical animals and fires at a scapegoat. At intervals afterwards he will say, "Oh, what am I doing?" and "How could I . . . miss both times?" and "It's like a knife, the shame I feel." In these three bits of dialogue it isn't hard to trace the arc of his despair. "What am I doing?" or, What sort of person is doing it? "How could I miss?" or, Am I really as hapless as that? (Maurice Valency writes about the "Chekhovian effect" of the shots going wild: "The external man is comically inept, but the ineptitude reveals the depth of his pain."[25]) "The shame I feel" or, I see what I am.

Vanya will try again to do something "decisive," to make something work, when he steals the morphine, and he won't succeed any better. Taken together, the two failures make up a central perspective on the play, specifically on the relationship between its naturalistic events and its aesthetic reality. Had Vanya succeeded in killing the professor or in taking his own life, the first action would have been an excessive response to the provocation, the real or imagined grievance, and the second an equally excessive reaction to the earlier ineptitude. Both would have been melodramatic and either would have been artistically reductive.

This is something Chekhov had to have seen when, years after writing *The Wood Demon*, he cannibalized it for characters and situations to serve in a transformed tale. While he was working on the earlier piece he had remarked in a letter that he knew of "only two ways to end a play," to get his hero "married" or killed off at the curtain.[26] He had gone a long way past such conventions with *The Seagull* and now he would leave them entirely behind. Astrov (Khrushchov) won't have his bride, Vanya (Yegor) won't die; fate in the new drama is much too ambiguous for such closures. Vanya's remaining life, within the text and along that line we invariably project beyond it, will be spent in one of the most ambiguous activities in all of Chekhov's writing: work.

Chekhov said about *The Seagull* that "Nina is the play," and while we can't quite say that about Sonya and *Uncle Vanya*, her importance to its structure, tone, and vision is hard to overestimate. Why, then, we might ask, didn't he give the play her name, as he indirectly did with Nina and *The Seagull*? Well, he most subtly did in fact get Sonya into the title. He could have called the play *Vanya* or *Voynitsky*, or invented a sobriquet for the character, as he had for Khrushchov and Nina. But he called it *Uncle Vanya*—*uncle* pointing up the relationship to Sonya. It's worth noting that in the stage directions he's always "Voynitsky," and in the dialogue "uncle" only to his niece. The two of them, separated by age, sex, and temperament, will share the same destiny, the "work" that will allow them precariously to continue beyond their losses.

For a considerable time work remains in the background as a theme, emerging only sporadically. Astrov very early speaks of being "overworked" but later, a little boastfully and conveniently forgetting Sonya, says that "I . . . work harder than anyone around here." Still later he will deliver his long speech to Yelena about the declining countryside in part as a sermon on the necessity of work. Vanya only half guiltily remarks that since the Serebryakovs' arrival "Sonya does all the work and I just eat, sleep and drink." At a later point she will berate him for this: "I have to do everything myself, and . . . I'm worn out." Serebryakov, whatever else is true about him, does work a great deal, to Vanya's intense irritation, and Marina goes about her duties.

At the beginning of the third act another note is sounded. Sonya replies to Yelena's complaint about not having "something to do" with a suggestion that she might "help out around the place, or go teach school, or go be a nurse." Yelena's response is rather different from that of a willfully indolent woman. "I don't know how to do those things. . . . It's only in earnest novels that people go in for teaching and nursing peasants." Her words introduce a troubling question about work's universal "nobility" and hint at one aspect of Chekhov's own complex view. I'll come back to this apparently offhand and self-contained remark in a little while.

Throughout the first three acts the subject of work continues to be only intermittently and marginally present. In the clamor over Serebryakov's plan for the estate, for instance, Sonya, "choking back her despair," pleads with her father for some understanding, stressing to him that "Uncle Vanya and I worked round the clock." But only with the fourth act, as love completes its thematic task and recedes into regret, does work come forward to replace it, taking on its predecessor's urgency and, too, its dubiousness as a "solution."

In an especially elegant demonstration of craftsmanship in this regard, Astrov, resigned to having failed with Yelena, drops his amorous campaign and accuses her and her husband of doing "nothing" and "infect[ing] us all." He is wrong about Serebryakov (whom nobody ever seems to credit with "real" labor!), and he then goes on to cheat himself and Yelena out of another portion of truth when he explains away his own recent idleness by the fact that he "fell hard" for her. Not so; scapegoats abound. With her in his sights he was more than ready to do nothing "for over a month"; she didn't "infect" him as he claims. The larger point is that work is always ready to cede to love as the agency of salvation or renewal, until the game is played out, after which work will once again claim its right to define how we're supposed to live.

As the play draws to a close, work becomes an almost hysterical necessity for Vanya and for Sonya a mode of uncomplaining but far from simple resignation. As the harness bells ring on the carriage taking the professor and Yelena away, Vanya says, "I've got to get busy with something right away. Work! We've got to get to work!" The repetition has an obsessive, nearly cataleptic quality, and a little later he will do it again: "Work, work. . . ." Just before the end we see the two of them bending over the estate's accounts. Sonya has brought a candle and they write quietly.

"Work for these people," Bentley writes, "is not a means to happiness, but a drug that will help them to forget."[27] This is only partly true: work may help Vanya, but nothing indicates that it will narcotize Sonya or, for that matter, that she needs or wants forgetfulness. (I might parenthetically remark that critics of Chekhov, even the best of them like Bentley, are given to talking about "these people," "life in the provinces," or "the mood of the play," as if it were all one thing, without inner variousness.)

But Bentley's observation has the virtue of contradicting Yermilov's official Soviet idea that "the theme of *Uncle Vanya* is the life of 'little men,' with its hidden sufferings and self-effacing toil for the happiness of others,"[28] and his more broadly preposterous notion that "we know that in [Chekhov's] opinion, as expressed in his characters, only work . . . is capable of creating human beauty."[29]

We know nothing of the kind. What the stories and plays tell us (*Three Sisters* is especially useful in this respect) is that Chekhov's attitude toward work was highly ambivalent, that he never saw it as existential fulfillment, that he detested as a literary pose the notion of working with ideological fervor for the sake of others (compare Yelena's remark about "earnest novels"), and that while he himself worked all the time, he regarded this more as a compulsion than as a virtue or a ground for it. In this respect Trigorin does speak for Chekhov when he says the same thing to Nina.

Chekhov's notebooks are particularly rich in comments on work, on busyness and "idleness," and so may reduce the burden of interpretation on critics who can't distinguish between what characters say and what authors mean. That there are a number of characters in the plays who fill everyone's ears with exhortations to work doesn't at all mean that they should be taken at face value.

On the contrary; such sermons or stump speeches are almost always give-aways, revealing obsession, wish-fulfillment, or pious abstract policy.

From Chekhov's notebooks: "My ideal: to be idle and love a fat girl."[30]

"To be idle involuntarily means to listen to what is being said, to see what is being done; but he who works and is occupied hears little and sees little."[31]

"When a decent working-man takes himself and his work critically people call him grumbler, idler, bore; but when an idle scoundrel shouts that it is necessary to work, he is applauded."[32]

And here is a pertinent excerpt from the long story "Three Years," of 1895. A character named Laptev, who clearly has Chekhov's sympathy, says to an-other: "One must arrange one's life in such a way that work is necessary. There can be no pure and joyous life without work." A little later he thinks about this little speech. "Why had he lied, saying he had grown up in an atmosphere where everyone without exception worked? Why had he spoken in that edify-ing tone about the pure and joyous life? It was neither interesting nor clever, but mere cant—typical Moscow cant!"

In *The Wood Demon,* before Khrushchov sweeps Sonya into his arms and wedding bells prepare to ring, Chekhov has her say: "Misfortune has taught me to forget my own happiness and think only of others. Life should be an act of constant self-sacrifice." In *Uncle Vanya* such Dickensian abnegation, with its tacit promise of reward in this world, yields to a true heroism, muted and entirely without cant.

Sonya in the new play is free of her predecessor's sententiousness; she will work for others, but not because she's forgotten her own happiness; her life will be one of sacrifice, but not because of any moral imperative. In Chekhov's mature writings ethical abstractions are always coercive, in the most profound way inhuman. In the light of this Sonya isn't now abstractly altruistic; she will give her love—converted from passion or, more accurately, with eros having disappeared into agape—to a specific person, her uncle, her fellow sufferer. The process of pulling him out of his despondency, more nearly a paralysis, starts when she urges him to give back the morphine. "I'm just as unhappy as you are," she tells him, "but I won't give in to despair."

We remember that during the uproar over Serebryakov's proposal she had to "choke back her despair." With her world careening in front of her she turns to Marina, in an apparently unremarkable scene whose resonances will keep on sounding. To her "Nanny! Oh Nanny!" the old nurse croons, "It's all right,

Uncle Vanya

137

love, it's all right. It's just like the geese, they cackle for a while and then they stop . . . then they stop. . . . You poor dear, just remember, God is good." For Sonya, as for Astrov and Serebryakov, Marina is a source of comfort, offering them the undemanding affection they knew in childhood. But for the girl she's something more—a counselor in patience, a shrewd tutor in endurance. The geese will stop cackling. They cackle, then they stop cackling: the way it is.

As the end approaches, everything slides gently into place around a couple of moments of different kinds of tension: getting the morphine away from Vanya, and Astrov's and Yelena's last meeting. Except for the professor's unconsciously, and cruelly, funny remark that "you must get down to work! All of you!" the mood now is quiet, somber, about to become elegaic, one is tempted to say, except that the word is too literary for Sonya's last great speech. In the final minutes the dialogue, the objects on stage, and the sounds seem to compose themselves into a frieze in which each element has its own justification and is discrete from the others yet in intimate connection to the whole. We are a world away from any conventional gallop or even trot toward a dénouement.

Astrov looks at the map of Africa, which has so mysteriously appeared on the wall at the beginning of Act Four, and says, "It must be hot in Africa right now. Really hot." The critic Nils Ake Nilsson has pointed out that it's a mistake to look for deep semantic or semiotic meanings in Astrov's words or in the map itself, whose function is a rhythmic or compositional one.[33] Africa, remote, unknown, a wholly other life, isn't a comment but a contrast, a piece of counterpoint.

Everything here functions beyond the logic of narrative and development: the harness bells, Astrov's glass of vodka, Telegin tuning up and then softly playing his guitar, Marina knitting, Vanya's mother writing in some margin, the watchman tapping, Vanya's calculations on the abacus, sighs, interjections, the candle burning on the table. In the end is the beginning. All has come full circle, and this is the unstated environment for Sonya's last speech.

In the scene near the end when he's pressing Vanya about the morphine, Astrov says that "the only thing [you and I] have to look forward to is a little peace and quiet when we're finally in our graves." This is often taken as presaging Sonya's last speech, and I suppose it does in a way. But though the doctor and the young woman both speak of the grave and of potential solace beyond it, their tones and intentions are wholly different; where he's cynical she's without stratagems, where he banters she flowers into eloquence.

Although on an immediate level the tenor and language of Sonya's final monologue have a strong religious cast, it would be a great mistake to understand them as simple piety or conventional resignation looking toward future beatitude. The "calm" and "rest" she speaks of will of course be deferred, but this is only on what we have to see as the narrative plane; aesthetically they're in the present, in the form of invocation as much as prediction, as part of the subtle, elusive beauty that adheres to the other side of grief. As we hear the words they transfigure the moment with a sort of painful radiance, at the same time as they cast back on the whole play an intense reflection of both its sadness and the truthfulness of its feeling. Sonya's lines and gestures here can't be confined to those of a character with a particular psychological nature but issue from her larger status as the agent of aesthetic grace. Their rhythms, intonations, repetitions, and respirations are more than their "local" meaning.

This is why Magarshack's idea that *Uncle Vanya* isn't about "frustration" and despair but about "courage and hope" is a sympathetic one but fundamentally misleading. In reversing the conventional view of the play as a group portrait of "losers," it puts it back on the naturalistic level it so clearly transcends. *Uncle Vanya* isn't "positive," it doesn't leave us with any sort of optimism, but then it doesn't leave us pessimistic either. Everything that has been suffered will remain, Sonya's words wipe out nothing of the past. What she does wipe away are Vanya's tears, in this moment. Utterance is pitched beyond despair and hope, beyond psychology or the objective situation. What she's expressing is the culmination of Chekhov's effort all along, the "burden" and "lyricism" of sorrow.

The burden is where we would expect it to be, in so many having "wept and suffered," in the losses, defeats, injuries, and awarenesses of self-injury— Vanya's shame. It's in the way gestures have fallen short of their objects, words of their intended hearers, love of what it wants to gaze on. It reveals itself most delicately in Sonya's saying that they will work for others but without knowing "a minute's rest" (how different this is from self-congratulating sacrifice) and in her "weary" voice when she speaks of the peace beyond. Nothing better indicates that Sonya isn't transcending or escaping the burden through religiosity than the way the heaviness accompanies her litany of hope.

But the full music establishes itself, the rhythm moves between sorrow as sorrow and as an unexpected, unwished for but liberating opening to the inmost self. Lyricism doesn't transform or redeem the weight of sorrow, it doesn't even physically lighten it. What it does is place it, environ it, bring it into intimacy with the soul which, tested by grief, learns about itself. At the same time lyricism makes visible the hidden and speaks of how grief makes us human; the beauty that inheres in sorrow is our recognition of mortality, which happiness obscures.

The lyricism is in Sonya's wiping away Vanya's tears, laying her head in his hands; it's in her words "the diamonds of heaven," "a flood of compassion," gentleness like that of "a loving hand," the "angels singing"—all those words that testify to her having, out of her sorrow, become capable of uttering them.

"We'll rest. I know we will." But rest, peace, is already there, besieged, infinitely fragile, in Chekhov's art. We mustn't fail to see how throughout Sonya's speech and her comforting of Vanya, with its final faint suggestion of a secular pietà, the others take no notice. And this is because for them the scene isn't a highlight, a revelation of character or a dénouement, but simply the play, to whose music they've contributed, sending out its final notes. So they go on strumming, knitting, scribbling in margins, doing their unself-conscious, humdrum things, as "the curtain slowly falls."

> About suffering they were never wrong,
> The Old Masters: how well they understood
> Its human position; how it takes place
> While someone else is eating or opening a window or
> just walking dully along . . . .
> (W. H. Auden, "Musée des Beaux Arts")

THREE SISTERS
or I Can't Go On, I'll Go On

When in the winter of 1901 Chekhov was told that some people were complaining because the ending of his new play was very much like that of his previous one, *Uncle Vanya*, he wrote to Stanislavsky that this was "no great misfortune. After all, *Uncle Vanya* is my play and not somebody else's."[1] He wasn't a plagiarist, that's to say, he could resemble himself if he liked. It probably would have been all right with him, too, if he could have foreseen that in years to come the plays would be thought similar in more than their endings. If people couldn't see that while the two dramas had considerable continuity of feeling and idea they occupied separate imaginative spaces—neighboring ones, to be sure, but entirely distinct—well, that was their problem.

Three Sisters was not a transposition of *Uncle Vanya* to different circumstances or in any way repetitive of the earlier play's basic textures and rhythms; it simply didn't exhibit any sharp thematic break with its predecessor, the way *Uncle Vanya* had done with *The Seagull* and that play with *Ivanov* before it. When it came to technique, a great deal was new but mostly invisible; for the rest there were extensions—consolidations, we might call them—of methods already in hand.

That Chekhov hadn't offered a wholly new dramatic tale in no way testified to his imagination having become sluggish or to his having decided to mark time for a while in the choice of subjects. *Subjects* were not the point anyway, since at the deepest level they were (and are) essentially pretexts, occasions for the mind to declare itself, locations for the exercise of vision and craft. If the new play had affinities with *Uncle Vanya* and if that didn't trouble him in the least, it was because he had come at last to accept himself as a dramatist. He was able now to go this way and that, to "advance" or move sideways, to double back on himself in pursuit of afterthoughts or reprises, to refine or risk what might look raw or puzzling, doing any of it as he pleased, after fifteen years of struggling with his materials, with the deadly conventions of the stage, as he had thought of them, and with his own recurring doubts about his talent as a playwright.

It's true that he wrote in September of 1900 to his sister, Maria, that "I find it very difficult to write . . . *Three Sisters*, much more difficult than any other of my plays,"[2] another time to his wife, Olga (whom he had in mind for a central role), that "it looks at me gloomily, lies on the table and I think about it gloomily,"[3] and again that "there are a great many characters, it is crowded, I'm afraid it will turn out obscure or pale."[4] And after he'd finished he wrote to a friend that it *had* turned out "dull, verbose and awkward."[5]

But for reasons we'll look into later the new play *was* more difficult, and words like "gloom" and "fear" and the negative judgments he pronounced on the finished manuscript were by this time very nearly reflexive, signs of an invincible modesty and of standards beyond anyone's comprehension, rather than indications of deep and permanent self-doubt.

Chekhov had once written in his notebook that "dissatisfaction with oneself is one of the fundamental qualities of every true talent";[6] dissatisfaction on the part of other people didn't faze him now, as it had earlier, when, for example, the disastrous receptions of *Ivanov* and *The Seagull* on their first performances brought him close to giving up the theater, during the time when he was still in effect serving an apprenticeship, although at an immeasurably higher level of skill than the word usually connotes.

Uncle Vanya had brought him into the fullness of his powers as a dramatist, and although even *that* fell short of what he could conceive, it must have seemed to him that he had nothing much more to learn, in the ordinary way, about his craft. All that remained for him now was to extend his hard-won dramaturgical prowess to the things he had still to say—to compose—about time and work, loss, hope, grief, and endurance, all those states of the soul and governances of being whose atlas he had steadily been compiling.

"All that remained for him" and "the things he still had to say." I sound rather as if I were drawing up a preliminary sketch for his obituary, and this isn't far from the truth.

When he wrote *Three Sisters* during the summer and fall of 1900 he was well into the final stages of the illness from which he was to die less than four years later—the consumption, as they called it then, the tuberculosis which he, a doctor, most perversely refused to diagnose in himself despite all the evidence. "I only get frightened when I see blood," he had written to his friend and publisher Alexei Suvorin in October 1888; "there is something sinister in the sight of blood pouring from one's mouth, like the glow of a distant fire."[7]

How darkly beautiful is the writing here, and how his own "sinister" eloquence ought to have shown him the truth. But if it did, he refused to acknowledge it. He had suffered the first such bleeding in 1884 but, as he told Suvorin, if it had been consumption he surely would have been dead by now! His logic in this area grew no better until the proof came. Before that, in exile in the supposedly salubrious climate of Yalta, the then fashionable health resort on the Black Sea, losing strength from month to month yet having enough left to plant trees around his house and cover his garden walk with stones he himself carried up from the seashore, making a couple of arduous trips to Moscow to consult with members of the Art Theater, he wrote *Three Sisters* and most of *The Cherry Orchard*, two plays in which his "health" had never been better.

His last two works for the theater, they are distinctly different in tone, theme, and what we might call their intensities of light and darkness. One, after all, is in Chekhov's special terminology a "drama," the other a "comedy," and this obviously reflects a change of mood. Yet we can be sure it wasn't one that mirrored his physical condition, but rather the reverse; *The Cherry Orchard*, the "lighter" of the two, came from his desk when he had less than a year to live and must have known it. But for all their differences, they share with one another, and with *Uncle Vanya* only slightly less fully, a methodological exactness and splendor of unself-conscious technique such as we would have a hard time finding anywhere else within the body of world drama.

The writing has become immensely assured, resilient, and apparently effortless. The dramatic construction in all three plays is remarkably intricate while seeming to be wholly casual, to some eyes even careless. Statement and implication, the overt and the tacit, the visible and the invisible, relate to each other without the slightest strain, with none of that coy or portentous hinting at "deeper" layers of meaning that disfigures the work of so many of Chekhov's imitators. And his famous economy has overtaken even the remaining stray bits of superfluity that can still be found in *The Seagull*.

We might observe here that the superfluous in drama (or in their own ways in all the arts) is always the result of a disjunction between theme and texture, where, in the most moderate cases, wisps of things rendered in excess of their aesthetic point stick out, and in the most severe ones plot or subject bulges out into the imaginatively gratuitous.

Chekhov's economy was never a matter of willed austerity, of niggardliness or the pinching off of dramatic life, but made itself known as amplitude within restraint. "The art of writing is the art of contracting," he once said. "I know how to talk briefly about big things."[8] This is what he meant by this notable definition he once gave: "When someone expends the least amount of motion on a given action, that's grace."[9]

The key word here is "given": an action with its own integrity and unblurred outline, aesthetically specific, with only such ambiguity as the textual surroundings call for. Haven't we always known that the richest ambiguity, the kind that, as in Chekhov, expands meaning instead of fogging it up, comes not from things ambiguous in themselves—if such isolation were really possible— but from context, the precarious or unheralded relationships of definite actions to other ones?

Against Chekhov's own murmurings, the miracle of *Three Sisters* is that despite having so large a cast of characters and therefore at risk of being, as he had put it, "crowded," it turned out neither obscure nor pale but intensely vivid, neither verbose nor awkward but verbally just what it needed to be and dramaturgically full of grace.

Apart from the grossly inflated *Platonov* and the immodestly hefty *Wood Demon*, *Three Sisters* is Chekhov's longest play, nearly a third longer than both *Uncle Vanya* and *The Cherry Orchard*, and it covers by far the longest span of time, something over four years. Since no direct mention is ever made of how much time has passed from the opening curtain to the end or between any of the acts—a silence whose great significance I'll take up later—we have to deduce the play's fictional length from internal evidence. This is made up of Tuzenbach's remark near the end that he has loved Irina for five years (at the opening he and his fellow soldiers are shown to be already on intimate terms with the Prozorov family), the indicated ages of Natasha's and Andrei's children, and, centrally, Irina's having her twentieth birthday party in the first act and in the third saying she's now twenty-three.

It also has the largest cast, again except for *Platonov,* and along with *The Cherry Orchard* is one of two plays that don't have a name or a sobriquet for a title. It's the first, then, not even to pretend to try to focus our interest on the destiny of a single protagonist. The title offers a group of them, a collective; in this respect, and clearly in this respect alone, it's rather like *The Trojan Women* or *The Merry Wives of Windsor.* Then, too, it's the only one of Chekhov's full-length plays that isn't set on a country estate and, as I've had occasion to speak of before, one of only two he subtitled a "drama."

These are some of the basic facts with which we can start to work out an approach to this very beautiful play, of which I once wrote that while it may not be the greatest drama ever written, it would be hard to establish that it isn't.

For reasons that I can't do more than touch on at this point, novelists have often been more astute observers of drama than playwrights themselves, and than narrowly professional theater critics and scholars. Dramatists have their biases and agendas and the specialist is more likely than not to be tone-deaf and colorblind, saddled with received wisdom about the nature of dramatic art, whereas the writer of fiction (the poet, too, I might add; W. H. Auden on Shakespeare is an example) is more likely free to see the art beneath the history and the sensual behind a cloud of theory.

We've all heard, to cite something close to this book's concerns, how nothing really *happens* in *Uncle Vanya, Three Sisters,* and *The Cherry Orchard,* and been told to the point of exasperation that this deficiency is somehow compensated for by a special Chekhovian "atmosphere." As far as I know, it was a novelist to whom we're indebted for being the first person to point out the flaccidity and irresponsibility of any such view of Chekhov, any reading of him that stresses atmosphere over substance.

Writing on Chekhov in the *New Statesman* in 1920, a time when his plays were still exotic, baffling birds to the British, Virginia Woolf had this to say: "It is, as a rule, when a critic does not wish to commit himself, or to trouble himself, that he speaks of atmosphere."[10]

If a critic does wish to commit and trouble himself, he has to start by scrapping every trace of an idea that Chekhov's art is essentially or even peripherally about the creation of atmosphere or its near relation, "mood." These are entirely empty artistic categories, best left to the composers of music for

Hollywood. Do we speak of, much less celebrate, the atmospheric quality of Mozart's chamber music or Goya's *Disasters of War*, or call attention to the mood of the *Oresteia*? These are densely wrought works, solid creations, not auras. (The great Russian director Yevgeni Vakhtangov was once asked, "Isn't [a mood] a theatrical achievement?" "No," he replied, "there should be no moods in the theater . . . there is absolutely no such thing as a theatrical mood."[11] Which is another way of saying that moods are too cloudily subjective to be shaped into drama.)

We're also called on to get rid once and for all of the related judgment that Chekhov's plays lack "action," a subject I've been addressing throughout this book. With *Three Sisters* in front of us, presenting us with a minimum of physical activity but an abundance of psychic and emotional eventfulness, we have to look more carefully than ever into the revolutionary new meaning Chekhov gave to the concept and nature of dramatic action. As always we have to take the kinds of intellectual risk he took, make conscious for ourselves his likely intuitions, following him as he goes against the force of habit; for to move against habit is the basis of all originality.

And so I want now to cite another novelist on originality, though only indirectly on Chekhov's. Henry James once praised Ibsen's *Hedda Gabler* by saying that it offered "that supposedly undramatic thing, the portrait not of an action but of a condition."[12] The perception was extraordinarily acute, but it applies with even more liberating pertinence to Chekhov, especially to the last three plays (James seems never to have commented on Chekhov, apparently not having known his work at all).

In contrasting an "action" with a "condition," James clearly meant to distinguish a conventional idea of drama, Aristotelian in origin and having undergone many permutations through the centuries, from what he rightly saw as Ibsen's changed vision and consequent innovations in method. To put it very briefly at this point, the depiction of an action, such as the great majority of plays have always concerned themselves with, has traditionally involved movement centering on physicality, or external eventfulness, progression from exposition through plot development to dénouement, the ushering in of some sort of change, a sense of resolution. Against this, to render a condition implies the presentation of something nearer stasis than vivacity and centered on the internal, and also implies a lack of steady progression and an absence of explicit or definitive change. Why all that should have been considered undramatic is easy to see, but James added the crucial qualifier "supposedly."

He had seen that to "portray" a condition, a state of existence, could indeed be dramatic in a newly uncovered property of the word. We have to guess at some of his meaning, since he didn't exhaustively explore the structures and procedures of the Ibsen plays he wrote about, which, moreover, exemplify his ideas less fully than Chekhov's plays do; but we can follow the arc of his thought.

The dramatic quality lies not nearly so much in ordinary plot as in the portrayal itself, in the aesthetic movements, the way the *thing,* as James was so fond of calling any particular artistic enterprise, was brought off. The imagination seeks its subjects beneath a thin skin of material events; motivations, the springs of conventional physical behavior, and so of psychological drama, rise mostly from the pressures and, most often, the painfulness of inner recognitions; conflict, the energizing principle of traditional theater, largely takes the form of struggle toward and away from those awarenesses.

A condition, a state or situation of moral, psychic, spiritual, or metaphysical existence, more usually an amalgam of several or all of these—for how really are they to be distinguished from one another?—was something one could discover as a "subject" outside the sanctions of tradition and artistic habit. Ibsen's portrayal of the condition of tyranny by the moral past in *Ghosts* is an example of such a new imaginative stance; egoism swallowing up humanness in *John Gabriel Borkman* is another.

Intuiting its proper signs, shaping its necessarily oblique revelations (what so many critics have mistaken for arid "symbolism" in Ibsen's last plays and for a static "suggestiveness" in Chekhov's), listening to its own instructions as to how everything is to be organized—the book of dramatic rules or precedents is of little use now—you find yourself fashioning what James, in another splendid observation about Ibsen, called a "thinkable thing."[13] The remark moves unimpededly to cast light on *Three Sisters,* as does still another of James's perceptions about Ibsen: that his plays' real subject was "the individual caught in the fact."[14]

Playwrights as different from one another as Pirandello, Brecht, and Ionesco, as well as a theater prophet like Antonin Artaud, have all said that the dramatist (and by implication any artist) is a type of philosopher and that consequently plays are to be valued for their philosophical substance, which is not to say for any specific ideas, certainly not any special intellectual "system," but the way they're suffused with thought. And this thoughtfulness, in the exact sense of that word—a weighing of experience—implies, as Artaud said, the power to set further thought in motion. This is what we take away after the immediate sensual or emotional experience of seeing or reading certain plays, the ones we most value, and it's what James meant by his terminology: a "condition," the "thinkable," capture by the "fact." In the presence of a depicted condition, "thinkable" means *worth thinking about*; the condition is the "fact" against which our individuality or selfhood struggles.

To put it as swiftly and unceremoniously as I can, I think the condition which *Three Sisters* portrays (to once again use James's sweetly unfashionable term) is that of living within time. I mean being caught in it, resident in it, experiencing it as chronology or duration only in its most superficial or apprehensible manifestations but more deeply as a place, a habitation; being rocked in it as the cradle of all we do; knowing it as wholeness, indivisibility, but more often in fragments; trafficking with it as myth; projecting everything ahead to await its presumably transforming arrival as future and simultaneously seeing everything disappear into its wake as past; time, the "double-headed monster of damnation and salvation," as Beckett, whose *Waiting for Godot* has such profound affinities with *Three Sisters,* called it in his essay on Proust;[15] time, which flattens out all distinctions, refutes and covers over all meanings except its own; time, which leaves us, like the sisters at the end of the play, with only one possible response to its inscrutability: "If only we knew!"

From an imaginary text:

> A friend of Chekhov's: "Tell me, Anton Pavlovich, what are you working on right now?"
> A.P.: "Oh, I'm trying to write a play about time as a condition, as, well, you know . . . a condition."
> The friend: "Can you, uh, tell me a little more about it?"
> A.P.: "Yes, well, I've got a whole crowd of characters all stuck in time and they have to undergo its effects—excuse me, that sounds too, um, academic!—they have to keep going to some unheard, maybe dismal or at best melancholy music—and that sounds too arty!—well, then, they have to just live, just live. . . ."
> The friend (dubiously): "I see. And what's the dénouement going to be, how will it all end up?"
> A.P.: "Well, I think it's going to end up the same way it began, only different. (Pause.) I mean something will be different and something will be the same, and I'm having the devil of a time trying to sort that out. (Pause. Takes off his pince-nez and rubs his eyes.) I suppose that's the reason I'm afraid, as I told Olga, who, by the way, sends you warm greetings, that the whole thing is going to turn out pale and obscure."
> The friend (without conviction): "Oh, surely it won't!"

I think it more than safe to assume that Chekhov didn't consciously set out to write a play about time as a condition, nor was he likely to have thought in such terms at any point, unlike Proust, who surely must have had rather more than a skeletal idea about doing something with time and its relation to memory before he started on *A la recherche du temps perdu*. But the difficulty Chekhov spoke of almost certainly had to do with what *Three Sisters* was turning into, nothing like a piece of philosophy in dramatic form, as I hope I haven't in any way made it sound, but a play whose philosophical or metaphysical implications couldn't be shrugged off, even if he had wanted to do it.

Memorable plays aren't likely to spring out of polished ideas or from carefully outlined plots. I suspect that most begin in the mind as a kind of music without words, a rhythm of potentiality without details, following on an isolated image or memory or an equally isolated fragment of conversation or some kind of sound. How can we know where *Three Sisters* began in Chekhov's imagination?

Maybe he started to write the play after hearing a clock strike twelve somewhere ("The clock struck that morning just the same way," Olga says in the first speech, referring to their father's death a year ago), or when he remembered or reread the opening lines of Pushkin's *Ruslan and Lyudmila*—"Beside the sea there stands a tree, and on that tree a golden chain . . ."—words he will give to Masha. Or, it might be, when in Yalta, his self-styled "Devil's Island,"[16] his "warm Siberia,"[17] he had a sudden pang of yearning for Moscow, where Olga was. (In 1903 he would write to her: "To Moscow! To Moscow! That is not said by THREE SISTERS but by ONE HUSBAND."[18]) In the story "Peasants," written in 1897, just two years before the play, we find this: "Oh Lord, he went on in anguish, if only I could have a glimpse of Moscow! To see Mother Moscow, if only in my dream!" And even closer to the play in 1899, the story "The New Villa" had an unhappy little girl, "pale and shaking all over," cry out, " 'Let us go away, Mamma!' " To the mother's "where?" the girl replies, with a rhythm to her speech suggestive of Irina's to come, "To Moscow . . . let us go, mamma."

He would have been likely to have heard the music of a regimental band going by, for the tsar's nearby summer palace required military personnel. In perhaps the sharpest clue of all, he had written from Yalta to a friend, Lydia Avilova, in January 1899, that "I am just like an army officer stationed in some godforsaken provincial hole."[19]

However it began, the play doubtless took shape in the usual way of Chekhov's writing, with the work sometimes seeming to dictate itself to him and at other times having to be coaxed, until various strands of plot suggested themselves, possible relationships sent out feelers, characters began to take on traits, and organization gradually rose from the chaos that precedes creation. But at some point the new play must have begun to present problems stemming from the absence of precedents for what he found himself at work on.

As he made his way through the obstacles and dilemmas, he wasn't likely to have seen them the way we do, with the advantage of hindsight, or posed to himself such questions as How do I make inner reality perceptible? or What do I do about giving some animation to those scenes in which people are just sitting around? Those are the questions we ask ourselves, after the fact. How did he do it? How did he bring off this seemingly intractable thing so that it looks so effortless and incontestable?

Which is another way of saying that if the play was about a condition, something presumed to be undramatic, how did the drama materialize? I said before that in Henry James's formulation the implicit idea was that ordinary motivation now exists mostly in interior struggles; how do we recognize them? And in my whimsical invented dialogue I had Chekhov saying that the play was going to end as it had begun but also differently; what does this mean? Most arduous for our understanding, how could Chekhov have *Three Sisters* not only move through both real and fictive time, the way all plays have to do, but also exist as, so to say, a replica of time itself? How could time passing be made to feel as though it was most often standing still? And how might these beings trapped in time solicit and occupy our consciousness as other than *case histories*? Let us begin to examine the text.

Any play as an imaginative artifact is clearly more than just the sum of its governing methods and techniques, still less of its thematic pronouncements. But we still have to start with those things, working our way from the outside inwards, from broad compositional procedures and unmistakable motifs to the finer mysteries and revelations of sensuous details, all that the text intimately holds. How much more necessary than usual is this in the case of *Three Sisters*, with its disregard of ordinary construction and its subversion of ordinary statement in an effort to "dramatize" time?

The first speech is Olga's in the living room, with "the table . . . being set for lunch" in the dining room at the back. "It's a year ago today that Father died," she begins by saying, "May fifth, on your birthday, Irina." After the three specific references to time in this single line of dialogue, we'll hear eight or nine more in the next minute or two: citings of particular hours, days, spans of years, all of them fastened to remembrance, as later for a while they'll be attached to hope and still later to resignation. A little further along the word "Moscow" will appear in the dialogue a dozen times too, in the space of just a page or two of text.

Time and place, memory and the city, the past and the future, with Moscow, where the Prozorovs were born and grew up and where they yearn to return and whose name is spoken in these early minutes with joy and longing; Moscow—amulet, icon and grail, and also place fused with time—ruling abstractly over the constellation of tenses and desires. In such an unassertive way of disclosing his scheme, with no themes directly announced but with theme in the texture, Chekhov quickly lays out the far boundaries of his play, the polarities of its design, and the broad outlines of everything he expects it to encompass.

Bearers of these first oblique indications of pattern and subject, every character, even the most marginal, is introduced within a very short time; Natasha is the last to come on stage, but still she appears well before the end of the first act. As was true of *The Seagull* and *Uncle Vanya* and will be of *The Cherry Orchard* too, nobody will arrive later on to bring significant new information or by his or her actions complicate or alter the dramatic circumstances. Whoever is going to be there is there, whatever is to happen is present in embryo.

All the characters are going to be involved in what for want of a better word I have to call a plot, but the play itself doesn't have any discernible plot line, any central narrative sequence we can confidently extrapolate as its "story." The closest thing to this is Natasha's predatory taking possession of the Prozorov house. But her act of usurpation is carried out in an extremely oblique manner, behind everyone's back, we might say, in the interstices of other activity, with nothing directly said about it as a process and nothing consciously acknowledged by anyone except for one hermetic outburst by Masha. And so it never emerges as a clear narrative pattern until we become aware of it as a fait accompli, and even then Natasha's hegemony is communicated in images rather than as anyone's conscious appraisal—the famous fork on the bench near the end, about which she gets so angry, and her plan to cut down the noble old trees.

If, as I intend to show later, *Three Sisters* does have a story, it can only be the implicit, negative one of the Prozorovs' failure to get to Moscow, but this can scarcely be said to make up a plot in the accepted sense, which is to say the way plot was looked on before Chekhov began to write, and to this day mostly still is.

In effect, then, by traditional criteria the play is composed of a number of subplots without anything for them to exist *under*. Yet even this is misleading, since "subplot" denotes a secondary story, complete in itself, related to the major narrative or dramatic action most often by ironic contrast or by that story's being transposed to a minor key, and reaching its dénouement simultaneously with its big brother. But since there isn't any central story line in *Three Sisters* and no conclusive or even ascertainable climax, the plot elements or narrative fragments, as we can think of them, remain throughout like clusters of particles suspended or drifting in a solution. The difference is between purposefully telling or spinning a story and simply allowing its details to accumulate. Or between using time as a vehicle of plotted narration and supplying it with data whose uses are unpredictable.

"One thing after another," Georg Büchner had the beleaguered central figure of *Woyzeck* say at a moment of special indignity. The phrase is one we use to describe the way the troubles and crises of our lives never seem to let up; it's a cliché enunciating a kind of rueful fatalism and is employed by Büchner as a bitter understatement. But "one thing after another," as I once wrote, can also be read as a principle of dramaturgy, a description of Büchner's method as well as a piece of his theme, for in *Woyzeck* events more often take place literally *after* other ones, with a large degree of independence, than through a chain of remorseless cause and effect. As different as it is from Büchner's play, Chekhov's goes forward in much the same manner.

To remove visible causation, to allow occasions the freedom to at least seem to arrange their own schedules, is to contribute to a feeling of relative motionlessness. One central impression of this is created by the scarcity of physical actions that are the results of previous ones and that in turn cause still others, all of which usually serves to consume time, to give the sense of its being filled with movement and so with extension. We've all had the experience of days that pass swiftly when our bodies are engaged, while an hour alone with our thoughts can seem an eternity, although not necessarily one filled with tedium.

It should strike us at once that, as happens in all of Chekhov's last four plays, nearly every important physical event or material sequence of *Three Sisters* takes place off stage: the fire, the duel, Andrei's gambling, Chebutykin's drinking, Natasha's affair with the unseen town councilor Protopopov, Olga and Irina at their jobs, the suicide attempt of Vershinin's wife. We are either only told about them, in some cases without verification, or we get just a fragment of their physical reality, their sounds: the muffled shot, the fire alarms in the town, Protopopov's sleighbells at the door. But either way they remain at the edges of our awareness, part of its static information, never becoming the substance of palpable encounters.

Then, too, our sense of time passing is heavily affected by the way Chekhov conceives and arranges the separate acts. Unlike in Ibsen or for that matter in any naturalistic or naturalistic-seeming drama, the four acts of *Three Sisters* have no externally necessary relation to one another; we're aware of no apparent reason for one act to end where it does and the next to begin where *it* does. Another way of putting it is that the acts don't *cause* each other but are allowed to exist without obvious narrative connection or any firm continuity of thematic logic.

I don't at all mean to suggest that the acts are entirely isolated from one another, which would be nonsense; a skein made up of character, iconography, subjects raised, and hints of destiny slowly uncoils as the play's largest composition. Still, each of the acts has its own special weight, its particular coloration and sense of the general condition; each has its distinctive emotional tonality and chosen function within the play-as-dramatic-field. More than that, the four acts aren't held together by the relative suspensefulness we feel, say, in *Uncle Vanya*, with its growing emotional tension, or in *The Cherry Orchard*, with the fateful auction hanging over everything.

That nowadays *Three Sisters* is hardly likely to be performed in four acts but in two or, more rarely, three doesn't disturb the point. Blackouts replace intermissions or scene changers go visibly to work while the drama waits, but the large dramaturgical units remain, four blocks or expanses of activity without a ponderable flow of time to unite them.

(The four acts of *Three Sisters*. The language and rhythm of this sentence irresistibly bring to mind Gertrude Stein's and Virgil Thomson's *Four Saints in Three Acts*. The connection is more than a verbal coincidence, for the opera's joking title actually reveals an aesthetic premise much like the one we find in Chekhov's construction. In the same way that Stein's libretto isn't an ordinary story, certainly not one about the lives of saints, but the essence of "saintliness" as she conceives it—as verbal reality, not spiritual subject—distributed throughout a work whose traditional formal divisions it both obeys and mocks, so

Three Sisters isn't a conventional tale but a distribution of the women's situation, and that of the group of which they're the center, throughout a play which only nominally follows a traditional act structure expressly designed for traditional tales. *Three Sisters* in four acts.)

Here are some of the ways the acts differ from each other. Act One is entirely occupied by Irina's birthday party, introduces everyone, announces amorous connections—Andrei and Natasha, Vershinin and Masha as a probability—and breathes the idea of Moscow into the air. Act Two has no really dominant activity or occasion, unfolds languidly in some stretches, animatedly in others, and sees Natasha's takeover of the house begin. Act Three is played against the backdrop of the fire, is full of late-night weariness but ends with passionate outbursts by Andrei and Irina, and has much to say about work and its discontents. Act Four is the physically most eventful and the most melancholy of all: Tuzenbach's death in the duel, Natasha's triumph, the departure of the brigade, and with it the end of Masha's and Vershinin's hope of love.

I wrote in an earlier chapter that after *The Wood Demon* Chekhov gave up dividing the four acts of his plays into scenes, in favor of constructing each act as one unbroken cinemalike "take." This helps guarantee their internal unity and the integrity of the way they distribute the sense of duration. There are no novel-like shifts of setting, no alternations of focus—"cross-cutting"—or temporary exclusion of one element of plot for the sake of another. Plot itself, or rather dramatic activity, is continuous and of an even consistency, never "thickened" by sudden physical complication or given locomotion by event following quickly on event. The result is that time in each act feels whole, without divisions, and so is relatively static.

On the simplest level of fact, the first act takes place in the living room of the Prozorov house and begins a minute or two after noon. The second act is in the same place, starting at eight in the evening. Act Three is played in the bedroom temporarily shared by Irina and Olga and begins some time between two and three in the morning, and Act Four takes place in the garden, starting, like the first act, at "noon." The stage directions give us these times, after which we're left to our own chronological devices.

Each act would seem to cover an hour or an hour and a half of imaginary time, although Act Three might be supposed to last a little longer. But in another demonstration of how duration is presented in *Three Sisters*, we're hard pressed to give even rough estimates of how long, in fictive time, what we've been watching or reading has taken. My own guesses are based on deductions, not on how I've physically experienced the play.

The first two acts are separated by an interval of something like two years, the second from the third and the third from the fourth by about a year each. But once again we have to infer these time spans, and again something strange makes itself felt. The data of our inferences—*this* must have happened, or *that*—have the effect of adding to what we actually see and hear a greater weight of "timelessness." It's as though everything that has taken place in the intervals between acts, the rumored or implied events, has taken up invisible positions in the present, has *gone on happening*, as it were, and in this way stretched time out.

At the end of the play's first speech Olga is talking about their father's funeral: "It was raining, raining hard, and then it started to snow." Irina says, "I don't want to think about it." Olga ignores her and goes right on remembering: "Father got his [brigade] eleven years ago and we left Moscow and came here. . . ." But before she starts this second piece of dialogue a stage direction tells us that "Baron Tuzenbach, Chebutykin, and Solyony appear in the dining room" at the rear, and after she finishes, with an expression of desire "to go back home," we hear the doctor say, "The hell you say!" and then Tuzenbach, "You're right, it's all a lot of nonsense." Olga then resumes, or rather, because she's never really stopped, simply goes on talking, complaining of overwork at her school and of feeling her "life and strength . . . slipping away," and ending with the hope of "going back to Moscow." Irina, who hasn't responded to anything Olga has said for a long time, suddenly picks up on this, saying, "Moscow! . . . Selling this house and everything and going back to Moscow. . . ." Olga replies with "Yes, going back to Moscow! as soon as we can," and the two then have their first real, if brief, exchange.

In the text a stage direction now reads: "Chebutykin and Tuzenbach laugh." After another short exchange between Olga and Irina, again about Moscow, another stage direction says that "Masha whistles under her breath." Olga and Irina go on talking (Olga ends by saying, "If I'd gotten married . . . I would have loved my husband," to which Irina doesn't reply) and Tuzenbach says to Solyony, "Nothing you say makes any sense! I can't take it any more," then sits down at the piano and plays "quietly" while continuing to talk.

The thematic elements introduced in this segment of the opening are clear enough: Moscow; Tuzenbach's initial arousal of Solyony's enmity; the ironic foreshadowing of Irina's ultimate acceptance of a marriage without love in Olga's guileless remark that she would have loved her husband. But something much more broadly significant shows itself in the sequence.

Those sudden apparitions beyond the columns in the other room, which we catch out of the corner of our eye, and the mysterious utterances of the baron and the doctor, obviously part of a conversation that has begun out of our hearing and included Solyony; Olga talking right past Irina's question; Masha off to the side reading a book and whistling, as if in a different play; the way, if we read the whole text to the point where I've stopped, we hear subjects raised and abandoned, the commonplace mixed with the fervent, abrupt shifts of mood (in the morning Olga felt "such a wave of happiness inside me," and a moment after reporting this, and with no transitional phrase such as "but now I feel . . . ," she speaks of her headaches and lost youth), the disconnectedness and switches of topic and tone—all this, in a page and a half of text and maybe three minutes of stage-time, is a microcosm of how the play is largely going to unfold. The same rhythm of detail-ellipse-detail, then a breaking off to turn elsewhere, also marks the larger units of discourse and behavior.

A central difference from conventional drama of the time, as well as from that of our own, is that from the outset the dialogue never stays for very long in a familiar pattern of statement and response, spoken instigation and rejoinder, exchange of information, and so on—what Strindberg called a "mathematical" arrangement. There's some of this, naturally, for without it the play would appear as a series of hermetic or atomized moments, but it never becomes the prevailing mode. As early as *Ivanov* Chekhov began to slip around the formula, and now he dispenses with it for whole stretches.

He starts with very nearly a group of soliloquies, except that, classically, soliloquies are delivered by persons who are alone on the stage or who think themselves alone. But Olga isn't alone; she has an ostensible listener in Irina, and Masha is also within earshot. Yet the sense most of the time is of great distances separating the three, with Irina standing "lost in thought" and Masha off in her own world.

Olga is allowed to go on without interruptions, or anything she would acknowledge as one, even when we would surely expect some reaction from Irina, as, for instance, when her sister says that "it's as if I'd gotten old all of a sudden" or confesses her regret at not having married. "No, you're not old!" and "It's not too late for you to find a husband," Irina might have said if this had been a conversation. But of course there isn't any conversation and Irina isn't the listener, we are; she stands dreaming until the sound of "Moscow" periodically wakes her. Meanwhile the soldiers make their ghostly entrance, are credited by the women with no bodily reality, and utter their enigmatic words.

We find such seditious loops of technique throughout: a sly, subtly organized frustration of our expectations operates whenever the play threatens to become too predictable, too accommodating to our habits as spectators. As with all theatrical "realism," we anticipate coherence, order, development, recognitions when something is there to be recognized (why doesn't Olga at least nod to the soldiers or throw them a glance?), connected and substantial conversations; we want surprises if we're adventurous onlookers, but surprises of a material, not a procedural, order. But all too often here we get disjunction, ellipse, gaps in dialogue or between dialogue and physicality, the sudden intrusion of the seemingly irrelevant, the arbitrary or inappropriate.

Questions won't be answered, promising conversations will be cut short, provocative news met with silence, subjects changed without warning; a passionate speech will be followed immediately by a pedestrian one that ignores it; reveries will take their places on either side of a recital of facts. Solyony will unaccountably go "chicky, chicky, chicky" and Chebutykin, apropos of nothing, will throw out "Balzac was married in Berdichev."

Consider a few more examples:

At one point Olga responds to Masha's sadness by crying and saying, "I know what you mean." Whereupon Solyony comes out with, "When a man talks philosophy you get philosophy or at least sophistry."

Tuzenbach delivers an impassioned little speech about how the earth will one day "be beautiful and wonderful," so "we have to get ready for it, we have to work." Upon which Vershinin, completely ignoring him, comments admiringly on the Prozorov house.

With nothing detectable to occasion her words, Masha says: "I don't know . . . habit can be very strong." (A mysterious utterance. There isn't anything to which the word "habit" seems to connect.) And then she ends with a salute to the "military" as the "best brought up and best educated people" in the town. Vershinin's reply: "I'm really thirsty, I'd love a cup of tea."

Fedotik gives a detailed description of a pen-knife he's bought for Irina. The next line is Rodé's: "Doctor, how old are you?"

Solyony says about Bobik, "If that child were mine, I would have sautéed him in butter and eaten him long ago." Natasha: "Oh, that man is so crude and vulgar!" Masha: "How wonderful it must be not to know whether it's winter or summer. I think if I lived in Moscow I wouldn't care what the weather was."

All of these discontinuities and elisions, and even more their presence in larger units of dialogue, are designed as a continual disruption of any smooth flow of conversation, of shapely narrative or thematic progress, and one function of this is to replace a conventional logic of dramatic construction—the portrait of an action—with a composition more in accord with time's nature as our condition. Time has no logic, no reasons or rationale; it doesn't proceed smoothly, it doesn't *proceed* at all but simply is. And it doesn't have a plot.

To anticipate an obvious objection, one it might be tempting to make to everything I say about chronology: since *Three Sisters* is ostensibly a realistic play, not a fantastic or surreal one, certain events have inescapably to come before or after others: Irina's party has to come before the soldiers leave town, the duel has to come after Tuzenbach's proposal. Time has to elapse in some rational order.

And it does, who would deny it? But as I continue to stress, the experience of its moving is forever being subverted by the way things *feel*, the way time's extension seems continually to be broken up, arrested, incited into a languorous resumption only to slow down to a crawl before indolently picking up and then cranking down once more.

Not that we're conscious of time at all as we watch, since it's withheld from us not by the usual "suspension of disbelief" as in other plays but because its rhythms are different from those of our ordinary movement through our experience or, much more salient, the way we construct that movement as we go along, as anticipation and memory. There it's all upsweeps and descents, highlights and flatnesses, insulting dead ends and a liberating regaining of momentum, the elation of aspiration and the repression of what doesn't fit. In fact, of course, time's rhythms in *Three Sisters* are those of our truest lives, which habit and egotism—the hunger for importance and, precisely, for *drama*—obscure and falsify.

Sometimes made frantic by its obdurate invisibility, wanting to *think* it into the actual, we construct a logic for time, objectifying it as past, present, and future, rationalizing it as cause and effect. But *Three Sisters* isn't a play about causes and effects but about effects only. And so, on the level of theatrical actuality, the dramatization of time, the causes of everything are hidden or eliminated and we're left with as pure a state of noncontingency as it's possible to find in a play until Beckett, several generations later, will write as though

Chekhov, his more full-bodied, perhaps more "humane" ancestor, were informing every line.

That *Three Sisters* doesn't seem to be taking us anywhere is, once again, a matter of Chekhov's having written it so that we see time's effects not as rational or even irrational consequences, not as consequences at all but as an accumulation, like the sand that more and more covers Winnie in Beckett's *Happy Days,* where time is rendered in a visual metaphor. Eventful immobility, or movement around a still center, or a circle, or a series of flat planes rather than a more or less straight line—any of these images will help free us from an inherited, chronologically and narratively anchored way of looking at *Three Sisters,* a perspective disastrous to understanding.

Just as a dramatic motif or subject can have no location other than in the speech and behavior of characters, so characters can't exist on the stage except in connection to others. (Are you thinking of one-person plays, solo enterprises? In such cases the connections are to tactically invisible figures.) This might seem far too obvious to bring up, yet it's precisely the mark of inauthentic plays (there are no such things as good and bad art, José Ortega y Gasset wrote, there are only art and non-art) that their motifs seem to float above the characters in whom they ought to reside and that relationships in them are arbitrary and inorganic.

Themes, relationships, characters. From the beginning everything in *Three Sisters* is of a piece, mutual and reciprocal, the abstract embedded in the sensuous, physicality releasing thought. *Uncle Vanya* was the first of Chekhov's plays fully to achieve this nearly flawless unity, one in which themes unfold more as manifestation than as statement, in which themes, indeed, as I wrote earlier, are best seen as "ideas attached to bodies . . . notional presences." This continues in *Three Sisters,* but something is subtly different.

In *Uncle Vanya* there are some extended sequences, relatively long arcs of narrative, scenes complete in themselves between, for example, men and women sparring at love, or the hectic convocation at which Serebryakov announces his plan for the estate. The result is that themes or subjects are put forward in relatively substantial sequences, so that the parabolas of their unfolding make up detectable wholes, without major interference. But in *Three Sisters,* with its drifting plot clusters, the units of thematic exhibition are much smaller, often no more than two or three connected lines of dialogue, sometimes only a single interjection or isolated declaration, a moment spent on this or that character's preoccupation or some other subject before something breaks into the sequence or someone moves out of it. The camera dwells for a short time somewhere, then slides or is jostled on.

A continuous traffic takes place, rather like that of farce, except for the far slower steps and antipodal intentions: people moving in and out of the setting, shifting the composition, changing the moral weather. Everything is interrupted, elided, replaced, allowed to put in another appearance, allowed slowly and extremely intermittently to accumulate, the way time does.

A sequence from the middle of Act Two:

Fedotik [to Irina playing cards]: "Do you want me to show you another way to play solitaire?" (He lays out the game.)
(The samovar is brought in and Anfisa attends to it. A little later Natasha comes in and also busies herself at the table. Solyony comes in, greets everybody and sits down at the table.)
Vershinin: "Listen to that wind!"
Masha: "Yes, winter's a bore. I can't even remember what summer is like."
Irina: "Look, the solitaire is coming out. That means we'll get to Moscow."
Fedotik: "No it isn't. See, you've got an eight on the two of spades. (Laughs.) That means you won't get to Moscow."
Chebutykin (reads his newspaper): "Tsitsikar. An epidemic of smallpox has broken out here."
Anfisa (going up to Masha): "Masha dear, tea's ready." (To Vershinin.) "Excuse me . . . I've forgotten your name."

All the notional presences—love, work, the future, Moscow—struggle to declare themselves within successive small tapestries of such design. The themes will lean on each other, interdependent; they will be elbowed away, stand mute, then reclaim their places, spasmodically filling in the whole field we will grasp as the drama.

If I were to be asked by someone who has never seen or read the play to say what it's about, what *happens* in it, and were given no time for reflection, I'd likely give some such answer as this: The characters include so and so, and so and so. Natasha and Andrei get married and two children are born, one or even both of whom might have been fathered by Protopopov, the town councilor with whom Natasha's been having an affair; she gradually takes over the Prozorov house. Olga reluctantly becomes headmistress of her high school and complains of headaches and being overworked. Solyony and Chebutykin have a dispute over the words *chekhartma* and *cheremsha*. Kulygin gives Irina an absurd book as a name-day gift, the same one he gave her last Easter. Singing and accordion music are heard from off stage. Irina goes to work and is disappointed in her job; she accepts the marriage proposal of Baron Tuzenbach, whom she respects but doesn't love. There's more music: a soldier and his guitar, singing, Tuzenbach at the piano, Andrei off stage with his violin. Chebutykin breaks a valuable old clock and asks if maybe he didn't break it, if maybe he and the others don't exist; he reveals that long ago he was in love with the Prozorovs' mother. Natasha tries to fire the old servant, Anfisa. Andrei gambles away most of the family's money. More music: two street players perform briefly on stage. A fire breaks out in the town. The house is mortgaged. Masha and Vershinin fall in love. Andrei confesses that while he still loves Natasha, she sometimes reminds him of "some kind of animal . . . blind and vicious and mean." Vershinin's wife tries to commit suicide. The baron is killed in a duel with Solyony. Ferapont, the old caretaker, says that there's a rope "in Moscow, hangs all across town. . . ." Andrei circles the house pushing a baby carriage. Natasha finds a fork on a bench. The doctor sits on another bench and sings "Tara-ra-boom-dee-ay," while the sisters lean together and wonder about the future. The soldiers leave town to the sound of a marching band.

As a bonus I might add some of the things that, as I remember, don't happen. Andrei doesn't get his longed-for professorship. Irina doesn't get married. Olga doesn't get married. Vershinin doesn't get the tea he's craved for hours. Anfisa doesn't get fired. The sisters don't get to Moscow.

Now a little earlier I offered a straightforward, organized account of the differences among the four acts. But that was after I had consulted the text again to refresh, and on some points correct, my memory. The heterogeneity and grab-bag quality of the citations I've just given represent my memory of the play as I've actually experienced it, a compilation, before the supervention of any organizing principle, of what sticks out from the dozen or so productions I've seen and the two dozen or more times I've read it. It's a sort of Jungian word-association exercise—what pops into your mind when you hear me say "*Three Sisters*"?—and its point is to indicate something of the way the play presents itself to our immediate consciousness as a series of discrete phenomena bound together with invisible wires.

I've mixed up the humorous with the serious, the seemingly trivial with the undeniably grave, physical events with dialogue. I haven't made any distinctions between events that have extension and those that are over in a moment, or between the ones that take place before our eyes and those we only know about by deduction (for example, Andrei and Natasha are shown as husband and wife, so they must have got married). And I've mostly scrambled chronology, which, even if it were possible to construct one with reasonable accuracy, would, as I've tried to point out, inevitably appear false, except in its broadest outlines; and even those contours, encompassing as they do almost nothing but irregularity and fragmentation—those floating plot clusters—would be hard put to retain their firmness.

In the few minutes of her presence at the end of Act One, Natasha will have revealed a good deal about her nature and the approach to the general situation Chekhov locates in her. It's not too much to say that the cumulative, differing, and sometimes warring senses of the situation, the condition, on the part of all the characters is what in fact will constitute the drama, every person "caught in the fact," each consciousness bearing upon the whole, each eliciting from the others direct or oblique refractions of the state of things.

Natasha's nature. To one extent or another she and her fellow dramatic personages have been revealing or, with the same outcome, trying to conceal, what they are like. At this point we can set down the revelations of character, the data of preoccupations and concerns, together with some collateral information about literary or factual origins or connections, which the first acts give us. The characters' "character" won't change radically, though circumstances do, and this is because nobody in Chekhov ever goes through a sudden, surprising, and permanent transformation. But we should remember, too, that no one is obliged to behave with perfect consistency and that our idea that stage personages have to act according to "type" is one of the products of our debilitating rage to classify.

Though they will all stay within the rough lineaments of their predilections and idiosyncrasies, the characters are free—encouraged is more like it—to go temporarily against their grains when the moment calls for it. What I mean is that Solyony, a "dark" character, can be extremely funny, Kulygin, pretty much a fool, can be admirable and touching, and Olga, kindliness itself, can snap and bark.

Chekhov never gives us careful, narrow typologies, strict divisions of human nature, but instances of varying consciousness, appetite, and behavior; he doesn't incarnate this vice or that virtue exclusively and uncomplicatedly in particular characters but assigns moral and psychological weights and leading tendencies, distributes behavioral nuances, and brings everything together in a web of relationships where individual identity is neither fixed nor volatile but in part, as befits the nature of drama, situational and in part the product, the creation, of the selves that surround it.

With those caveats we can go ahead. Natasha: vulgarity, the resentment and uneasiness of the social climber, acquisitiveness. (From the story "In the Ravine": "the inability of the good but weak to defend themselves from those who are armed with the strength of selfishness.") Olga: good sense, works hard, some weariness and irritability, warmth, a longing for Moscow. (A short story of 1897, translated as either "The Schoolmistress" or "In the Horsecart," is of exceptional interest: "For thirteen years she had been a schoolteacher . . . this life had aged and coarsened her." Chekhov's brother Ivan was a high-school teacher for a time in Voskresensk, near Moscow, where the family spent three or four summers.)

Irina: youthful hopes, a desire for work, like Olga a dream of Moscow. (From "A Visit": "Completely unaccustomed to work, she was now inspired by the idea of an independent life; she was making plans for the future—it was written in her face.") Masha: discontent, ripeness for love, intellectuality or at least sharp intelligence. (She has some affinities with Yelena of *Uncle Vanya*.) Vershinin: also readiness to be in love, affability, a touch of self-pity, a penchant for philosophizing. (From Dostoevsky's *The Possessed*: "The little widow suddenly burst out angrily, 'Why they dragged me from the flames by a rope when Vershinin's house caught fire.'" The Soviet critic Vladimir Yermilov says that Vershinin was modeled on an artillery colonel named Mayevsky whom the family knew at Voskresensk; Simon Karlinsky, however, thinks the man might have been someone named Yevgraf Yegorov.)

Andrei: naiveté about Natasha, instability, a drinking problem, strong hints of a lack of self-possession. (He has some resemblance to the husband in the short play *On the Harmfulness of Tobacco*.) Chebutykin: good humor but also increasing alcoholism, signs of anomie, moral indifference. (From "A Boring Story": "Of late I have become so indifferent to everything that it is absolutely all the same to me where I go—to Kharkhov, to Paris, or to Berdichev." From "The Two Volodyas": "'Tell me something I can believe in. . . . Tell me something, if it's only one word.' 'One word? By all means: tararaboom-deeay.'") Solyony: quarrelsomeness, a wicked tongue, a swagger like that of

Pechorin, Lermontov's hero. (From *The Brothers Karamazov*: "He [Papa K.] longed to revenge himself on everyone for his own unseemliness.") Tuzenbach: a pronounced innocence, a bit of windiness, mild intellectuality. (Trofimov in *The Cherry Orchard* will somewhat resemble him.) Kulygin: pedantry, a desire to please, inability or refusal to see Masha's contempt. (He is a little like a man married to an earlier Masha, Medvedenko in *The Seagull*.)

(Also: Protopopov was the name of a very bad contemporary literary critic. There is a village named Ferapontovo three hundred miles north of Moscow.)

A number of characters offer objective "signatures," as in every late Chekhov play. One of them might be the sisters' dresses, which remain the same color throughout, in the stage directions at least: Olga's blue, Irina's white, Masha's black. But I don't think too much should be made of this. The colors don't have heavy iconographic or symbolic significance, although such interpretations aren't uncommon: white for innocence, blue for sobriety or steadfastness, black for mourning, or more mildly, unhappiness . . . that sort of thing.

This seems too unsubtle for Chekhov, and so I think the color scheme is chiefly there for the eye, to offer variety, a composition, during the times all three of the sisters are together on stage—surprisingly on only three occasions: all through the first act, for a time in the second and a stretch at the end—and for simple identification otherwise. A Russian audience, for one thing, would know that, as a stage direction tells us, Olga's "dark blue" dress is the regulation one of a high-school teacher. (This is the only stage direction concerning clothing. That the sisters' dresses remain largely the same color and the soldiers wear their uniforms throughout adds to the impression of timelessness in a subliminal way.)

But other signatures do have pertinence to character and theme: Chebutykin never being without a newspaper; Solyony often sprinkling his hands with scent; Andrei playing the violin; Masha reciting or humming or whistling snatches of poetry and songs; Kulygin spouting Latin; Fedotik, a figure on the outskirts of the action, taking photographs.

The doctor's ever-present newspapers speak of an edgy need for distraction and an emotional distance from the others. Solyony's eau de cologne, the most programmatic item on the list and so maybe the play's one lapse from artistic rectitude, hints at his besieged vanity and—in the manner of Lady Macbeth, of whom it so obviously reminds us—at bad faith. Kulygin's Latin is pedantry incarnate but also a source of unwitting and rather endearing humor. Masha's murmurings reveal her itch to get beyond the mundane, her aspirations toward a more "poetic" life. Andrei's music adds to a sense of the family's refinement but, because he won't play for others, betrays the somewhat amateur and marginal status of culture in this house. And Fedotik's photos, the most casual and disarming of all these epiphanic objects and activities, speak of an innocent attempt to fix time.

Characters, characteristics; invented lives, inventions for the lives.

Some things won't change. Others will. Hopes will be ground down, desires thwarted, rapacity appeased. Bodies will become more distant from their souls, but they will be the same bodies, the same spirits. The balance of things will remain. It will all become different, yet not.

In the opening sequence we absorb Masha's isolation, the physical and temporarily emotional distance between Olga and Irina, and the unexplained arrival of the soldiers with their momentarily baffling dialogue, without having the time or inclination to question these things. And we're caught up in Olga's speeches and Irina's much shorter and fewer ones without noticing, or caring if we do notice, that they're mostly not stage conversation in any familiar sense.

This is how we will react to all the subsequent dramaturgy of discontinuity and disruption, unlike the members of the Moscow Art Theater when Chekhov first read them the play. They found it static and unpleasantly disjointed, we're told, and for a while had no idea how to perform it. Having found, as Stanislavsky was later to write, "a new approach"[20] to acting for *The Seagull,* they still had to regroup and think the whole thing through again for each Chekhov play that followed. The distance we've come since then attests not to our superior sensitivity but to our having been given the materials for a growth in sophistication, the steady elaboration of what Harold Rosenberg called a "tradition of the new." With the grip of the "normative" broken, we're not baffled at the way things begin but can be seduced into immediate acquiescence by the animation of the first words we hear, their depth of "felt life," which was Henry James's chief criterion for imaginative writing.

From the moment Olga begins by saying, "It's a year ago today," which entices us into her memories, we're in the presence of a substantial personality, a highly "agreeable" one, as Jane Austen, her eye on what recommends selves to others, might have put it. Olga's sensibility, her distinctiveness, will quickly establish their dramatic authority, and those of the others, right down to the deaf and addled Ferapont, will soon join hers.

In Olga we hear a voice without self-consciousness (a subtle mark of Chekhovian characters, most of whom seem simply to lean into the particular drama they're part of, or to elbow their way in, without authorial notations on the process). She moves easily between the matter-of-fact and the lyrical—"Moscow . . . full of flowers . . . and sunshine everywhere"—description and evocation, memory and desire, fretful complaints and generosity—"You do look lovely today . . . and Masha is beautiful too." Hers is a voice supple and changeful, unapologetic and open to whatever is going to be made of its possessor.

A voice, a persona open to what will be made of it: what a strange thing to say about a character in a play! Yet with this observation about Olga as we first encounter her we move to another level of imaginative reality and practice in *Three Sisters,* which is the way the characters permit us to apprehend their natures and lives. When I absurdly say *they* permit us, I'm speaking of course about Chekhov's own generosity as an artist, his "courtesy with respect to matter" (to quote once again Jean Genet's definition of talent). Chekhov puts no obstacles in the way of our knowing his creatures, although he makes us shed our biases and preconceptions in order to get at them.

None of the characters, not even the most marginal like Anfisa, Ferapont, Fedotik, and Rodé, has merely functional duties to perform, none is the embodiment of an abstract idea or an agency of exposition; each adds to texture and theme. We have to intuit a great deal about them, put things together, but the paths to intuition are clear. The characters never announce who or what they are but simply speak and behave, and we, who are in effect *allowed to be there,* have among our ruling tasks that of deciphering what they leave out. This is what I mean by our having to intuit. They make themselves known at every moment, but the important knowledge is chiefly of interiority; we have to follow their signs, using the stuff of our own experience as a guide. We're not *told* anything in *Three Sisters* but given mysterious yet lucid enactments.

Then too: the characters waste nothing on preparations, as characters do who are building up a dramatic plot in storylike fashion. They don't wear masks or disguises. They have no artistic or ideological axes to brandish. None of them speaks for the author because all do, meaning that none is privileged beyond the others.

Chekhov's lack of authorial solicitation (this is a *drama* you're seeing!), the limpidity of his writing, and the way the art is hidden are the sources of the celebrated and much misunderstood appearance of "lifelikeness" in his plays. And this in turn is the origin of the well-intended but pathetically naive idea that, as the reviewer Brooks Atkinson once confided to his *New York Times* readers, the plays hadn't "been written at all" but were simply *there*, "as life exists, without conscious purpose or design."[21]

The nonsensical notion that Chekhov's plays are all life and no art, that he didn't so much write them as come upon them, presumably to his great surprise, the way the poor cobbler in the fairy tale discovered all those exquisite shoes the elves had put together in the night—this, as I say, is meant as a commendation and is made possible by the artistry being so perfectly concealed. Put another way, the art, the design are so unobtrusive as to seem to be perpetually dissolving themselves, leaving the characters without "artificial" support; a shaping and unshaping is going on, disappearance in the midst of appearance.

For Chekhov's work of what we call characterization, the granting of mobility and attributes to expectant stick-figures, who may begin as mere names or as nothing but a moustache or a peignoir in the mind—this disappearing act, the magician in hiding, entails the elimination of anything we might detect as a marionette string, the covering up of every trace of the writer's controlling hand. We're dealing with slippery matters here, and a potential for criticism to seem naive; for the writer *does* control everything and invisibility isn't the same as nonexistence.

But something uncanny goes on in *Three Sisters*. Of course Olga is Chekhov's creation, his creature who can only do or say what the text calls for. Of course everything is predetermined. Yet Olga and to varying degrees of fullness the other characters give us a strong impression of laying out their own existences, and this isn't a matter of clever and resilient performers, though these are necessary in production, but of the writing itself. Alain Robbe-Grillet said of Didi and Gogo in Beckett's *Godot* that they are thrown on stage to ad lib for their very lives. A fixed text that feels as if it's being improvised? This, even more astonishingly than in Beckett, is one of the secrets of *Three Sisters*.

When I say that Chekhov fashioned for these characters what I've described as an openness to all that will be made of them, what *time* will make of them, I don't at all mean to suggest that he conceived them as passive or docile; this notion warps all our understanding of the play, as it does of *Uncle Vanya* too. I mean that he allows them their destinies without hints of preordination or any pressures emanating from an impatient plot. They live within time and time lives within place. They will move about in their setting, selves bumping up against externality and each other, doing what they can do, knowing what they can know, and chancing the rest.

Chekhov, we remember, had written to Lydia Avilova early in 1899 that he felt like an army officer stuck "in some godforsaken provincial hole." From everything we hear said about it by its characters, the play's mise en scène is just such a place, not nearly as physically far from Moscow as is Yalta, it's clear, yet spiritually much the same sort of universe away.

Here the officers are stationed and here they have met the Prozorovs, who feel exiled in the same way they do. (Chebutykin had known the family intimately in the past, Vershinin, who's just been transferred here, only slightly.) To appreciate the affinity the two groups feel for one another we should know that at this period in Russia army officers were for the most part educated men, many of them of good social standing, and therefore likely to be as interesting and attractive to people like the sisters and their brother as the family is attractive to them. Another link between them is their shared sense of being stranded in what in our own time we would call the boondocks.

To open the play with a birthday luncheon for Irina provided Chekhov with just the sort of generously elastic occasion he could best use. The party serves to bring everyone on stage—the Prozorovs and the soldiers, Natasha and Kulygin, Anfisa and Ferapont—without any other plot justifications, without, that's to say (delicious brusque phrase!), further ado.

It immediately sounds the note of time as a subject. It encourages memories, reflections, hopes, and confessions. In its atmosphere of conviviality slightly straitened by social convention yet wide enough to accommodate complaints, asperity, and even patches of darkness, it fosters the beginning of one relationship—Masha with Vershinin—sets going the elaboration of others, and brings into view the first sprigs of theme.

Now when we speak of the themes or motifs of *Three Sisters* we have to remember that as with any densely wrought work of imagination it's only by a violent act of excision, in which we pluck out a subject like an entrail before stuffing it back into the body, that we can talk about it in isolation. I may seem to be belaboring the point yet I'll take the risk, for nothing is more damaging to understanding than to ignore it. What criticism so often does to drama, or to fiction for that matter, is to speak of the ideas within a work, its motifs and themes, without their sensuousness, the intricacies of their relationships to physicality—to speak of them, really, as if they can be contemplated in isolation, detached from bodies and the meshings of character, detached, indeed, from each other.

Well, then, the theme or notion of love in *Three Sisters,* to turn to that first, has its only presence within the play's lovers or would-be ones and as it hovers over the objects of their desire. And love is almost always linked with another, larger motif, that of the future, the *idea* of the future, which in turn has its central location, in the play's geography of longing, in Moscow. In Act Three Irina says, "I kept waiting for us to move to Moscow. I knew I'd meet my true love there." And can't we think of Vershinin as Masha's Moscow, the "site" of her potential deliverance from the blankness of the heart?

Love, Moscow, the future. Set down this way they're abstractions, and our obligation is to restore them to their life within the play, where they move between being explicit and submerged, embrace each other at times and at others go off on separate little parallel journeys, notional presences, as I call them again, elements of the portrait of a condition.

In an earlier chapter I quoted something Chekhov once wrote down in his notebook: "Love. Either it is a remnant of something degenerating, something which once had been immense, or it is a particle of what will in the future develop into something immense, but at the present it is unsatisfying, it gives much less than one expects."

Whether or not it happened under the sway of this somber yet also wistful observation, love as a subject in Chekhov's plays steadily diminishes in weight and centrality, from *The Wood Demon,* where almost nothing else is at issue, to *The Seagull,* where it's substantial but by no means dominant, and *Uncle Vanya,* where its complications, if not its intensities, are reduced, and *Three Sisters,* in which it has to push against other subjects for attention. In *The Cherry Orchard* love will dwindle to a handful of connections, none of them distinctively passionate or thematically influential.

"Men have died from time to time and worms have eaten them, but not for love." But time still cradles it in *Three Sisters.* Something to notice at once is that those who love or desire within the play (Natasha's eroticism is outside it, as is Irina's objectless yearning) are with the exception of Masha all men: Vershinin, Andrei, Solyony, Tuzenbach, Kulygin, and even Fedotik, whose stream of little gifts to Irina are in gentle contrast to Solyony's importunities. Masha's and Vershinin's feelings are mutual, Kulygin's and Andrei's unreciprocated, as are Tuzenbach's and Solyony's, although there's a huge difference between Irina's positions toward them. As in *The Seagull* and *Uncle Vanya*, love and desire are of greatly varying seriousness and authenticity, and their manifestations occupy spaces ranging from Solyony's single abruptly squelched outcry—"I can't live without you. You're divine!" to which Irina icily replies, "Goodnight! Please go."—to the steady accretion of Masha's and Vershinin's romance.

Of these heterogeneous connections the two marriages are the most awkward and embarrassing for us to have knowledge of. We see from the start that Natasha thinks of Andrei instrumentally, as a means to her goal of social position and domestic control. She never says even one affectionate word to him but strategically exploits his misplaced passion while cuckolding him with Protopopov. Andrei will cling to the end to his public stance of love and admiration, although, in two spasms of despairing truthfulness, he will tell his sisters not to believe the praise he's just given Natasha, and confide to the doctor the devastating fact that she sometimes makes him sick to his stomach. Still, he will continue to insist that he loves her, as desperately formal and arid an avowal as it's possible to imagine.

There's nothing the least bit funny about Andrei's marriage, but Kulygin's releases a current of acrid humor. Poor, earnest, literal-minded, self-deluding sap, we think, as he keeps proclaiming his love for his wife in the face of Masha's sharp and sometimes brutal put-downs. "My wonderful wife. . . . I love you, my only . . . ," he tells her, which she interrupts with "amo, amas, amat," mocking his Latin. But he goes right on, "I'm happy. I'm a happy, happy man!" Masha: "And I'm bored. I am bored, bored, bored!"

Yet for all his oafish desire to please, his functionary's nerdiness (to use a word I think Chekhov would have enjoyed, considering the batch of prototypes he created for it), Kulygin is an essentially kindly soul. When near the end, fighting through her sorrow at Vershinin's departure, Masha at last gives her patient and uncondemning husband some recognition—agreeing that in his false beard and moustache he does look "just like the German teacher" and then saying, "Let's go home"—the thing is so subtle and oblique it can pass us right by. But we should take notice of it, for it's an understated element of a far wider acceptance on Masha's part, that "we have to go on living," as she says at the very end.

Tuzenbach and Irina. The baron almost casually makes known his feelings near the end of Act One; she tells him not to "talk to [her] about love," and nothing more is made of it for nearly two whole acts. Then, three years later in fictive time, Tuzenbach renews his suit and Irina, exhausted by her expenditure of romantic yearning and having seen that her Moscow dream lover was "all a lot of nonsense," accepts his proposal. She doesn't love him, she tells Olga (she will tell the baron too), but "respect[s]" him. "I will marry him, I promise," she cries, and then, most significantly, for it shows that the city has a wider hold on her than just as a venue for romance—moving now as a theme to futurity itself—she adds, "only please let's go to Moscow. . . . I beg you . . . Olga. . . . Please!"

That Irina doesn't love Tuzenbach but will marry him out of deep respect prepares the way for one of the play's most affecting moments. He is going off to the duel, which he suspects will be fatal, as we do too. Irina is vaguely troubled, having heard rumors of an incident with Solyony, but knows nothing. He tells her again of his love and she, acknowledging that she doesn't love him in return, pledges to be his "faithful" wife. He speaks lyrically of the waywardness of things, remarks on the "beautiful trees" all around them, notices a dead tree that "still moves in the wind with the others." So, too, he'd still "be part of life," even if he were to die.

They stand irresolute. She suddenly says, "I'm coming with you" and, alarmed, he backs away. Then, in one of the most heartbreaking little speeches I know about in drama, he says: "I didn't have any coffee this morning. Ask them to fix me some, will you?" and goes off. I didn't have any coffee this morning. Where has emotion been rendered with more painful astringency than that? A displacement, an inspired shifting of feeling onto innocuous words that, impregnated with grievous fatality, will remain in our memory more securely than any direct rhetoric of loss.

Something to note: had this been a scene between two lovers on the eve of their wedding, the risks of sentimentality would have been overwhelming. As it is, that Irina intends to marry the baron out of affection and esteem instead of passion radically undercuts the potential reign of the melodramatic. Having given up dreaming to reach for a measure of possibility, having allowed a perhaps more noble aspect of her nature, at least a more realistic one, to take over, and been, as she'd said a little earlier, relieved and soberly inspired by it, she experiences a loss that is all the more ironic, all the more sorrowful an exemplification of how life—time—defeats our logic and our plans.

Masha and Vershinin. This is one of the quietest liaisons in Chekhovian drama: no crises, no misunderstandings needing to be cleared up, few ardent declarations (only one on Masha's part, and that one to her sisters). The romance threads its way through the play like an underground stream that only occasionally comes into view. It has a restrained music, not just the "tram-tams" and "tra-ras" the lovers use to communicate in semisecrecy but a general rhythm of mostly gentle rises and falls, a minor diapason. When they part, the scene touches us strongly but is of a more conventional order than Tuzenbach's and Irina's last moments.

The only real textual puzzle concerning their affair is why Olga should be so opposed to it. "I'm not listening," she says when Masha tells her sisters what she feels for the colonel. "I don't care what you're saying." This has been interpreted as an indication of Olga's primness or even prudery, but I don't think that holds up. It's more likely that she foresees the hopelessness of the situation—both of them are married and divorce is all but impossible—and so can't bear to hear about it. Then, too, she might be jealous of Masha. But prudery, no; after all, Irina, about whom no suggestion of puritanism has ever been brought forward, remains silent throughout Masha's "confession," as though tacitly sharing Olga's attitude.

One more point. Bound together with the strongest ties of understanding affection, sometimes, as at the end, seeming to coalesce into a single organism, the sisters do have their occasions of disharmony. Which is all to the good artistically; what would we do with a portrait of flawless mutuality, programmatic support?

And a note on style. The way Masha first reveals her attraction to Vershinin is a model of Chekhovian wit and economy. Feeling "in a depressed mood today," she announces her intention of going home. But before she can do it Vershinin arrives and fills all the sisters with excited delight by his evocations of Moscow. Much animated talk ensues until the colonel embarks on an extended aria (one of the play's longest speeches) about the dullness of the Prozorovs' town, the special brightness of the sisters in such an atmosphere, and his hope for a transformed future which obliges us to "dream of it . . . prepare for it." When he finishes, Masha ("tak[ing] off her hat") says, "I'm staying for lunch," a remark about which no one comments as it slips elegantly into the tapestry of the whole.

In the plays from *The Seagull* to this one, men seem to love or desire more ardently and aggressively than women. This is partly to be accounted for by social custom, the male as active suitor, but it's also a cover for their craving more desperately to *be* loved. On the whole, men in Chekhov need more, they move more disconsolately within their finiteness, they wish more hungrily to be delivered from the responsibilities of self. Which characters best outlast the loss or failure of love, remaining more or less intact? Nina, Sonya, the sisters. Which are most injured by its absence or defeat? Konstantin, Vanya, Andrei beneath his glum bravado, even Astrov, so empty of self-knowledge in this area.

It's precisely Irina's having freed herself from the illusion of love's necessity that enables her to "settle for" Tuzenbach, a defeat from one perspective perhaps but surely a kind of maturing. An even more arduous process of discovery and self-instruction empowers Nina to go on with her life after Trigorin's defection and, melancholy and pain-ridden as the acceptance may be, helps Sonya survive the death of her hope of "another." But Vanya is crushed by his failure, or rather by the abyss he sees in himself in its aftermath, and Konstantin is brought to suicide in the wake of his.

Psychic or moral differentiation along lines of gender is never close to being programmatic in Chekhov. If many of his most admirable characters are female, his most "villainous" one is a woman too, Natasha. Some of his women remain sentimental and naive about love and are inconsolable in its absence (Arkadina says she would "die" without it!) and some of his men stand stolidly outside its urgencies. But the broad pattern of differences, shadings between the ways men and women act, is there, in certain dispositions, an impulse here, a restraint or moderation there.

Men also tend to philosophize more than women. In *Three Sisters* nearly all the speeches about the future, those which claim to have some vision of it, are by Tuzenbach and Vershinin, as they are by Astrov in *Uncle Vanya* and will be by Trofimov in *The Cherry Orchard*. Perhaps because men are more disgruntled, have heavier grievances, shadowy and imprecise as they mostly are (the imprecision or vagueness of many complaints in Chekhov—"I'm bored," "I'm tired," "life feels empty"—are existential mutterings, not bills of particulars for lawsuits, and women, of course, express them too), they tend more readily to project life into a more satisfying future, for themselves or others; they wrap time to come in rhetoric. Those who, like Tuzenbach and Vershinin, don't appear unhappy have still a hidden dissatisfaction, we intuit, an itch to launch themselves, through words, into something distantly better.

Women, voluble enough in general, stay closer to sources, to the way, indistinctly as they see them, things are. They're less given to abstraction, they distance themselves a little less from the reality of present, inescapable life. Moscow, for example, which the women in *Three Sisters* crave more than the men, is at least a real place, for all its Avalon-like residence in the mind.

As an explicit subject Moscow makes two robust appearances very early in the play and then subsides to an occasional reference or an exhalation, while remaining a constant undercurrent of aspiration. The first appearance, we'll remember, is at the outset, when it comes up a dozen times between Olga and Irina, and the second, also in a dozen or so citations, comes a little later, in the conversation set going by Vershinin's entrance. (Something worth noticing about Vershinin's arrival is the way he seems almost to have been magically evoked by the sisters talking of Moscow.) Here the city takes on specificity, a physiognomy, for the only time: the Old Basmanny Road, Nemetsky Street, the Novo-Devichy (New Virgin) Cemetery, where the Prozorovs' mother lies buried (as also did Chekhov's own father, Pavel, who had died in 1898).

From then on it's Irina who chiefly keeps the city in consciousness, although Olga will join her once or twice. For a while their optimism, or pretense of it, holds steady. "Oh my God, I dream about Moscow night after night," Irina says, ostensibly to Masha but really to her own listening morale. "We're moving in June so that leaves . . . February, March, April, May . . . almost half a year!" (which, we deduce, makes it January as she speaks, the only other time, after the reference to May at the beginning of the play, we're given a specific month or even season). She ends the second act alone on the stage, with "longing," in a fervent apostrophe: "I want to go to Moscow! Moscow! Moscow!" And then, as I've cited, closes Act Three with a plea to Olga, "Let's go. . . . Please!"

But as time wears on and invisible impediments assert themselves, the sisters (and Andrei more opaquely) pass into doubt and then despair. A little before her third-act curtain speech Irina will break down for a moment in front of Olga: "Life goes by and it won't ever come back, and we're never going to Moscow, never, never. . . ." And only a few minutes before the end Olga will say to Vershinin at their parting, "Things never work out the way we want them to. . . . And of course I'll never get to Moscow."

Why should this be so? Why has Moscow been shut down to them in both dream and actuality? Why, in short, don't they *get there*? This is a question I want to address closer to the end of this chapter, for reasons that I think will become clear.

In Chekhov's last four plays (as in much of his later fiction) the future has varying status as a subject for discussion, a locus of speculation, a presence, and an idea. In the two comedies, *The Seagull* and *The Cherry Orchard,* time to come is relatively "open," beckoning in a nonprescriptive way; in the plays they flank, *Uncle Vanya* and *Three Sisters,* it will become indistinct, then closed off. The noteworthy thing is that it's in just these two plays that talk about the future is at its height, as if while time to come is being undermined, emptied out in the deeper dramaturgy, in the dialogue it keeps recommending itself most earnestly as justification or compensation for present disappointment, pain, and darkness.

In *Uncle Vanya* and much more in *Three Sisters* the future is talked about, sometimes rhapsodized over, chiefly as a sort of relocated golden age, lying not behind us but ahead. "In two or three hundred years," Vershinin says on one occasion, "life on earth will be unimaginably beautiful, astonishing," and he repeats the prediction at another time. To foresee such a transformation can retroactively redeem the present by encouraging our persistence, reaching back to us to assure us that we were right to hope. For this is what hope says: in a future that will contain me I'll be happier, different, better. And if the change doesn't begin until time has left me behind, I'll still be connected to it through the long chain of being. "A new life will come one day," a character in the long story "Ward No. Six" says, "and justice will triumph. . . . I may not live to see it . . . but somebody's grandchildren will."

Several points need to be made about this complex of ideas. To begin with, one persistent way of getting Chekhov wrong has been to take certain assertions of some of his characters at face value, snatching them out of context and assuming that they represent the author's own thought. The perversion ought always to have been obvious, yet at one point in his career Chekhov felt compelled to write: "If, say, a character in one of my plays or stories claims that one should murder and steal, that doesn't entitle [anyone] to parade me as an advocate of murder and theft."[22] We saw earlier in the book how persistently characters' complaints about being "bored" and about their "stupid" surroundings have been mistaken for truthful sentiments and for Chekhov's own opinions about his creatures' lives, when in fact they are more often neither.

Where ideology enters, Soviet (to stick to the now outdated word) criticism of Chekhov has been especially guilty of distortion in regard to the subject of the future in his plays, wishing to turn him into a prophet of the age that followed his, the Bolshevik millennium; Vladimir Yermilov, whom I've quoted before, among many other similar comments had this to say: "Chekhov's characters postpone love and happiness to the future, for those who come after them, for only in the future will love and happiness be worthy of the names, when they are purged of vulgarity and filth."[23] (One can feel the self-righteous ideological pressure behind these words.)

This is pernicious nonsense. Every piece of evidence we have, most impressively from the plays themselves, as it should be, but also from Chekhov's obiter dicta, establishes with certainty that the future held no such promise for him. He wasn't any kind of optimist, nor certifiably a pessimist either, but practiced the strictest realism about time to come: *we can't know*. It's some of his characters who, as an aspect of their natures, hence of the plays' aesthetic design, breathe optimism and, as we'll see in a moment, he continually undermines their glowing forecasts.

From his notebooks: "Before the dawn of a new life has broken, we shall turn into sinister old men and women and we shall be the first who, in the hatred of that dawn, will calumniate it."[24]

From "An Anonymous Story," where the speaker clearly does represent Chekhov's thought: "But one wants to live apart from future generations and not only for their sake."

From a letter to Maxim Gorky: "We all hope that life will be better in 'two or three hundred years' [the phrase here is a forecast of Vershinin's rhetoric] but nobody bothers about making it better tomorrow."[25]

In another instance of misreading by Chekhov's countrymen and -women, this one before 1917, M. N. Stroeva, in her well-known essay "*Three Sisters* in the Production of the Moscow Art Theater," reports that Stanislavsky told the actors how "important" it was "to stir up the audience"[26] during Vershinin's speeches on the future, and says that for him "the purpose and goal"—presumably of both the speeches and the play itself—was "to find a true path to happiness, to a free and bright life of labor."[27] But then Stanislavsky was capable of writing such drivel about Chekhov as this: "His dreams of future life speak of lofty spirit, of the World's Soul . . . of the wonderful life for whose achievement we must work, sweat and suffer two hundred, three hundred [those time spans again!] and even a thousand years."[28]

We can be sure that Chekhov had no such dreams of future life and that he would have flung himself into the Volga before being guilty of even thinking about the "World's Soul." But the clearest reproof to Stanislavsky is the way that in *Three Sisters* nobody's oratory about time to come is allowed to take imaginative or intellectual control. Instead, each such utterance is immediately counteracted or subverted by what accompanies or follows it.

When Tuzenbach, agreeing with Vershinin that "life on earth will eventually be beautiful and wonderful," adds that "we have to get ready for it, we have to work," the colonel, as if uninterested in anyone's prognostications except his own, interrupts with a remark to the sisters, "Yes. What a lot of flowers you've got. And a beautiful house!"

When Andrei says to Ferapont, "The present is awful, but when I think about the future, I feel better. . . . I can see freedom. . . . I will be free from laziness, from drinking too much, from eating too much . . . ," the deaf old caretaker's response is to say that "two thousand people froze to death" in either Petersburg or Moscow, he can't remember; the daffy irrelevance negates the intended effect of Andrei's words, leaving them hanging exposed in their insincerity.

In the most subtle and consequential of such actions, Chebutykin will come close to canceling out Olga's final speech in which she says that though they'll all be forgotten, their "sufferings will turn to joy for the people who live after us." As she's speaking, with the sisters "standing close to one another," the doctor, across the stage, sits reading his newspaper and singing "Tara-ra-boom-dee-ay." The play's last words are Olga's—"If only we knew!"—but Chebutykin is almost simultaneously saying, "What difference does it make? What difference does it make?"

An incident in which I was involved is worth recounting here. In 1965 the Moscow Art Theater gave a program of plays, including *Three Sisters,* in New York. I was the drama critic of *Newsweek* at the time and went to a party the MAT gave after the last performance. My enthusiasm for Chekhov evidently impressed the MAT's artistic director, for he interrupted our conversation (a TASS correspondent was serving as interpreter) to whip out a medallion with Chekhov's face on one side and stylized wings, the Theater's seagull emblem, on the other, pinned it on my lapel and said, "Now you're an honorary member of MAT." (I learned that the medallion had been struck in 1960 for the centenary of Chekhov's birth.)

Fine. I thanked him. But then I said: "I've been wondering why in your

Three Sisters you cut out Chebutykin's final words, leaving Olga to give her last speech without, shall we say, competition." He glared at me, then turned abruptly away. I suspected the reason, of course, and the TASS man, an early proponent of glasnost, confirmed it. For the Soviets the profound ambiguity and irresolution of the last scene, as Chekhov wrote it, were most unwelcome; they wanted to see the play, as I wrote some time later, as "an unequivocal declaration of faith in a future which they themselves were to bring about."

Hope, desire, expectation all presuppose time to come, populating it, filling it with details, matter-of-fact or more likely fanciful. When hope fades, carrying expectation with it, the future darkens, is denuded, nothing remains on which to rest an eager bewitched gaze. For the Prozorovs, Moscow recedes and then starts to turn blank or rather into six abstractions, the letters *M O S K V A*; the future, of which for them the city has been the chief repository, has been retreating toward the present.

For Irina, the youngest, the future has been the most seductive suitor. She is like the character in "A Woman's Kingdom" whose "healthy instincts of a young woman flattered her with the false message that the true poetry of life had not yet arrived, but lay ahead." For Andrei, the dream of a professorship in Moscow has ebbed with his own deterioration. Olga has said, "Things never work out the way we want them to," and this isn't disgruntlement but a sober assessment. A religious proposition I know of is that God doesn't give us what we want but what we need. We shall see that it may also be an aesthetic truth.

("The individual is the seat of a constant process of decantation, decantation from the vessel containing the fluid of future time, sluggish, pale and monochrome, to the vessel containing the fluid of past time, agitated and multicolored by the phenomena of its hours."—Beckett, *Proust.*[29])

"Man must work, work in the sweat of his brow," Irina says early in the first act, "that's the whole point of his life. And all his happiness. How wonderful it must be to get up at dawn and pave streets, or be a shepherd, or a school teacher . . . or work on a railroad." Tuzenbach later joins her in this paean to physical toil and sentimentalization of those who do it: "Working people must sleep very well." And then, typically, Chekhov shuts down the subject for a while by having Fedotik tell Irina, "I was down on Moscow Street today and I bought these for you at Pyzhikov's. Crayons. And a little knife. . . ."

People in *Three Sisters* do work; we're not dealing with a class of drones here. Except for Masha and Chebutykin, who's a self-confessed goldbrick, everyone does presumably useful things. The soldiers have their unspecified military duties, the servants their tasks, Andrei is at the council office, Olga and Kulygin are teachers, Natasha has the household and children, and Irina holds several jobs before the end. Why then is there so much talk about the "necessity" of work and, oddly enough, in the circumstances, about "laziness"?

"We must find a way to join love of work to love of higher things," Vershinin says; and another time, "Happiness doesn't exist as yet, it will never exist for us. . . . Our task is only to work and work; happiness is reserved for our descendants." Tuzenbach proclaims that "there's a storm gathering . . . wild, elemental . . . it will clean out our society, get rid of laziness . . . and this prejudice against working." (A ripe text for the Soviets!) "I intend to work, and in twenty-five or thirty years we will all work." "We have to work, we really do," Irina echoes him. "The reason we're unhappy . . . is because we don't know what it means to work."

Is this true? In reality work's meaning for most of them is anchored in a romantic notion of "meaningful" and "selfless" labor, an emanation from the social atmosphere of the time. Beginning in the 1860s Russia witnessed the spread of ideologies of labor, leftist or simply idealist repudiations of a socio-economic structure marked by indolence and parasitism at the top and exhausting toil at the broad, poverty-stricken base. "We come from families who thought they never had to work," Irina says, and much of her and Tuzenbach's and Vershinin's hymning of physical work issues from a cloudy and naive wish to atone for this "aristocratic" past.

But something else affects them. A figure in a notable Chekhov story, "My Life," is a doctor who owns a run-down farm. "We talked," says another character, "about physical labor, progress and that mysterious unknown awaiting us in the remote future. The doctor didn't like farming because it interfered with our discussions."

The characters in *Three Sisters* behave in rather the same way. The work they invoke so ardently is still to come and, like the future itself, its reality exists only in their conversation; its solicitation is that of an idea, a piece of ideality. And again like the future their talk about work serves to relieve or deflect present discontents, to project them onto an agency or principle of healing; to think that "by the sweat of our brows" we can be secured against unhappiness is in this dispensation a source of solace and a boost to morale. But it isn't hard to see through.

Chekhov makes abundantly clear in the play, as in *Uncle Vanya,* where

Sonya has no illusions about the curative power of work, and throughout his stories and in his letters and notebooks, where blessed "idleness" figures as a counterbalance to grimly programmatic toil—"Life does not agree with philosophy: there is no happiness without idleness and only the useless is pleasurable"[30]—that work has no privileges, it isn't "the answer." Whatever work's necessity (the least interesting thing about it to the imagination), it neither transfigures nor transforms. Like love, it most often doesn't satisfy, it doesn't make up for the evictions of feeling, the ousters of portions of the soul. It doesn't provide solutions for dilemmas of a fundamentally ontological and metaphysical kind. It doesn't ennoble or redeem.

This is what Olga's complaints about her job and, much more forcibly, Irina's about *hers* are designed to show. Olga is worn out by her teaching ("The Schoolmistress" offers an especially fine sketch of the process), and Irina, the young panegyrist of labor in the early going, has only to experience it to change her song. "Whatever it was I wanted or was dreaming of," she says in Act Two, "this [her job at the telegraph office] is definitely not it. It's work, but there's no poetry in it, no meaning." And later, after changing jobs, she wails: "Oh, I'm so unhappy. . . . I can't work anymore, I won't. . . . I hate everything I have to do there . . . my brain has shriveled up."

Doesn't Irina appear to disavow all this near the end, when on the eve of her scheduled wedding she says she feels "happy, less depressed" and feels "like working again"? It's not that there's anything inauthentic in what she's saying, but the cheerfulness and renewed desire to work would seem to be products of her decision to marry Tuzenbach, and as such they feel more compulsive than wholly free.

The inference is that Irina is determined to follow up her relinquishment of formless romantic desire by reinstating the purposeful in her life; hence the wishfulness rather than conviction that we intuit here. At the same time her altered consciousness in this scene is an example of Chekhov's gift of resiliency to his characters, the license to double back on themselves or appear as entirely, if briefly, new.

Irina, we feel, won't be any happier in her new job as a teacher than in the others—Olga's experience is cautionary here—but this won't be due to her being especially hard to please or to any other characterological defect. The defect is in the nature of things.

As an aspect of his general strategy Chekhov wished to expose—to demystify, in current usage—the way we turn objects and activities into abstract ideas, essences, as we turn unrealities like the future into places. Roland Barthes wrote about "this disease of thinking in essences, which is at the bottom of every bourgeois mythology of man."[31] Except that it's even more flagrantly a disease of every *antibourgeois* mythology, Barthes was right, and Chekhov saw the matter long before him.

As an abstraction, a construction of the mind, work will possess any quality we endow it with. So when we put our *hopes* into it, making it promise relief from whatever it is that spiritually ails us, Chekhov will turn upon it his neither accusing nor even admonitory but simply clear and untraducible gaze: "There's no poetry in it, no meaning."

The indistinct hours and days crawl on, time's more and more indistinguishable units. Elements of stories, those subplots for which no covering master tale has been provided, have introduced themselves; now they fade away for a while, reemerge to add a detail or two to their claims on our attention, duck down again, and finally—mock dénouements, false climaxes—solidify their membership in the artistic whole as the play ends: Natasha bestriding the known world, Solyony firing the barely heard shot which sends Tuzenbach to his place in Irina's astonished and undemanding heart and among the swaying trees of memory.

In the fictive time between Acts One and Two Natasha has laid the ground for her imperium. The first ominous note is struck when Andrei mildly protests her decision to keep out the carnival players, telling her it ought to be up to his sisters—"It's their house, it's up to them"—and she says that it's up to them "*too*" (italics mine).

From then on her manner becomes increasingly officious and she moves in swift little forays to squeeze out the Prozorovs. She gets Olga out of her room, first in with Irina and then out of the house altogether to the school, gives Irina's room to the child, Bobik, maneuvers Andrei out of the marital chamber, and provokes Masha, who for some years has been living elsewhere with her husband but whose real "home" has always been here, to swear she'll never set foot in the place again.

But as I said before, all of this is done at long intervals (surprisingly, Natasha is on stage only a half-dozen times or so, and never for very long) and with such apparent offhandedness, surrounded by so much competing business, that we and her victims are continually caught off guard. Meanwhile with growing self-absorption Natasha carries on her affair with Protopopov, brandishes her

Three Sisters

children as armaments for her own ego, inflicts her pretentious French on everyone and steadily emasculates her unresisting husband.

At the end she revenges herself on the sisters for Olga's earlier criticism of her clothing by telling Irina that she needs "something more stylish" in a belt and announces that her first act after everybody has left will be to "have them cut down all these old trees" around the house. The spoliation is complete.

An episode in Act Three beautifully indicates Natasha's calculating moral sense, as well as Olga's contrasting generosity. With the fire jangling in the night, Olga comforts the exhausted eighty-year-old Anfisa and helps her to sit down. When Natasha comes in she berates the maid for daring to be sitting "in my presence," then asks Olga why she "keep[s] that old woman around." In the ensuing dialogue Olga, shaken by Natasha's behavior, tells her that "I get depressed when I see someone treated like that, I get physically *sick*," whereupon Natasha "kisses" her and tells her how "sorry" she is.

The subtle point here, easy to overlook, is that the sorrow Natasha expresses isn't for her cruelty to Anfisa, to which she's wholly blind, but for having "upset" Olga, a breach at this point of her pretense of affability. But when Olga, ignoring the gesture, says that Anfisa "has been with us for thirty years," Natasha returns to the attack: "She *cannot work*, she just sits around or she sleeps," to which Olga responds, "Then let her sleep." A moment later, as the fire-alarm sounds again, Olga says, "I think I've aged ten years tonight." The context makes clear that she isn't referring only to Natasha or the fire but to a complex of enervating, intractable things.

If the story of "Natasha and the House" unfolds in widely separated, discrete narrative particles, that of "Tuzenbach, Solyony, and the Duel" is distributed in even smaller, more isolated units. In the opening scene Tuzenbach tells Solyony he talks "nonsense" and a bit later, though apparently not in response to that, Solyony threatens to shoot Tuzenbach or Chebutykin (it isn't clear which from the text). Several times he irritates the baron with his "chickie, chickie, chickie"'s, yet Tuzenbach will tell Irina that "I feel sorry for him."

Some time later Solyony confides that "whenever I'm alone with someone, I feel all right, just ordinary, but when I'm in a group I feel depressed and shy . . . stupid." When the baron tells him that in spite of everything "I still like you," he says, "I don't have anything against you, but I have the soul of Lermontov." Soon after, he swears to Irina that if there are any "happy rivals" he'll kill them.

Three Sisters

Then, for many pages of text, scarcely anything, until the mysterious incident and the shot.

One clue to Solyony is of course his linking himself to Lermontov, the early nineteenth-century romantic writer who was killed in a duel at twenty-seven. Solyony thinks of himself in a literary way, making himself into a character in the word's several senses (might his cologne-doused hands be a conscious echo of Lady Macbeth?), striking poses, quoting, to no discernible point, Krylov, Pushkin, and Lermontov himself. All this is an aspect of his radical estrangement. He doesn't fit and will do anything he can to make a place for himself in the consciousness of this group, among whom he feels so clumsy. So he employs Swiftian or otherwise outrageous humor (one of his targets is Natasha, which wins him a few points with us!), gets into absurd quarrels about words or facts, and practices intimidation.

He wants to be distinctive, to make himself unmistakable, for otherwise he feels blurred, a smudged portrait. Like all those at the darker end of Chekhov's spectrum of moral existence, he is less actively, criminally evil than destructively incomplete: a crimped soul, a man itching for his "due," which nobody can give to himself. His discontent is therefore of a different order from that of his fellow characters except for Natasha, with whom, at odds as they are, he shares some central traits: unappeasable appetite, acquisitiveness, a feeling of having been excluded from what the others know or intuit to be superficial but which these two see as vital. Solyony eats up all the candy and bites off a life; Natasha, like a cormorant (Robert Brustein's memorable word for her), devours the sisters' goodness and consumes their patrimony.

Solyony is the play's chief source of irrationality, its way of unbalancing matters lest they become too stabilized; he's the dark imp of the unaccountable, the agent of the unforeseen. His presence is jumpy, divisive, as is Natasha's. And though neither is at the center of the stage action, both are as much as the others at time's center, two of the inevitabilities that hang there. Natasha, Solyony's colleague at another extreme, is cold rationality itself: whoever left a candle burning must be identified, forks must be in their proper places, "useless" old servants must be lopped off and trees, whose only justification is their beauty, chopped down.

She and Solyony give *Three Sisters* the edge of danger, the component of the directly inimical it needs to give some specificity to the otherwise barely visible, immensely attenuated depredations of time. Part of time's trap for the others, two of its teeth, they're caught in it themselves. They injure the others and are "injured" by their own lack of sentience; in a play which is in great part about the ouster of illusions, they're the embodiments of illusions—that you can fill in your own missing substance through a raid on others, that the self is sufficient and everything is calculable.

If Solyony seems beyond anyone's power to curb or control, why at least don't the others oppose Natasha? Why don't the sisters in particular *do something* about her? Well, what are they to do? Their brother, so centrally implicated, clearly lacks the will. Are they to try to "bring him to his senses"? I put the last clause in quotes because its pronounced ring of the archaic indicates just how far *Three Sisters* is from ordinary psychological drama. Asked to rewrite Chekhov's play so as to fill in its baffling omissions, a conventional dramatist, a "play-doctor," would move with alacrity to have the sisters wise up Andrei, while taking steps against Natasha themselves, perhaps not to defeat her, as in a melodrama, but to make themselves *felt*, and to provide what's so much needed: conflict, tension, development, confrontation, change—everything *Three Sisters*, whose silences must infuriate psychology majors and all proponents of things forthrightly explicable, so grievously lacks.

Nowhere in Chekhov's plays is his understanding keener of the way emotions and the objective world must query each other, how what we feel has sometimes to hesitate and turn reticent in the face of other feelings and "facts." In "An Anonymous Story" someone speaks of "the tact, the delicacy which are so essential when you have to do with a fellow-creature's soul." How especially delicate the sisters have to be when the soul is that of their beloved brother. That he allows Natasha's rapacity to go unchecked is proof of Andrei's interior collapse, his loss of will and self-esteem. If the sisters were to try to rouse him from his funk, the cave-in would be all the more costly to him and to their love for him than silence is. When he does stir himself for a moment and tells them not to believe his defense of Natasha, it's too late, time's accumulation has gone too far, and the poignancy of this belatedness adds itself to the prevailing winds.

But something else is true of all this; "something else" is always true in Chekhov. I have been writing in this section on a psychological plane, exploring possible motives in the realm of emotions and relationships, and while I think my ideas are sound, they're insufficient. If we're to have the fullest understanding of *Three Sisters* it's imperative to discover why.

Chekhov agreed with Tolstoy that any invention is to be permitted the writer except one: nothing in the realm of the psychological can be made out of thin air. And he added to this that a basic test for the psychological in drama is its plausibility. This is to say that characters must not behave in ways that "real" people don't or, more important, can't. But this is a minimum consideration, ensuring only that you can move ahead unimpeded by objections on the level of fact: "But people aren't *like that!*" The famous last line of Ibsen's *Hedda Gabler,* Judge Brack's "But people don't do such things!" after Hedda's suicide, illustrates a subtle but central aspect of the matter. People do kill themselves, they can, and Brack's astonished comment doesn't establish that plausibility has been betrayed but testifies to the action being unimaginable only in his narrow world of sophisticated rationalism and genteel corruption.

What any good writer does, of course, is bring plausibility out of often unsuspected corners, displaying it for the purpose of being able to go past it. For with this flank secured the writer moves on, goes deeper, into a domain where the imagination transforms the merely plausible into the revelatory, what lies beyond ordinary perception and so constitutes the artistic "thing" itself.

An incident in Act Three superbly exemplifies what I mean. It's just after Natasha's outburst against Anfisa. Exhausted by the fire, a number of the characters gather in Olga's and Irina's room. After some desultory conversation Chebutykin, clearly drunk, picks up and then drops a valuable porcelain clock that had belonged to the Prozorovs' mother. When it shatters he offers a bizarre denial: "Maybe I didn't even break it. Maybe it just looks like it's broken. Maybe we don't even exist, maybe it just looks like it." When nobody responds, and as if to make himself "real" again, he says, "What are you all looking at? Natasha's having a little affair with Protopopov, but you can't see that. You just sit there and you can't see that Natasha is having a little affair with Pro-topopov." Singing, he goes out, and the next lines are Vershinin's "Well . . . (Laughs) This is all really very strange, isn't it? (Pause.) When the fire started I ran right home; as soon as I got there, I realized our house was safe and sound . . . my two little girls were standing in the doorway. . . ." And the casual talk goes on.

It's not that they haven't heard Chebutykin or "taken notice" before this. That they don't respond and then allow Vershinin to change the subject comes from a covert understanding among them not to be drawn into the matter, an entente the doctor has broken. The affair is there, a factor in their lives, part of the climate, but there isn't anything they can do about it and they won't insert themselves into it with judgments, moral nosiness, or cluckings. Even more important from the standpoint of the entire design, Chekhov, as I once wrote, "won't allow the affair, potentially so rich in melodramatic energy, to move from the edges of the play, where its shadowy presence will be real but where it cannot draw attention to itself at the expense of subtler things."

This decision doesn't annul or negate the psychological—at least as much moral—reading I gave before; it assimilates it into a larger aesthetic scheme, where a more complex truth solicits our patronage. *Three Sisters* isn't about solving or confronting anything.

Our inquiry into why nobody opposes Natasha has given heart to a flock of questions of roughly the same order. Why does Olga find teaching so exhausting? Why is Irina so dissatisfied with her jobs? Why do they both complain about feeling "old" when they're still in their twenties? Why is Chebutykin such a disaster area? Why is Masha so unhappy before she meets Vershinin, and why for that matter did she marry Kulygin in the first place? Why, for his part, does he swallow her insults and go on stubbornly adoring her? Is Ferapont senile? What's wrong with Andrei? What's wrong with most of them? What is it the sisters can't know? And then, crown of this list, why don't they go to Moscow?

We should notice that all these questions are basically psychological except for the last two, which are philosophical and aesthetic, which means that they contain elements of mystery rather more reverberant than the puzzles of the first batch. Yet those are ultimately aesthetic and philosophical too, or rather the answers to them are, for we won't get more than a glum satisfaction if we stay within the readibly calculable workings of the uninflected mind.

I wrote earlier that *Three Sisters* is a play about effects, not causes, and though our natural impulse is to pursue causes anyway (actors most naturally have that bent; they want their motivations!), as I just did with Natasha versus the others, I managed to emerge from that inquiry on a different plane. Too often understanding of this play, as of *Uncle Vanya* and *The Cherry Orchard,* remains stuck at the level of what *ought* to be explained and seems possible to explain according to our *previous* knowledge. (So many italics here! Well, italics rub attention's nose in the point.) But our previous knowledge, what we *think* we know, is always put in question by imaginative works; art is one corrective to the pretensions of the behavioral sciences.

I've already answered some of the questions of behavior on the level of plausibility and now need, at the risk of some repetition, to give them a little push into artistic idiosyncrasy. Olga complains because teaching *is* enervating, Irina because her jobs *are* uninteresting, but in the more "thinkable" dimension of Chekhov's dramatic scheme they gripe because work is being shown to be no sort of solution. As for their feeling old before their time, being in your twenties is no bulwark against a sense of premature aging unless you believe that chronology outweighs what time has put you through.

Ferapont may well be senile, but if so, what then? Are we to dismiss his remarks as meaningless? But they have "meaning" within the whole: they're profound and liberating moments of irrelevance, delicious bits of counterstatement to "seriousness" when it becomes self-conscious. Besides that, the fact that he's deaf says something about Andrei, who is able to talk most freely precisely to a man who can't hear him. Masha is unhappy because her husband is inferior to her in psychic size, acuity, and capacity for the poetic; she married him because he was there. Kulygin dopily worships her because he's a masochist, if that's what you want to think; might it not be, though, that *in the play* he's strategically a site of dogged, old-fashioned, unthinking but not at all contemptible fidelity?

If we stick to psychology, the cases of Andrei and Chebutykin might seem harder to crack. The doctor's misanthropic callousness—what difference, he says, does "one baron more or less" make?—his self-indulgence only a bit tempered by his love for Irina (her mother's reincarnation?) and drunken indolence . . . all this indeed makes for the portrait of a soul in disarray. As do Andrei's failure of will and morose self-pity, although he too is slightly redeemed by his evident, if beleaguered, love for his sisters. But neither man strains our credulity in the least; if we don't clinically know why they act as they do, the behavior is well within our sense of the possible.

So why do we need to explain them? The play explains them, in its own terms, discovers their actions within the whole, fits them in as it does Solyony and Natasha, uses them for complication, contrast, elements of what we might call negative vivification. They are among the drama's givens, parts of its human substance. They take their places within this intricate arrangement of qualities, tendencies, emotional weights and measures, likelihoods and unlikelihoods, figurings and miscalculations: logistics, human geometry.

Why should we scrutinize them for their psychic histories, the origins and classifications of their maladies? Their psychic and spiritual illnesses arose before the play begins, in the nonworld from which all dramas emerge; the dramatic world exists only from the opening curtain, after which we see only what the characters do and are *now*. And in this dimension of present fictive time their neural classifications have only an extra-aesthetic and diversionary interest: they aren't fever charts but presences among others.

We've never fully learned the lesson that to want to know the "practical" reasons and causes of everything, to want motivations to be determinable along quasiscientific lines and characters to be wholly explicable—sometimes wresting the explanation from whatever obduracy thwarts our satisfaction—to want this is to try to turn the drama back into what it has already transcended: the understandable in ordinary perception. Chebutykin and Andrei, neither "dark" figures like Natasha and Solyony nor ones of varying "lightness" in the chromatic scale of Chekhov's moral imagination, move with no more mystery, but no less, than the fellow beings with whom they share this world of time's erosions.

Each character affects the others, each is sometimes the proximate but never the sufficient cause of other people's behavior. In the rudderless lifeboat in which they bob, some have a more intense hope of being rescued, some less; they range themselves within and against fate in shifting moods of alarm, surprise, bewilderment, rage, and quietism. The signals they give are in languages and codes we alternately translate and decipher.

A world of time's erosions. "Where is it? Where did it all go?" Irina cries out to Olga near the end of Act Three. And then she adds, "We're never going to Moscow." When time begins to crumple into its only true existence, the present, it means that its two extensions, past and future, are losing their constructed reality, the future through a diminishing of hope, the past by the sapping of memory. Forgetting: a way of withdrawing from one or another self that once seemed possible.

The process is distributed throughout; the characters forget from different angles and with different things at stake. Masha can't remember Vershinin at first, can't recall the author and title of a song she's humming, and is beginning to forget her mother's face. Vershinin has a hard time with faces too; Andrei's ambitions grow dim; Chebutykin has lost his knowledge of medicine. And in the most affecting of all these evanescences, because its very commonplaceness points up the indiscriminate action of time in wiping out its own traces, Irina says, "I've forgotten everything. I can't remember the Italian word for window or ceiling . . . every day I forget more and more."

The Italian word for window. Like Tuzenbach's "I didn't have any coffee this morning," Irina's most matter-of-fact citation is at the heart of Chekhov's method. Drama, as we've seen so often in this study, doesn't live in the supposedly "dramatic," the stock of materials the imagination can readily draw upon for predictable effects. The great expansion of theater's possibilities that Chekhov brought about arose from his having freed the reputedly undramatic from its exile, welcoming it with all its unheralded nuances, its revelations in tiny, *not yet considered* figures, its modest beauty.

The all but undetectable operations of time are of such a nature. As the play moves along it becomes ever more clear to us that nothing sensational is going to happen, in the exact meaning of that word: full of the striking, the out-of-the-ordinary dazzling us with intensity. The one risk in this regard is Tuzenbach's death, and so the shot is "muffled," the event takes place at the far edge of consciousness and its repercussions are left almost wholly implicit; a lesser playwright would unquestionably have called heated attention to the sorrowfulness and irony of the thing.

For the rest, time piles up its effects in the smallest increments, silent instances of disappearance, things slipping or chipped away. Everything is unspectacular, unremarkable, as though these lives haven't so much been cruelly stolen from as misplaced, misappropriated: time not as busy thief but as amphitheater for our inadequacies, our miscalculations and bungling.

The losses are material, psychological, and spiritual, and how are we to separate all that? The Prozorovs' house is slowly taken from them and with it their immediate past, the way-station between their heritage and what they have been hoping for. Masha and Vershinin have to part; their bodies will mourn in the emptiness that will supervene, which their souls will have to fill by other, greatly subdued means. Tuzenbach is killed and Irina is left with a corporeal gap to cross and a crimp in her newly won self-possession, all before she has even modestly gotten started on her mature life. Olga will go on working and wondering, surviving her headaches. Andrei will recover nothing.

The physical sufferings and subtractions aren't the "subject," but they're not beside the point either. If they weren't part of the "story" the play would lose solidity, it would verge toward abstraction, as a set of values under siege or humane principles worn down. It would then be a play of ideas, in the worst sense, a juggling of insubstantial, even though serious, matters; it would truly then become the arid lesson in metaphysics its boldly detailed sensuous textures in fact keep it from being.

Three Sisters

But if it were centrally about material failures or defeats, palpable things gone wrong, it would lack all mystery, would be a chronicle merely of bad luck or weakness or incompetence or culpable victimization. (In the 1920s a writer named William Gerhardi offered an opinion whose variations can be heard to this day: "Good God! How can there be such people? Why can't people know what they want and get it?"[32]) A drama of that kind fits comfortably into the zone of psychology and sociology where problems and solutions abound; and in which blame is more likely than not to be meted out. In light of all I've been saying, what standing could such a *Three Sisters* have?

Fate, everyone's "lot," to use a good gruff old word, isn't deserved by those who lose out, but it isn't undeserved either. Destiny here is pitched beyond such considerations of blame and innocence, as it always is in Chekhov. Need I repeat that this doesn't at all mean he was unconcerned with moral outcomes or uninterested in ethical distinctions, as for opposing reasons so many of both his admirers and his detractors have thought? Within his moral schema behavior, the materialization of the soul's thinking, its impulses and aspirations, all struggle against an indifferent Nature, indifferent Time. How does one assign blame to that? The play doesn't take us to moral conclusions, though it touches intimately on moral reality as nothing other than one face of reality itself. Yet "the individual caught in the fact" is not an ethical proposition but an ontological one.

In our own vocabulary of existence as competition, our lexicon of ratings, we speak confidently of successes and failures, more grossly of winners and losers; we label material triumphs and defeats and, more subtly, build hierarchies of goodness and evil, into which structures of morality sentimentality settles like a blight. In regard to all this Chekhov once wrote to a friend that "classifying people as successes or failures is looking at human nature from a narrow, biased vantage point. Are you a success or not? Am I? What about Napoleon? And your Vasily? Where is the criterion? You have to be a god to distinguish the successes from the failures without making a mistake."[33]

He would not put himself in the way of such perilous judgments or create the materials for us to make them. Does Tuzenbach deserve to die? Does Cordelia? Are Natasha and Solyony successful, as it might appear? Was Iago? What is the criterion? The art changes the terms. It isn't too much to say that no playwright after Shakespeare did more than Chekhov to give drama that fertile indefiniteness, the sense of values behind values, by which consciousness is made to expand. The mind wants its certainties, the imagination overthrows them. The narrow, preconceived view Chekhov spoke of in that letter is just what falls away, or ought to, when we fully assimilate *Three Sisters*; originality, as I wrote earlier, is the defeat of habit, and nothing is more habitual than our way of judging and the way we raise up expectations as a form of projected judgment.

With *Three Sisters* our temptation is to pronounce a particular sort of judgment, on the Prozorovs mainly but also on Chebutykin, Kulygin, and even Vershinin. In this judgment, however much we may be moved by some of them, these are inefficient people, unsuccessful ones; to us, technocrats of human living as we are, the failure to get to Moscow is the crowning piece of evidence, the culminating defeat in a chronicle of incapacity and culpable loss. All this induces us to think of the play, despite the humor that keeps breaking in to discompose our categories, as melancholy, if not deeply dispiriting.

Melancholy it is, in part, though "sorrowful" is better, again only in part. Dispiriting? Only if, precisely, you're unable to see beyond notions of failure and success that have only a utilitarian status, the idea of what, outside the spirit, *works*. But how the spirit itself "works" has been in question all along, as it always is in Chekhov.

When *Three Sisters* was in rehearsal at the Moscow Art Theater, Chekhov gave Olga Knipper, whom he had married not long before this, some pointers about playing Masha. "Don't make a mournful face," he told her, "angry, yes, but not mournful. People who carry grief in their hearts a long time and are used to it only whistle and often sink into thought. So you may be thoughtful during conversations."[34]

Remarkable advice, if at first sight a little eccentric. But only at first; assimilate the idea of whistling out of grief and being thoughtful about pain and deprivation, think of meditative anger as a possible response to suffering, and you will have put your finger on an essential aspect of Chekhov's originality. If the fundamental imaginative principles of *Three Sisters*, its aesthetic rationale, can be located in any such circumscribed resting place, it's in those words: "You may be thoughtful."

Has a more subversively liberating permission ever been granted to an actor and through her to a character? This very thoughtfulness, so unlikely a source of the dramatic because so much better suited to the portrait of a condition than of an action as I've been defining those terms, is just what distinguishes the kinds of life on exhibition here from the baser composition—by which I mean more alloyed, as in metallurgy—of conventional dramatic existence. Such existence is regularly contaminated by a lack of consciousness, a strain of unknowingness about the emotions being summoned up (this is why unimaginative actors are forever asking for those "motivations") and their place in the whole. But now the character is charged with reflecting—literally passing on the spirit's rays of involvement, not moping or mooning—on what is being undergone. With this gift we are in a Shakespearean dimension.

We can assume that Knipper listened well, since from all reports she was a splendid Masha. She quarreled with Chekhov on interpretations from time to time, but not when she saw that they were at the exact heart of his mature artistry.

To act a dramatic character is to give explicit signs of mind and spirit at work, signs that emerge from consciousness repeatedly fed from unconscious sources. This is what thoughtfulness is, as distinct from abstract thinking: the surprise and seriousness of the mind when feeling passes into awareness. To be "thoughtful" in Chekhov's meaning encompasses more than the particularities of Masha as a character; it's advice to all the players. For the actor must feel entrusted with a "thinkable" thing, if the text has composed one, and must know that to get at that requires you to see that in the humming, redolent silences beneath what is directly done and said lie as many of the thing's truths and nuances of truth as have physically been offered.

This is usually called the "subtext," but the problem with such a term is its suggestion of some tangible whereabouts, which you might be able physically to reach in some manner, by digging, say. This is just what results in all those labored excavations for "meaning" or "authenticity" that go on in various corrupt forms of Stanislavsky's system and, for that matter, sometimes within the system itself. Wouldn't it be more useful to think of the subtext as the "latent" or "implicit" text, a dimension rather than a place? Within it the real is invisible and toward it everyone, the reader or audience member and, surely, the performer, sends out feelers of intuition to take possession of the unsaid. And the unsaid, or rather in this perspective the *not yet said*, is just what so many of Chekhov's most fugitive yet perfectly solid states of being, including thoughtfulness, are all about.

We have seen that in *Uncle Vanya* Chekhov had rendered what he called "the subtle, elusive beauty of human grief," something not yet "understood" or "properly described" and which requires for its articulation a grasp of the coexistence within sorrow of a "burden" and a "lyricism." In *Three Sisters* he again moves among some of the details of such a theme—to put it better, such a proposal for the mind—and, applying lighter or darker tones here and there, doing some thickening, some reapportioning and elaborating, carries it not into a deeper place but a wider one. He takes everything into a greater range of experience, more to be *gone through,* enough to press up against the absolute boundaries of what time encircles, makes possible and impossible, announces, hides, and will not answer for.

But *Three Sisters* isn't simply an expansion of *Uncle Vanya,* for besides the significantly different mise en scène and its inhabitants, the quantitative change is the agency of a qualitative one. The lyricism of *Uncle Vanya* is muted and pacified, so to speak, becoming a more attenuated music. The staccato excitabilities of the earlier play are gone, its kinds of tension flattened out, so that nothing builds toward a climax. The actual existence of time—which in *Uncle Vanya*'s far smaller compass shows itself until the very end, when Sonya projects it into an unchanging future, as a local pressure rather than an entire habitation—now becomes the Jamesian thing itself.

Because there is more time for it, fictive and metaphysical, the thoughtfulness is more prominent, more evenly distributed. It belongs not only to Masha but to everyone touched by grief, which means all the principals except for Natasha and Solyony; to be thoughtful means not to know, and those two, as the very token of their human insufficiency, act as if they know everything. But they too are part of the rumination Chekhov had begun long ago: What in the flow and substance of our lives is it most necessary to come to terms with?

Sorrow is one of those things. In *Uncle Vanya* it's acute, sharply discovered, often remarked upon; it pervades the entire last sequence on the stage. In *Three Sisters* it's more implicit, further below the surface; it unfolds in a more leisurely way, we might say, it's scarcely to be distinguished from everything else. Yet there's no gloom, or rather when that threatens it gets a ready opposition: Fedotik gives Irina the most sweetly trivial of gifts; Kulygin blunders into humor; Masha whistles.

These tiny clues tell us that the play (I'll leave *Uncle Vanya* behind now, though much of what I have still to say fits it too) contains a counterpoise to pure sorrow and, a most salient point, that the sadness itself isn't to be defined or experienced as a contrast to what we think of as "happiness." The play certainly isn't a tragedy, either by any formal criteria or in the debased usage by which we call tragic anything distressing, from a bus crash to a fallen soufflé.

There's no pushing against limits in *Three Sisters,* no straining against the terms of existence; nobody is brought down by hubris or the necessity of an impossible choice. Sorrow is inherent, permanent, not the result of some fateful decision or irrevocable event. It isn't to be "corrected" or made palatable through wisdom; it's not to be sublimated or transcended or have anything at all done to it. It simply is there, the burden and the lyricism. Time passes or stretches out, time surrounds, and things are lost in it, continuously, without fail. Nothing is salvaged except as traces in the spirit and through the valor of the art. For the play's beauty lies in the recognition it gives, the enactment, of deprivation and diminishment as our condition, the essence of what we go through and, in struggle and doubtfulness, either come to terms with or evade.

How we go through it, what we do during the only real time granted to us, the present, that confluence of what is no more and what is not yet, is the play's story. It's anything but a tale of futility and ineptitude, and we can only think it is if we judge its people as failures against notions of success that have no status in literary or dramatic creation: to have satisfying loves, "fulfilling" work; to reach particular Moscows; to get, in short, what the will has vaingloriously settled on.

If God satisfies not our wants but our needs, art, when it's honorable, does the same. What is it we want for the characters, especially the sisters, so nearly our surrogates? To succeed as we ourselves would like to? But in an important sense they *have* succeeded; the art changes the terms. They've moved from potentiality to actuality; they can't know the future but they know what they are now. And for us they offer imagined incarnations of the qualities that reign over every other virtue in Chekhov's theater: stamina, endurance, going on. (Played as only a thread of drama on the periphery but quietly representative of such general perseverance is the disaster that befalls Fedotik; he loses all his possessions in the fire yet remains upright, even philosophically rather cheerful.)

"I can't go on, I'll go on." The crowding together of the two halves of this sentence from Beckett, without even a "but" or a "yet" to separate them, only the neutral comma, renders almost exactly the morale of most of the lives in *Three Sisters.* They can't, they do. It's unendurable, they endure. The negative and the positive are as nearly simultaneous as the nature of syntax will allow. In the midst of successive losses they survive, in part through goodwill that leaps periodically over the worst of the conditions—*the* condition—to issue in camaraderie and affection; they do it with the help of the humor that surrounds them, the surprises of rueful wit or simply unapologetic laughter. The humor, it should be seen, isn't there to "balance" or offset the sadness but to give grief another dimension in thoughtfulness, a way of self-recognition as continually reviving animation, not paralysis or pallor.

As I near the end of this chapter the parallels with Beckett, of which I've cited so many, offer themselves once more. (I ought to say here that I haven't been using Beckett to praise or validate Chekhov; if anything it's the other way round, since Chekhov is the anterior touchstone.)

Just as Didi and Gogo are the very ones for whom Godot doesn't come, so the Prozorovs are the very ones who don't get to Moscow. The French title of Beckett's play is *En attendant Godot— While Waiting for Godot*; one regrets the erasure of that first word. For the play is "about" what the tramps do while Godot doesn't come, and in the same way Chekhov's play is about how the sisters live while not getting to Moscow. Had they gotten there—and after all there's nothing really to stop them, nothing physical or moral requires them to stay mired in the provinces—they would have been in a different play. As it is, the "provinces" they're stuck in are the precincts of the lives they necessarily *do* lead, not of the ones they, and we on their behalf, might have wanted.

And so they have no choice but to be in the play devised for them, to live as Chekhov, in his dramatization of how time even-handedly devours our substance while continuing to prop us up, has chosen for them. Why they don't get to Moscow is, then, a question only to those for whom everything in art, as in life, is utility, satisfaction, recompense, and everything not seized and exploited, all that doesn't work to our ostensible advantage, is defeat. But the play proposes other values and offers a different perspective: what it's like to be alive here, now, beyond social situation and idiosyncratic fate, in *this* drama of inconclusiveness and acceptance of mystery. "What's keeping us here?" Hamm asks Clov in *Endgame*. "The dialogue," Clov replies. What keeps the sisters where they are? The text.

The women will go on, we're free to think, immersed in time, suffering and recovering, making do, craning their necks now and then to try to catch a glimpse of that stretch of the unknown and unknowable that lies before them. "My dears, my dear sisters, life isn't over yet. We'll go on living," Olga says just before the end, and then, as Chebutykin "softly" counterbalances her with

"Tara-ra-boom-dee-ay" and "What difference does it make?" she adds, "If only we knew!" Both she and the doctor have it wrong: they can't know and it does make a difference.

At the end of the long story "Three Years," written in 1895, a character says to himself, "One may live another thirteen, another thirty years. . . . Something still awaits us in the future! We shall live . . . and we shall see." And the last line of another notable Chekhov story, "The Lady with the Pet Dog"—which I quoted earlier in this book (in a slightly different translation)—is this: "It seemed as though in a little while the solution would be found and a lovely new life would begin for them; and to both of them it was clear that the end was still very far away, and the hardest and most difficult part was only beginning."

Chekhov began this story in August 1899 and had not yet finished it when he started on *Three Sisters*. So during the period of overlap he was doubly occupied with rendering presence and duration: what is, has been, and un-fathomably is still to come. Once more the structure of a sentence tells us more than any loud thematic pronouncement. The not yet extinguished hope of the lovers kept from mutual happiness by fateful circumstance is followed on the page not by a "but" but by the "and" of a grave recognition of unlikelihood; the aspiration and its enemy would exist simultaneously except for the neces-sities of linear composition.

As for the sisters? Hope still, empty yet persistent; time, difficulty, the future. We shall live and we shall see. Stamina.

THE CHERRY ORCHARD
or "An Aperture into Eternity"

As I prepare to write about Chekhov's last play, images from the other ones crowd around as councilors, voices making themselves heard with reminders of continuities, themes and variations, persistences among change. There is a sense in which the last four plays, even more closely the last three, make up a single action of theatrical discovery, imagination adding to itself until the dramatic "field," as we can think of it, is filled in.

An incremental vision, a vision in phases; there are, after all, four separate plots or situations, and so four different prevailing manners, tempos, and dramatic weights. But such are the resemblances and reoccurrences—of person, condition, and motif—that the four, certainly the last three, move together in our minds, not blurring, nothing like that, but linking up, creating imaginative tandems, or one extended family. Some details of the plays' ostensible stories keep reappearing but, beneath that, the group is held together by the "story" of style, the way that in each successive play the artifact is newly configured, having lent a certain irreducible human substance to its own reshaping.

Here is another way of putting it: light falls from different angles, with different intensities and at changing times of the artistic "day," the career. In *The Seagull* Chekhov at thirty-five considers human hopes and predicaments; at forty-four in *The Cherry Orchard* he considers hope and predicament again, adding perspective, modifying, suggesting something new. Between these two plays two others, *Uncle Vanya* and *Three Sisters,* mysteriously gain in richness from having been so framed.

Arrival and departure. Gathering and dispersal. The end in the beginning and also, in two cases, a new beginning in the end. Chekhov's last four plays have among other repetitions and resemblances this large structural pattern.

At the outset characters arrive or have just arrived from beyond the immediate mise en scène to set things in motion. Everyone who will figure at all measurably in the action is given a stage presence before events have gone very far. At the end a surprising number of them will move on, going out of the picture, but whether they go or stay, most of them will bear the marks of encounter, interchange, or simple propinquity, and they will have been altered in some essential aspect of self-awareness, which for the most part will be left to us to intuit. A few, generally Chekhov's "negative" characters—and this is a chief reason for classifying them that way—will be hardened in what they were when they started.

Life will resume, in that theoretical realm beyond the text, within the contours of natural probability. The artificiality of conventional dramaturgical design, whose effect is to seal off stage-life as hermetic, in a mode of the exemplary or inimitable, has been replaced by an openwork structure which resists climax, definition, or resolution, rejecting the dragooned shapeliness of a narrative frame for the display of heightened emotions, *important* truths. The truth distilled in these plays, modest, lowly, oblique, is rooted in the recognizable rhythms of our lives, with nothing set off by obvious "construction," nothing inflated beyond its familiar size, yet with everything transfigured by an imagination whose chief instrumentality is its penetration into the strangeness of the familiar.

Arrival. In *The Seagull* Arkadina and Trigorin have recently come to Sorin's estate; in *Uncle Vanya* Serebryakov and his young wife have come to Sonya's. In *Three Sisters* Vershinin has just been transferred to the town and Natasha makes her first appearance at the Prozorovs'. And in *The Cherry Orchard* Ranevskaya returns at the opening from five years in France, along with her daughter and some servants, and Trofimov has come to the estate two days earlier.

The newcomers and returnees enter an atmosphere which their arrival or its imminence has helped create: charged with expectation, a little unstable, flecked with a sort of moral danger. Each new presence will emit rays of understanding or will block off such gleams; each will move toward the center or rather will lend substance to the composition of plays that sometimes seem to be all center and no periphery.

Departure. At the end of *The Seagull* Nina leaves for her new, sober life as an actress and Arkadina will head back with Trigorin to the corrupt and enticing "city." At the end of *Uncle Vanya* Serebryakov and Yelena make tracks for somewhere they hope is less stressful; Astrov, we strongly suspect, won't come to the estate again. *Three Sisters* closes with the entire regiment, among whose members are half the play's characters, marching away. And at the end of *The Cherry Orchard* Ranevskaya is off to Paris again, Lopakhin will "spend the winter in Kharkov," Varya is leaving to stay with the Ragulins, whoever they may be, Carlotta is looking for a "place," Anya and Trofimov are going somewhere. In fact, so thorough is the dispersal here that as the curtain falls only Firs can be said definitively to "remain."

The last three plays, still more tightly connected by style and tonal arrangements, additionally possess several thematic elements in common, ones likely to be obscured by larger matters or by being so large themselves as to make us miss their position in a sequence. In each play a house, an abode, is threatened or lost. Sonya's estate comes close to being taken from her by her father's selfish scheme; Natasha usurps the Prozorov house; along with the orchard, their ancestral home is lost to Ranevskaya and her family.

In each of the plays, too, trees are objects and emblems of despoliation. Astrov fights against the ongoing destruction of the local forests. Natasha announces her intention of having the beautiful firs and the maple at the house cut down. And of course the last sound in *The Cherry Orchard* is of an "axe chopping down the . . . trees."

Details change, moods do, perspectives vary, vision becomes deeper or more acute, embodied existences grow more complex in some instances, technique grows more supple, but something reigning at the center of Chekhov's imagination and thinking remains constant. Among the last four plays we find another most significant similarity, both structural and thematic.

At the end of each, women, much more prominently than men, are seen facing one or another kind of future, carrying the implicit spiritual and aesthetic tales beyond their formal closures. Nina is moving toward the seriousness and responsibility of an authentic vocation. Sonya has started on the itinerary of sorrow and unfulfillment which stretches out in front of her. The sisters await whatever they might, without prospects or illusions, come to "see." And Liubov, incautiously perhaps but uncoerced, will go toward a resumption or reconstruction of her recent past, while her daughter Anya, sustained by an unspecific ardor, having not yet been advised by experience to stop hoping, stands before an open stretch of time as possibility.

With varying states of morale, then, with metaphorical doors having been slammed or left ajar, all of them are going to go on: continuance, endurance, movement across the indeterminacy of the years.

It remains to be noticed how the types of future I've described enter centrally into Chekhov's designations of the plays. He called *The Seagull* and *The Cherry Orchard* "comedies," subtitled *Three Sisters* a "drama," and gave *Uncle Vanya* the deceptively neutral and ironic label "Scenes from Country Life," though he could easily have called it a drama too. As for his three earlier full-length plays, we see that he left his first, which we call *Platonov,* without either a title or a subtitle, but it's as uncomedic as can be imagined, and that he called his next two, *Ivanov* and *The Wood Demon,* a drama and a comedy, respectively.

Two dramas—on the simplest level plays without anything we might think of as "happy" endings—to start with, then two comedies, followed by two more dramas; after *The Cherry Orchard,* a comedy, we could have expected another one, if Chekhov had lived and the orderly alternation had continued. (He left mention of a plan for his next play, something partly to do with Arctic exploration, strangely enough; but even that subject doesn't rule out a comedy in the Chekhovian mode.)

The evidence seems to be that his imagination, as it moved within the frame of his usually steady temperament, became darker or lighter by turns or, more precisely, his sense of possibility in regard to the lives he invented rhythmically dilated and contracted. This brings us to the relationship between comedy and the future I've spoken of before. To summarize it here: In Chekhov's special meaning, comedy has everything to do with an opening toward time to come such as the dramas by their very nature won't provide.

The slight change of morale from the dramas to the comedies appears mainly as the presence of a tenuous principle of potential movement, a lifting of the cover of permanence we feel about fate in the more "serious" works, those sorrowful yet also humanely funny plays of stasis. Tremors of potentiality stir Nina and, as we shall see, Liubov and Anya; they can safely be advised that things won't necessarily be the same; seize the day, they should be told; be prepared, though, to give up something in order to gain something else.

The only glaring discrepancy between comedy and drama as genres in Chekhov is his transformation, after the intervening *Seagull,* of *The Wood*

Demon into *Uncle Vanya.* The movement is from a contrived comic effort in which everything ends in celebration and projections of happiness for several pairs of lovers, to a predominantly solemn work whose interlacings of humor give way finally to a lyrically anguished, pitilessly "closed" ending.

The ill-conceived *Wood Demon* was Chekhov's only venture into what we think of as classical comedy. Working in an exhausted convention, he went against his abiding sense of the comic; when he recovered it he went back to its true meaning for him, that of a seriousness with only a slightly different face from that of the dramas, a countenance upon which a glint of liberating light from the future was allowed to fall.

A "loophole" in the fortifications of time, a sense of possibility not yet used up or been supplanted by unforgiving "facts": this is what enables certain Chekhov characters, central among them the women I've cited, to cross over to the "unreal" future, in the faith that by refusing to romanticize it or hungrily predict it, it will become real, as successive, repeatedly undertaken present times. Approached this way, time may grant some portion of what it ordinarily conspires with our human weaknesses or existential errors to deny. On this *other side,* beyond the segments of their invented lives that have been registered on the stage, in this domain of speculation for us and abstract next act for them, the characters can go forward with a guarded optimism.

Yet something troubles me about this idea. Optimism is never an authentic attitude or condition in Chekhov, any more than is pessimism. The terms imply a kind of satisfaction or complacency on the one hand and depression or despair on the other. These states are too settled for Chekhov's liking, too unambiguous; they hint at those unwarranted and unwarrantable assumptions about the future he was at such pains to undermine or counteract in his characters, as we've seen most clearly in *Three Sisters.*

No, it's the spectator or reader who out of the limitations of our vocabulary makes these ascriptions, and so I use "optimism" here to describe with an unsubtle word a much more complex state of mind. For characters like these women the future isn't fated to be the exact extended replica of the present. Their mood is comprised of a capacity to resist resignation, whether through innocence in Anya's case, a renewal of rough *élan vital* in her mother, or Nina's clearsightedness about the need for humility and devotion. Such strength as that and a sense, privileged in Chekhov, that time as a condition, with its remorseless wearing away of our substance, may be tactically outfaced, made provisionally to relent, before it once again resumes our diminution.

The Cherry Orchard

You defeat or cheat time only at the cost of some sort of sacrifice, the yielding up of a part of the self or of its internalized possessions—for Nina it's her romantically nourished ego, for Liubov and Anya the beloved trees—in the interest of another, perhaps more valuable part. Nina stands ready for an accession of new experience, as do the Ranevskayas, Liubov with some awareness of the kind of life she'll have, Anya with an animation and faith that lack all specificity. They will have ceded something, as I say, because as in all true comedies of high seriousness part of what you enter the action with has to be surrendered: a misconception, willfulness, a false outlook. But they're destined to be given an increment. In the cases of Sonya and the sisters, however, nothing will be added because nothing is going to change.

To look at *The Cherry Orchard* is to see not so much change itself as the postulation of change: *this* may happen if *that* does. I'll give away at this point my ruling idea about the play: only if they let the orchard go will new or renewed life become possible.

For reasons that aren't hard to find, *The Cherry Orchard* is almost surely Chekhov's best-loved play and so, we can guess with some confidence, very likely his most often performed. It was also his first to be translated into English, or at least rendered into it in some fashion, having been published as *The Cherry Garden* (the Russian word *sad* can be translated as either "orchard" or "garden," but for what it's worth, Shakespeare several times uses "orchard" for what we would refer to as a "garden") in 1908 in New Haven, of all places, the work having been carried out, as Avrahm Yarmolinsky tells us, " 'under the supervision of the Dramatic Department of the Yale Courant,' " of all publications.[1]

But Chekhov has had a way of popping up in unlikely venues and strange guises throughout the English-speaking world. The first production of any of his plays in Britain or the United States was of *The Seagull* in Glasgow in 1909, and among a number of peculiar adaptations a titular favorite of mine is something called *Three Sisters of West Virginia*. But the most bizarre such reworking, certainly the best known, appeared in 1950 when Joshua Logan transported *The Cherry Orchard* to a Louisiana plantation, setting it in 1905 (only a couple of years off, actually) and calling it *The Wisteria Trees*. (Taking off from a Turgenev title, Noel Coward called the production "A Month in the Wrong Country.")

Logan saw the original as a social and psychological study, a realistic work whose universal qualities made it legitimate and easy, he assumed, to transfer it from one set of historical circumstances to another. *The Cherry Orchard* is indeed "universal," but hardly in the unfortunate, soap-operaish perspective Logan adopted or for the reasons he seems to have discerned.

Mentioning Logan reminds us that from the beginning of its life on stage and in the critical and popular minds the play has swung between interpretive polarities: naturalism and poetry, social lament and social prophecy, most controversially comedy and something very close to a tragic mood. The views have multiplied. As early as 1911 Arnold Bennett called it "one of the most savage and convincing satires on a whole society that was ever seen in the theater,"[2] but eighty years later Peter Brook saw nothing satiric about its "microcosm of the political tendencies of the time."[3] Frequently the effort has been made to reduce or eliminate the distances between the larger oppositions by trying to combine or yoke them: Stanislavsky's "poetic realism," for example, or some variety of the tragicomic. One way of not having to make exegetical choices has been to stress the play's "musical" nature, which is fine as far as it goes but can be at the expense of any intellectual substance, leaving us with a set of hovering notes, program music without a program.

What we might call "the comic versus the melancholic" became a debate at the start. Anyone with more than a routine interest in Chekhov is likely to have at least heard of the contretemps between him and Stanislavsky, who along with Nemirovich-Danchenko directed the première at the Moscow Art Theater in January 1904, less than six months before Chekhov's death. Ill as he was at the time of the opening, he had enough vigor to denounce what he saw as Stanislavsky's depredations. (Nemirovich, always more finely attuned to Chekhov's artistry, seems to have had a subordinate directorial position but to have promised Chekhov that he would "keep an eye on" Stanislavsky.)

"Is it my *Cherry Orchard?*" Chekhov asked. "With the exception of two or three parts nothing in it is mine. I am describing life, ordinary life, and not blank despondency. They either make me into a cry-baby or into a bore. They invent something about me out of their own heads."[4] For his part Stanislavsky wrote later that well into rehearsals "the blossoms had just begun to appear when the author arrived and messed up everything for us."[5]

The quarrel included particular questions of interpretation but went deeper, to the roots of spirit and tone. Stanislavsky's analysis, though faulty, was actually not quite as wrongheaded as Chekhov supposed. Though he insisted on seeing the family as "spoiled aesthetes," a persistent misreading, he at least didn't regard the central action as the result of deplorable human lapses. The fateful encounter he saw, along with many since him, was between a representative group of improvident and historically doomed gentry and a member of a new socio-economic class, aggressive and vulgar but, again, historically necessary. He seems to have arranged the play's moods and thematic emphases so as to fashion a fundamentally lugubrious tale, picking his way between the political extremes that quickly afflicted understanding and wrapping the whole thing in his special brand of poetic or, as some have seen it, poeticizing realism.

"I invented all sorts of *mises en scène*," Stanislavsky later wrote, "the singing of birds, the barking of dogs, and in this enthusiasm for sounds on the stage I went so far that I caused a protest on the part of Chekhov."[6] No wonder. Stanislavsky himself reports that after seeing the way he had handled *The Seagull*, Chekhov had said to someone: "Listen. I shall write a new play and the first words will be 'It's wonderful, this calm! No birds, no dogs, no cuckoos, no owls, no nightingales, no clocks, no sleigh bells, no crickets.' "[7]

Still, this wasn't his main complaint, which concerned the mournfulness, the "weepiness," as he called it, that ran through the production. And so while his general gratitude to the Art Theater for giving his work a home remained intact, he added this bit of pique to the negative dossier he had also been compiling.

Since this primal dispute, the vane of interpretation has gone this way and that. Sociology has ruled, pathos has prevailed, the poetic has triumphed over the realistic and the other way round. The grimly or sweetly melancholic has been a perennial view, but the comedic took some time in getting established.

Eva Le Gallienne's 1928 production might have been the first to do justice to *The Cherry Orchard*'s lighter aspects, and since then the movement in that direction has picked up. Indeed in recent years some directors have turned the play into an exercise in knockabout zaniness, their textual justification lying mostly in the pratfalls and gaucheries of Yepikhodov and Trofimov, the broad humor of Semyonov-Pishchik, and Carlotta's parlor tricks. They may also have been encouraged by some letters and conversations of Chekhov in which, offhandedly and almost certainly as a defense against the grim view, he referred to the play as a "farce"[8] and "a vaudeville"[9] and told Olga Knipper that it was "happy and frivolous."[10]

He was overstating it, no doubt for tactical reasons. But he didn't help things and after him the disputes and conflicts of perception have kept on, resulting in some silly comment, some perspicacity, and one or two strokes of revelation.

Nearly all the mediocre, respectable critics of the period jumped on the play, mostly from political stances on the right and left—a sharp division in Russian cultural discussion then as later. Right-wingers objected to what they saw as a "parodic treatment of cherished stereotypes"[11] (Liubov, Lopakhin, Trofimov), as Joe Andrew tells us in his useful study *Russian Writers and Society*. On their side, leftist commentators denounced Trofimov for "justifying capitalist exploitation" and Lopakhin for "idealizing the decadent aristocracy." One representative review, by Vladimir Korolenko (supposedly a friend of Chekhov's), described Ranevskaya, who has always been a prime target of denigration of whatever provenance, as an "aristocratic slut, of no use to anyone, who departs with impunity to join her Paris gigolo." Then, freely mixing his metaphors, Korolenko adds, "Chekhov whitewashed her with a sort of sentimental halo."[12]

But some rather heavier guns sent off broadsides too. Maxim Gorky, who, as I've had occasion to speak of before, combined an often fawning adulation of the man with an ideologically induced blindness to some of the work, wrote the following in his 1905 memoir of Chekhov:

"There's the weepy Ranevskaya and the other former masters of *The Cherry Orchard*, as egotistical as children and as flabby as senile old men. They missed their chance to die in time and now they are moaning, seeing and understanding nothing—parasites who lack the strength to latch on to life again. The miserable student Trofimov talks prettily about the need to work and spends his time in idleness, entertaining himself with stupid ribbing of Varya, who works tirelessly for the benefit of these drones."[13]

I'll be touching again on this tirade of Gorky's and the strain of criticism it represents with such moralistic nastiness, but let's turn now to a couple of reflections by other people Chekhov knew, remarks that in contrast to critiques like Gorky's offer accessions of understanding.

Nemirovich may have been the first to celebrate *The Cherry Orchard* as a play that went far beyond social portraiture, certainly of the kind in which judgments reign and psychology fuses with politics to justify one or another pre-existing "position." "The entire play," he wrote, "is so simple, so wholly real, but to such a point purified of everything superfluous and enveloped in such a lyrical quality, that it seems to me to be a symbolic poem." (Several generations after Nemirovich's paean, Francis Fergusson would write an essay which no Chekhov commentator can ignore. It was called "*The Cherry Orchard*: A Theater-poem of the Suffering of Change," and it was noteworthy both for its reinforcement of the idea of the play as poetry and for its highly original thoughts about change as necessary pain.)

Meyerhold, who had started as an actor (he played Konstantin in *The Seagull* and Tuzenbach in *Three Sisters*) before breaking with the Art Theater to become an innovating director and bold theoretician, took his reading even further past sociology. In the process he struck at Stanislavsky's weaknesses and, in the tersest possible manner, announced a truly radical way of looking at all of Chekhov's mature plays. "To Chekhov," he wrote, "the characters of *The Cherry Orchard* were a means to an end and not a reality. But in the MAT the characters became real and the lyrical mystic aspect . . . was lost."[14]

The characters not a reality? What are we to do with this eccentric, to say the least, assertion? Well, to begin with we might praise it. In saying that the characters should not have become "real," Meyerhold performed two closely related acts of liberation. He released *The Cherry Orchard* from any obligation to verisimilitude and so helped it escape from a particularly deadly type of interpretive scheme: a reading of it as a photograph without mystery, evidence to confirm what from their different vantage points the literalists, the moralists, and the warring ideologues thought they knew. At the same time he freed attention to go where it belonged, to Chekhov's artistic calibrations. This is what Meyerhold meant by the "end" toward which he said the characters were a "means."

Meyerhold knew as well as anyone that Chekhov was in a sense a "realist." The question, as it always has been, was this: in what sense wasn't he one? That he wasn't a fantasist, a deviser of dreams to be staged, didn't make his realism a matter of the transcription of actuality. He was faithful to appearances, yes, but for purposes beyond them; the fidelity wasn't to any obviousness of surface or to readily available likenesses (as the sweet old term in portrait painting had it) but to the rhythms, tensions, flexions, and interplay of the deep human world.

When Nemirovich said that *The Cherry Orchard* was "wholly real," he surely didn't mean it was realistic—where in that case would the poetry reside?—but that it wasn't fanciful, wasn't *false*. He might just as well have said it was wholly "true" rather than real, and in fact the Russian word he uses wavers between those meanings.

Meyerhold understood that the characters' "unreality" consisted in the first place in their having been imagined, *made up,* not plucked from the world outside the play to serve as theatricalized envoys from a social drama antecedent to this one or as bearers of messages pertaining to correct (or incorrect, for that matter) political behavior. It lay in their not being ends in themselves, not being creatures conjured from nothingness, or rather from dumb matter, only to be hacked and whittled and shaped and colored and then displayed as specimens: a gallery of impersonations of the *tendencies of the times.*

If we see them instead as agencies of a vision wider than the "times," we'll be closer to Meyerhold's meaning: an invented set of existences, pretending to represent nothing, whose relationships and the milieu they inhabit, whose walls they beat against, compose the dramatic "reality," the artistic end. Then they're free to participate in something other than a dramatized report, a staged term paper in history or sociology, as it were. *The Cherry Orchard* is an action of the creating mind, not the product of some reproductive faculty; it's an amendment and corrective to our ordinary, congealed, codified, and presumptuous knowledge.

In Stanislavsky's attempt at a fussily poetic realism (of which the weepiness was doubtless a part; does anything work better than tears to persuade an audience that it's watching "real life" on the stage?), Meyerhold saw the loss of the lyrical and mystical, which is to say he noted the disappearance of a dimension of mystery. It will help us now to remember that understanding of both *Uncle Vanya* and *Three Sisters* has often been crippled by an inability to see that they too are mysteriously poetic constructions beyond the naturalistic.

Chekhov's real subject in *Uncle Vanya,* we'll recall, was what he spoke of as the "burden" and "lyricism" of grief and loss. In *Three Sisters* that subject reappears, more mutedly and, we might say, subterraneously, enclosed in the special mystery of Time as a human condition. The music and enigmas of *The Cherry Orchard* are of a somewhat different order, as befits its status as a comedy, and they will make themselves known to us in what we're about to explore.

Here are some questions which from the beginning any serious inquirer into *The Cherry Orchard* ought to have asked and which many have:

Are Liubov and her brother "irresponsible?" Are they "feckless" (a favorite epithet for them until maybe a generation ago, when the word began to fall into archaism, though you can still come upon it here and there)? Are they and Trofimov and Yepikhodov "parasites?" Is Anya one? Carlotta? Pishchik? Firs? Is anybody "decadent?"

Whose fault is it that the estate is lost? Could the loss have been prevented? What then?

Is the cutting down of the trees (a) tragic, (b) piteous, (c) saddening?

What sort of person is Lopakhin? Is he the villain of the piece? Why doesn't he ask Varya to marry him?

What is the meaning or significance of the famous "breaking string?"

Where *The Cherry Orchard* began in Chekhov's imagination and how it took shape are no more clearly visible than these things are for the other plays. (He's reported to have said to Stanislavsky at some point, "*Vishneviy Sad.* Listen, it's a wonderful title.") Yet as is true of the earlier works we do have some possible origins, or seeds of origins, not so much in his life as in his stories and the immediately preceding plays. We can, for example, detect *Uncle Vanya* and *Three Sisters* urging thematic elements of their own on the new play's creation, as in the matter of the endangered households and the menaced trees I spoke of before.

Ronald Hingley thought he had found a source for the play in Chekhov's life. He tells how in 1876, when Anton was sixteen, his mother went into debt after having been cheated by some builders she had hired for a small house. A former lodger, one Gabriel Selivanov, offered to help her but secretly bought the house for himself. "By dispossessing the Chekhovs," Hingley writes, "Selivanov had supplied the future author with a theme, the loss of a family home, which was to inspire his play *The Cherry Orchard* a quarter of a century later."[15]

I very much doubt this and am not persuaded by Simon Karlinsky's agreeing with Hingley on the matter. The family lived only briefly in the house and the circumstances of their leaving are thoroughly different from the play's. More important, Chekhov had ambivalent if not actively hostile memories of his home town, Taganrog, and it's a long stretch to think he had any attachment whatever to that particular house, which, moreover, was as far as one can imagine from being an ancestral seat. Finally, in the play the estate isn't taken from the family by any devious or immoral means, such as Selivanov employed.

A year or so after the incident Chekhov's family moved to Moscow, where Anton soon followed. If the matter of the house meant anything to him, assuming he even knew the facts about it, it might have been as a lesson in the untrustworthiness of contractors or of soi-disant friends. But as an inspiration to a play . . . I don't think so.

Much more reliable connections are to Chekhov's stories,"Late-Blooming Flowers" and "Other People's Misfortune" among them, and especially "A Visit to Friends," which he wrote in 1898 (and for some reason didn't include in his *Collected Stories* of 1899–1901). In the latter tale Podgorin, a lawyer, is urged by old friends to help them prevent the loss of their estate, Kuzminki, which is due to be auctioned in August (the date matters because the auction in *The Cherry Orchard* is in August too). Several of the characters in "A Visit to Friends" have resemblances to persons of the play, most notably a woman who cries out to Podgorin, in very nearly the same language Liubov will use to Lopakhin and Trofimov, that "I cannot live without Kuzminki! I was born here, it's my home, and if it's taken from me, I shan't be able to go on, I shall die of despair." Seeing no way to help the charming but "ineffectual" family, though not for that reason alone, Podgorin steals away one night.

The story has other narrative lines apart from the fate of the estate, but can anyone doubt that Chekhov drew on it for his play? He had made the same sort of raid on his own material on other occasions, among them, for instance, his use of "A Boring Story" and "The Neighbors" for important elements of *The Seagull.* There are, too, behind *Three Sisters,* the half-dozen stories in which someone stuck in the provinces cries out, "Moscow!" And just as he had done with the earlier borrowings, he put what he had taken from "A Visit" to new and more complex uses.

For quite a while I've been considering a digression on exposition in Chekhov's plays, and now, just before we move toward the full life of *The Cherry Orchard* as the text contains it, seems as good a time as any. The fact is that some people who may otherwise admire Chekhov have expressed dissatisfaction with the way he lays out information, mostly in the early moments. It seems to them obvious and mechanical and so they question the completeness of Chekhov's originality. I think they're missing something essential, although I recognize what has provoked them.

The data given out in the first scenes of the plays comes mostly in *The Seagull* from Masha and Medvedenko, in *Uncle Vanya* from Astrov, Marina, and Vanya, in *Three Sisters* from Olga and Tuzenbach, and in *The Cherry Orchard* from Lopakhin and Anya. The information is of several kinds. There are citations of events that have preceded the plays: Father died a year ago, the Serebryakovs have made their appearance, Liubov has been abroad. And news of impending events: Nina is going to act in Konstantin's play, Liubov's arrival is imminent, Vershinin is coming to call on the Prozorovs. And simple facts: Astrov is a doctor, Serebryakov is a professor of art, Lopakhin's father was a peasant, and so on.

In another dimension, where the line between exposition and dramatic substance gets rather hazy, are the data of feeling and personal condition: Masha is mournful; Olga is exhausted from teaching and yearns for Moscow (as does Irina); Nina and Konstantin are in love (Medvedenko tells us); though he's rich now, Lopakhin still feels like a "poor boy from the country."

Now most of this does constitute exposition in the material or technical sense. But something is different about such information in Chekhov, and to find it out we have first to ask what purpose exposition has traditionally served. Briefly put, it's an instrumentality of naturalistic, or naturalistic-seeming, drama, where it has a practical function and nothing like a poetic or expressive one. It sets the ground more or less painstakingly for the action to follow, making up a who's who and a what's what; it forms a pre-logic for the ensuing tale, closes up potential gaps, prepares the way for causal sequences, makes everything narratively rational. Smaller or larger building blocks of material detail are hauled into place as a foundation for plot. The effort usually shows, unfortunately; exposition is most often the enemy of mystery and of intellectual, if not purely theatrical, surprise.

Still, at a minimum and indispensably for any play that isn't surreal, "absurd," or a fantasy, it can also protect against confusion. It's for this modest purpose of establishing coherence and a rough order of eventfulness, not for the building up of a sequential plot, that Chekhov uses exposition. If his using it at all is held against his originality, we should remember that he was a realist, a symbolic or lyrical or "magical" one, as it happened, but in any case not an avant-gardist of our own day; Ionesco came *after* Chekhov, along with the idea that plays could begin in the middle.

And so his originality didn't consist in dispensing with exposition altogether but, in a sharp departure from conventional practice in his own time (and things are scarcely different in ours), in seeing to it that his expository material would appear in an atmosphere whose mystery and musicality it didn't diminish. So his "facts," the spiritual along with the objective, mostly have a different quality from the way information ordinarily functions. They emerge differently, are *surrounded* differently, and have different dramatic fates later on.

In Chekhov's plays material events are never the sufficient causes—and rarely even the proximate ones—of spiritual and moral activity, which flows almost entirely from inner promptings. They in turn make up the realm of the subjective or poetic, to which we gain access largely by continual movements of intuition, guided by the hints, allusions, and fertile silences, the rests which Chekhov's music lays before us.

All this is to say that facts don't generate the drama; if anything, it's the other way round. The drama doesn't hinge on the factual but surrounds and absorbs it, giving it new and usually unexpected fates, so to say, putting it to new uses of subjectivity in place of its ordinary status as objective.

Factual announcements don't presage anything inevitable or plot-driven; exposition doesn't anticipate anything determinable, the creation of suspense, for example, or a drama whose prevailing sights and sounds can be predicted from its early information. That Nina and Konstantin are in love, as we're told, doesn't mean that this is one of the experiences the play will render to us; if anything, *The Seagull* becomes in part the story of how they're *not* in love. Again, in *Three Sisters* the initial data about Moscow doesn't turn out to have been predictive of anything except loss, absence: exposition preparing the way for its own obliteration.

In Chekhov the struggles are internal, perception against perception, soul against soul, as Henry James said of Ibsen's characters in an observation that fits Chekhov's people even more closely. All the facts disappear into the web of enactments, the humming silences and echoing shadows.

Information in Chekhov, moreover, is almost never the product of a situation that seems urgently to call for it, and very seldom comes as a direct result of the interrogations or proddings common to realistic plays. Only rarely do we see exchanges such as the following invented ones:

> "You look tired, Olga." "I know, the school's getting me down."
> "Is Ranevskaya a nice woman, Lopakhin?" "Yes, extremely nice."
> "What do you think of the professor, Vanya?" "I loathe him."

Instead, a remarkable number of pieces of information that technically qualify as exposition seem to come out of nowhere, in the middle of a monologue, thrown into other people's conversation, dropping out of the sky. Casual and low-key mostly or, if not, encircled by lyricism, they don't feel tactical but incidental; they have a way of calling attention to things beyond themselves. And they keep to themselves, these facts, or stay in related clusters, almost never forming chains of progressive scene-setting. Nor do they have about them that peculiar air of apology we sometimes detect in conventional exposition: you have to know this, so forgive me as I go about telling it to you.

The opening moments of *Three Sisters* and *The Cherry Orchard* are especially often attacked for their purportedly clumsy or arbitrary expositions, although all the plays come in for their share of abuse in this regard. Olga's detailed "historical" account can make an attractive target. "On the fifth of May, your birthday. . . . It was very cold. . . . You actually fainted. . . . The clock struck [noon] just the same way . . . . Father got his [brigade] eleven years ago and we left Moscow and came here, it was the beginning of May then too. . . . Moscow was already full of flowers . . . there was sunshine everywhere. . . . Eleven years ago, and I remember it all . . . as if we'd only left . . . yesterday."

Lopakhin's monologue in *The Cherry Orchard* is almost equally vulnerable. "She's [Ranevskaya] been away for five years now. . . . She was always a good person. Very thoughtful. . . . I remember . . . when I was a kid . . . my old man . . . hit me . . . in the face, my nose started to bleed. . . . And Liubov Andreyevna, she wasn't much older than I was then . . . brought me inside the house, right through that door, and washed the blood off my face for me. 'Don't cry, little peasant,' she said, 'you'll survive.' Well, my father was a peasant, but look at me now, all dressed up, brand-new suit and white shoes. Silk purse out of a sow's ear, I guess. I'm rich now . . . but when you think about it, I guess I'm still just a poor boy from the country."

The most striking thing about these near-soliloquies isn't so much their rhetoric, intimate and sometimes eloquent as it is, but their circumstances and aftermaths. Olga and Lopakhin are presumably speaking to Irina and Dunyasha, respectively. Yet neither of the ostensible listeners makes any reply, neither gives more than a slight sign of having heard. The same is true of Astrov's "I don't need anything and I don't love anybody," spoken in the presence of Marina, and of Medvedenko's announcement of Konstantin's forthcoming play, to which Masha makes no response.

These silences should alert us to the way information is functioning. It's *we* who are being addressed, but not so much with cold facts as with the life and consciousness from which they emanate. In their speeches we really learn more about Olga and Lopakhin and the incipient tones of the plays than about plot elements, and the proof of this is that if we're listening well, having succumbed to the seductiveness of the proffered memories, memories of feeling encircling facts, the "objective" details slip unobtrusively into our awareness.

In this manner the facts and confessions disappear into the textures of the plays, dramatic elements like any others, no less poetic for being informative, no less mysterious for having been "laid out." The point to see is that we're forever being surprised, taken off guard by these data, and have no idea what will be made of them; we simply absorb them, after having caught them on the wing, and fit them, without giving them special markers, into the expectations we have for the wide unfolding drama.

Traveling a bit ahead of ourselves for an illustration, we might look at a speech of Anya's that comes not long after *The Cherry Orchard* begins. She is on stage with Varya and, "lost in thought," the significant stage direction says, she recapitulates the family's recent history in what could unreflectively be taken for standard exposition. "Father died six years ago," she says, "and a month later our little brother Grisha drowned. Such a sweet boy, he was only seven. And Mama couldn't stand it all, that's why she went away, just went away and never looked back. And I understand exactly how she felt. I wish she knew that. And Petya Trofimov was Grisha's tutor. He'll remind her of it all."

This little speech, instigated by their just before having spoken of Trofimov, has pronounced affinities to Olga's opening soliloquy. It begins almost identically—"It's a year ago . . . that Father died," we remember Olga says—and offers much the same fusion of objective or historical detail and singular feeling. Above all, like Olga's speech, it works to create or extend our sense of the character's governing spirit.

I wrote earlier of what "thoughtfulness" means in relation to a Chekhov character. That Anya is to speak while being occupied by thought is both an instruction to the performer and one disposition of the play as a whole. Her recital is to issue from a seriousness, a prior and ongoing contemplativeness that with its sources in sorrow and spiritual alertness lifts the "facts" into a poetry of statement cradled by emotion. How feeling surrounds and transfigures the factual is beautifully demonstrated almost in passing. Immediately after having reported the background and reasons for her mother's flight, Anya speaks of knowing "exactly how she felt." The historical action has a home and a defense in the daughter's consciousness. "I wish she knew that," Anya goes on. Liubov will come to know and it will be one thematic axis of the play.

Like Olga, Anya is really engaged in a reverie, and just as Irina did not respond in the earlier play, so Varya doesn't here. She doesn't have to; she knows the story and knows, too, that like Irina in Olga's tale she's included in it: "*our* brother," Anya says, and speaks of "Mama," yours and mine. So Varya can stand by while we ourselves, the true intended listeners, take "notes" on the little tale as it slips quietly, with its grave yet somehow light cargo of information, into the continuing life on stage.

In the realm of the practical, the expository as coherence and ground for what's to come, the speech gives a rationale for the mother's action which prepares us for her own later speaking of it and meliorates the bathos this will risk. It accounts in part for Trofimov. Most broadly, it links the past to the present without predetermining anything that might happen in the future.

The setting of the first act is a room still referred to as the "nursery"; since it clearly hasn't for a long time been used as one, the designation, conveyed to the reader by a stage direction and then on stage by Lopakhin moments after the opening, is an early, "establishing" indication of Liubov's sentimentality and nostalgia. Dawn is breaking, though it's still dark indoors. The time is May but out in the orchard "there's a chill in the air," though the trees are "already in bloom." How to show all this, finding the right line between the overdone and the visually scrawny, is a designer's test; the extremes of production that I have seen are the Moscow Art Theater's tedious opulence and the austerity of Peter Brook's recent offering.

Dunyasha with a lamp and Lopakhin with a book come onto the empty stage. (No other Chekhov play begins with an untenanted stage, nor does any end as austerely as this one will, with even the furniture mostly gone and Firs abandoned and alone.) Yepikhodov comes on and joins them in a rambling conversation around a longish monologue by Lopakhin. And so an exceedingly skeletal plot begins to unfold.

The early moments of every Chekhov play are little models of the way things are going to happen, microcosms of the subsequent dramaturgy in their deployment of technique and establishment of structural principles. But the beginning of *The Cherry Orchard*'s full action has a particular vivacity and amplitude as both foundation and forecast. All the marks of Chekhovian construction are present in abundance: the continual traffic on and off the stage; the alternations of pace and intensity; the frequently nonconsecutive or broken dialogue; the seemingly irrelevant interjections that reveal character or give body to texture; the abrupt movements of attention from men and women to objects and back to people.

Among many instances of such circuitry we might single out the tiny occasion when Varya says to Anya, "Oh, you've got a new pin, a little bee." To which Anya ("with a sigh") replies, "I know. Mama bought it for me." Then Anya moves away and the subject changes. A flicker of concentration on the jewelry, a note on its place within a contour of feeling, then the "camera" pulls back. Leonid Andreyev, Chekhov's admiring contemporary, called him a "panpsychologist" and said that in his theater "not only human beings but things perform."

Once again the process, in short, is the filling in of a dramatic space rather than the elaboration of a dramatic line.

After the short, somewhat desultory prelude, the main action gets started with an animation such as no other Chekhov opening can show. The stage is deserted again for a moment, noises off are heard, Firs comes on muttering something, then Liubov and her entourage sweep in. It's an irruption of personalities, with hers at the center at first, a swirl of greetings, questions, recollections, and rediscoveries, all the emotional plenitude of a homecoming. Quickly every substantial character will have been on stage, except for Trofimov, who will make his entrance later in Act One but whose presence in the house has been spiritedly talked about long before.

As the entire group comes on in a jumble of suitcases, boxes, umbrellas, and a small dog, Anya is the first to speak, asking her mother if she "remember[s] this room." "The nursery!" Liubov exclaims ("happily, through tears," that quintessentially Chekhovian operation which will occur again later on) and continues into full nostalgia: "My lovely, heavenly room! I slept here when I was a little girl. (Weeps) And now I feel like a . . . girl again." She kisses her brother and Varya, her adopted daughter, about whom, in an adroit, revealing shift, Chekhov has her then say that she "still looks like a nun." There's affection behind the remark, of course, but it tells us at the outset that Liubov has a tougher, unsentimental side, which she'll display on several occasions.

A slight, disconnected patch of dialogue now follows. Gayev says, to no one in particular, that "the train was two hours late. What kind of efficiency is that supposed to be?" Carlotta says to Pishchik, "My dog just loves nuts," to which he replies, "Really! I don't believe it!" after which everyone except Anya and Dunyasha goes out. The initial excitement has died down and the air and the tempo change.

The Cherry Orchard

Anya and Dunyasha on stage. Then Varya on, Dunyasha off; Anya and Varya together, with a "moo—oo—oo" in the middle from Lopakhin, "stick-[ing] his head in the doorway," Anya speaking from her adjoining bedroom; Dunyasha back; Varya going into the bedroom; Yasha on; Dunyasha with Yasha; Anya and Varya back on; Firs on and Dunyasha off (she's forgotten the coffee cream); and then Liubov, Gayev, Pishchik, and Lopakhin back on. Anya off to bed, after which the situation becomes more stable.

I've described this sequence of people being on stage and then disappearing, these rapid-fire entrances and exits, as though, minus the physical hurly-burly, it were a speeded-up swatch of silent film comedy or classical theatrical farce. For in some such manner this is the way it returns in memory: this character and that one, then this other one, now that one again, then these two or three, then those, a bustle of changing faces and voices. We will see this happen again, at a swifter pace and even a little hysterically for a time in the third act and more quietly in the fourth, after the relatively sedate traffic of Act Two.

The point I want once again to make is that this is one of the ways Chekhov prevents a linear, destination-bound plot from taking shape, as he steadily fills the stage with a multiplicity of shifting presences, with their differing densities and angles of vision. A revolving dramatic field, we might think of it, which as it turns gives us glimpses of successive arrangements of feeling and idea, connectedness and disconnection, participations near the center of the imaginative frame or farther away.

As the play slowly accretes we see themes beginning to range themselves alongside one another, relationships being established, all the sensuous detail of presence and conversation. We should remember that in the last four plays there are no formal scene divisions, but four unbroken acts in each, with no changes of time or place within them. It's the continuous movement of people on and off or a shift in the conversation from one pair or group to another that allows us to speak of discrete pieces of stage action, which, moreover, are at least as much verbal as physical.

When the focus of the homecoming turns to Anya, the spirit is at first wholly different from that of her mother's return. As Dunyasha fusses over her, Anya is "so tired [she's] dizzy." And she's self-absorbed; when the maid tells her that Yepikhodov has proposed, her response is, "That's all you ever think about. . . . My hair's a complete mess." But after ignoring Dunyasha's "he loves me, he really loves me," she suddenly perks up when her glance falls on the adjoining room: "My own room, my own windows. . . . I'm home, just as if I'd never left. . . . Tomorrow I'll get up and run straight out into the orchard." And she "joyfully" greets the news that Trofimov has come.

With Varya, Anya turns grumpy again, as the swift, complex portraiture advances. She complains of Carlotta, her hired companion for the trip to Paris; of the cold and snow there; of her mother's smoky rooms and the visitors; of her own "awful" French and Liubov's spendthrift ways. In an important memory, however, she speaks of having felt so sorry for her mother that "I just threw my arms around her and couldn't let go."

She's shocked and horrified when Varya tells her the estate is "up for sale in August." This is the first mention of the auction, but before they can discuss it—and so, strategically, before melodramatic suspense is allowed to build up—Lopakhin's "moo" diverts attention to him. "Did he propose yet?" Anya asks. Varya replies that though there's been talk, she doesn't "think anything will ever come of it. He's always so busy." In this way the ground is laid for the poignancy of Varya's dealings with Lopakhin at the end.

Anya again breaks out of her bad humor, going into her room and talking and giggling "like a little girl." "You know what? In Paris I went for a ride in a balloon," she says, whereupon Varya, in one of the play's many bits of discontinuous or autonomous dialogue, says, "Oh, darling, you're back! My angel is home." Then when Varya speaks of dreaming about seeing Anya "married to somebody rich" and, being able to "rest easy," "go[ing] off" to "live in the woods" or "visit . . . churches," Anya's own hermetic reply is, "Listen to the birds in the orchard."

Chekhov's methods have most often been compared to those of a composer, but we can liken them to a painter's too. A stroke here, another there; the extension of this line, the sudden swoop given to that; the gradual filling in of an area; stippling, swathes, darkenings and lightenings; wiping out (we know some of the things he erased); *building up*. In this regard something he wrote to his brother Alexander in a letter of May 11, 1889, is of exceptional importance: "A great deal of rewriting should not disturb you, because the more mosaiclike the results, the better."[16] In the writing of Chekhov's own plays such "results" essentially make up the dramatic *field* I've talked about as replacing a dramatic line.

Among the shapes and colors of character the sequence gives us, those concerning Anya stand out. Varya isn't far behind, and Yasha and Dunyasha have some measurements taken too, for even the most "minor" figure in Chekhov is continually giving off data about the self. And even the most minor of such data has significance: Lopakhin's single humorous interjection, for example, says something about his nature and his position in the play.

Anya's irritability can be mostly explained by her exhaustion, yet we sense she's moody beyond that, mercurial may not be too strong a word. The subtle thing Chekhov does with her in this early segment is to have her give off some "negative" glints so as to balance or slightly chasten the light of idealism that will fall on her later. She's very young, only seventeen, and in some ways unformed, impressionable. Her interests skip. She can be cold. But her good heart is evident, as is her deep attachment to the place.

Varya too has a good heart. Gorky spoke foolishly of her slaving for "drones" and Liubov says she looks like a nun. But though she herself speaks of "spend-[ing] all my time visiting churches," she's a good deal less austerely pious than all that might suggest. She's clearly devoted to her adoptive family and falls easily to weeping where they and the estate are concerned. In warning against having Anya speak "in a tearful tone," Chekhov said that Varya was the only "weepy" character, "because she's a crybaby by nature."[17] This seems a bit harsh, but he was probably making the point that sorrow wasn't endemic to the play and indeed, by having Varya cry rather immoderately, he created her in part as a contrast to Anya, who doesn't sob once. A brisk housekeeper and responsible steward, Varya's also interested enough in Lopakhin to resent his being too busy to notice her. All in all, she's more complex than is often seen.

Dunyasha is flighty, callow, a contrast with Varya. She starts with an apparent attachment to Yepikhodov, then flirts with Yasha who, fresh from Paris, seems to her a glamorous figure. We see him, in turn, in a tiny epiphany, as both lecherous and pretentious, speaking and walking "in an affected manner," grabbing and kissing Dunyasha, and telling her "You sure turned out cute, didn't you?" Theirs is one of the actual or sought for amorous relationships, and its fundamentally comic nature isn't out of line with the others; none has much weight or passion, except for Liubov and her unseen lover, about whose interchanges we can only guess. (Being unseen, the lover can't contribute to any potential melodramatic build-up; a more conventional playwright would surely have plopped him on stage for at least one or two heated scenes.)

As for Lopakhin, his moo is at the same time a reflection of his easy position vis-à-vis the household and a rather clumsy attempt to display it.

I've spent what might seem an inordinate amount of time on only six pages of text, but such circumscribed sequences can yield the most elastic results. The early moments are paradigmatic of how action and character inform one another, and of the way dialogue tends to accumulate, spreading over this surface and that, rather than existing as the girders and trusses of a plot. In this section, too, we can see how themes begin at the periphery before moving to pick up all the filings of attitude and emotion at the center (the quite casual and truncated announcement of the auction is an example). Now let's look even more closely at the way *The Cherry Orchard* constructs its life.

In the later part of Act One, Firs is on stage most of the time, and Liubov, Gayev, and Pishchik are on until near the end; Lopakhin leaves half-way through. Varya is there much of the time, Anya at the beginning and end. Trofimov comes on two-thirds of the way through. Carlotta makes a brief appearance. Yasha is on for a couple of stretches. (Only Dunyasha and Yepikhodov are absent.) So the stage is amply occupied during this time when the full range of character and relationship is laid out. The twelve named characters divide rather easily into two groups. We can consider half of them "major" and half "minor," remembering that in Chekhov these are relative terms. And so Liubov, Anya, Varya, Lopakhin, Gayev, and Trofimov are at or near the center; Pishchik, Carlotta, Yepikhodov, Yasha, Dunyasha, and Firs at varying distances away. Let's look at what each of the ten who are present in the second part of Act One says and does and therefore reveals, and how themes behave in their neighborhood.

(A note: As I said in an earlier chapter, this sort of anatomy does violence to the integrity of the whole and is defensible only if the characters are afterwards put back into context. There, we may hope, they'll lend themselves to us with less reserve, having been granted a provisional autonomy designed to encourage them to give up secrets. In our long view of the play these have to do with how the characters live on the stage as the "means" toward an artistic end, which Meyerhold held them to be.)

Gayev: He comes on practicing billiard shots, a "signature," and announces, to no ascertainable hearers, that he too grew up in this house and that he's fifty-one. He informs Liubov of some deaths during her absence and sucks on a piece of candy, another signature. Later he apostrophizes an old bookcase with what used to be called in Russia "jubilee oratory," florid praise of someone, usually an academic, who has held a post for a very long time. He constantly speaks from the fringes of the action and lives in a notably hermetic psychic world.

He displays, or at least makes gestures toward, his love of Anya and Liubov, yet in his sister's absence meanly says that "her behavior has not been . . . particularly exemplary . . . the fact is, she's what you'd call a loose woman." He calls Lopakhin's proposal for the estate "outrageous" and reveals his own wishful plan for saving it. He's by turns sentimental, testy, and windy. A bit of a dandy, something of a snob. "Ineffectual," an idler it seems, he's fine evidence for the "effete aristocracy, dying culture" reading of the play.

Firs: He resembles Ferapont of *Three Sisters,* though his part is richer; they're both nearly deaf and a little dotty and throw "irrelevant" remarks into the dialogue. Like Chekhov's other aged servants, he's both testimony to endurance and a block of detachment from the present. He's crankily devoted to Gayev, who, we sense, as the oldest member of the family reminds him most fully of the past. He has no theories. When he speaks of the orchard it's not about the trees' beauty or symbolic status; what he remembers from long ago are the "dried . . . pickled . . . and preserved cherries," the jam, sent out to "Moscow and Kharkov, by the wagonload." They were "soft and juicy," but when Liubov asks about the recipe his answer is, "They all forgot." The implications of this—to skip considerably ahead of ourselves—are that nobody seems to have maintained the orchard in one of its chief material functions and that consequently it has taken on a purely decorative existence.

Varya: She weaves in and out, extending our intimacy with her. She shows her usual efficiency (checks on the luggage, gives Liubov the telegrams). Gets angry when Lopakhin mentions the cottages. Weeps several times. Is "terrified" when Pishchik asks for a loan. Scolds Gayev for his garrulity. Scolds Yasha for his selfishness. Becomes lyrical once: "Look, mama, what wonderful trees! Smell the perfume!" Tells a long story about a rumor that she'd fed people nothing but beans, to save money, and is furious that such a story should circulate. Tenderly puts Anya back to bed.

Yasha: Adds to our sense of his pretentiousness and cruelty. Varya berates him for his treatment of his mother, behavior which is in sharp contrast to Liubov's generosity a moment before, when she lends Pishchik money they can scarcely spare.

Pishchik: He comes to mind visually like his near namesake, Pickwick. He's a wag, though his jollity is sometimes forced. In somewhat the same way as Telegin of *Uncle Vanya,* he's there in part to reduce tension, not exactly comic relief but more like comic displacement; and he's given to seemingly pointless interjections: references to his daughter are never acknowledged. His big early moment comes when he swallows all of Liubov's pills. Huffing and puffing, he's forever scrambling for money; in the end his optimism pays off, which we're entitled to read as a comment on fate in general: keep your spirits up and who knows? He speaks well of Lopakhin, which is important, as we'll see.

Trofimov: He's on only briefly but is a distinct presence, earnest and un-prepossessing in his student's uniform and "wire-rimmed glasses." As Anya had feared, he stirs in Liubov painful memories of her dead son, but the two tearfully embrace and engage in an exchange of gentle remonstrances on her part and self-mockery on his. He has some resemblance to Tuzenbach, which will mostly appear later, along with huge differences. When he sees Anya going off to bed, he cries, or breathes, "My sunshine! My own springtime!" This is the only such declaration of passion by anybody in the play.

Anya: In her short time on stage she deepens one element of our sense of her. After Gayev calls Liubov "a loose woman," she chastises him for it and for his general talkativeness: "We all love you. . . . But uncle dear, you should learn not to talk so much." But after he again swears that the estate won't be sold, she says she "feels better" thanks to him. The point is that she's subject to swift changes of mood, with the volatility of her youth, and is easily influenced. (As the play advances we see her grow more steady.) She's the pet of the household, the object of kisses right and left.

Lopakhin: "He's a fine man," Liubov says of him, reinforcing Pishchik. Yes he is, and it's essential for us to see it. His chief practical action in this sequence is to lay out the facts of the situation, stressing that in light of their debts the only way to prevent the auction is his plan of selling the orchard and leasing land for the building of summer cottages. We've seen Gayev's and Varya's reactions and will be aware of Liubov's throughout. The sense to establish here is that Lopakhin isn't a rapacious wheeler-dealer, not a "lout of a peasant, out for what I can get," as, he tells Liubov, her brother says he is. Everything in his speech and demeanor—if rendered intelligently by an actor—testifies to a spirit of generous concern for the family, especially for Liubov, about whom he feels "closer than family, even."

In the prelude he remembers how the aristocratic girl, not much older than he, had comforted "the little peasant." Since then their relationship seems to have been a fond one, transcending—or ignoring—class lines. "You've done so much for me," he says, and we can speculate that she may have helped him get started in business. Whatever the case, he tells her now that she "look[s] wonderful, just the way you always did," and tells her that he hopes she'll "trust" him "the way you used to." Peasant turned entrepreneur, awkward, kind and yet businesslike, nobody's pushover yet a man of heart—such is Lopakhin as we have him at this point.

Carlotta: The most mysterious of the characters. The stage directions describe her as "very thin and tightly laced"; "straitlaced" would seem appropriate too, if it were not for her cold wit and hints of potential sexuality. When Lopakhin tries to kiss her hand, she says, "I let you kiss my hand, first thing I know you'll want to kiss my elbow, then my shoulder." She exists to vary the texture of stage-life and, thematically, as the embodiment of a craving for roots among people whose drama is partly about the need to give up theirs.

Liubov: Even when she's not active she's never far from our notice. Much of her time is spent remembering, mostly with joy—Gayev's billiard shots, the bookcase and table, and of course the orchard—and once sorrowfully, when Trofimov rouses thoughts of Grisha. At one point she excitedly "sees" her own mother in the orchard, then quickly dismisses it as an illusion. But that she's had the vision at all says something about her temperament and condition.

Her temperament is that of a woman of warmth and openness, given to impulsive bestowals of affection; a bit scattered, a soft touch, part matronliness and part vivacity; sentimental, effusive. But she can also be tough, even harsh. More than in any other character the orchard lives in her, as memory and metaphor. Chekhov wrote to Olga Knipper about Ranevskaya that it would be wrong to show her as "subdued by suffering. . . . Nothing but death could subdue a woman like that."[18] Earlier he had written, "The central female role is an old woman who lives entirely in the past and has nothing in the present."[19] The play's movement might be thought of as encompassing Chekhov's change of attitude toward his own creation: from stymied, buried existence to irrepressibility.

Her condition, so inseparable really from her nature, is that of someone trying to escape the pain of a recent past (she tears up the telegrams from Paris) by recourse to a more remote, idealized one. Something essential to Chekhov's vision is subtly at work here. At the end of a passionate invocation of the orchard—"Oh, my childhood! . . . life was happy and it all looked . . . the same as this. . . . Autumn was dark and drizzly and winter was cold, but now you're young again, flowering with happiness"—she says, "If only I could shake off this weight I've been carrying for so long. If only I could forget my past!" We will come to see in this the irony that for all its beauty the orchard is itself part of the burden because it belongs to a past that can't be divided as she wishes—

The Cherry Orchard

between innocence and pain, "cold winter" and time of blossoming. The cherry orchard's passage in her mind from illusory place of succor to nostalgic icon to point of departure is the intellectual movement of the play itself.

The second act is much the most leisurely, with nothing like the homecoming to animate it or, later, the party, the unseen auction, and then the leave-takings. It's an odd sort of pastoral, bringing everyone out in *plein air,* making conversation alternately more intimate or indolent, or more oratorical, as though the challenge is to fill up all that empty air. The spaciousness is itself balanced, though, by some formal vestiges of time past, the closures suggested by the rocks that resemble gravestones, and the abandoned chapel.

The act brings attention to three previously little-seen characters, with a turn for Yepikhodov, a considerable speech or two for Carlotta, and prominence for Trofimov. And it contains a couple of disconcerting or somewhat ominous moments, the intrusion of the tramp and the famous sound of the "breaking string."

Chekhov's construction here is a highly supple weaving of large units and small, the continuous and the fragmentary. He gives arias of varying length, some of them of a confessional nature, to Carlotta, Liubov, Lopakhin, and Trofimov, as well as substantial speeches to Dunyasha, Yepikhodov, and Firs. Separating them at unequal intervals are less showy conversational sequences, many of them disjointed and nonconsecutive. Little untargeted interjections fly through the air. Pauses, always so charged in Chekhov, are particularly resonant here.

Several flurries of contention break out—between Gayev and Yasha, Gayev and Lopakhin, Lopakhin and Trofimov—and there's a raft of philosophizing, most of it by Trofimov. Amorousness twitches here and there. Voices echo in the stillness, as does music: the distant sound of the Jewish band and Yepikhodov's guitar at the beginning and end.

A shotgun slung over her shoulder, Carlotta opens with a soliloquy (none of the three others on stage gives a sign of having heard her), a personal history which leaves her as enigmatic as before. "I haven't got a birth certificate," she begins, "so I don't know how old I really am." Her parents were carnival performers, and as a girl she "did cartwheels and things like that." When they died "a German woman" took her in and "taught [her] a few things." When she grew up she went "to work as a governess." "Where I'm from, who I am, I've no idea," she says while eating a cucumber—a deft touch on Chekhov's part, for to be chewing on so homely and rather humorous a vegetable (the Russian word for it, *ogurets,* is as satisfying as the English) undercuts the potential bathos of her next words, "I feel like talking all the time, but I have no one to talk to. No one."

A little later she says that Yasha and Yepikhodov sing like "hyenas" and that "smart boys" like Yepikhodov are "all so dumb," laments again that she's "always alone" and doesn't "know who I really am. Or why," and "walks slowly off." Mournful and aggressive, acid and lost, Carlotta moves in *The Cherry Orchard* as a principle of the wayward and unlocated, an amalgam of insecurity and prim despair.

Dunyasha quivers through an unwitting self-parody; after having been taken in by the family as a young girl, she says, she's got used to their way of life, become "more delicate" and "more sensitive." "Just look at my hands," she says, "They're so soft and white, just like I was rich." A comic contrast with Varya, she declares her love for Yasha, whose chief attraction is that he's so "smart" and "know[s] so many things." He in turn displays his putative learning through his usual pomposities.

Yepikhodov, second only to Carlotta for bizarre behavior and speech, exhibits a revolver, wondering whether to shoot himself. "I'm a true product of the educational system," he says, but he doesn't "have any chosen directive in life." In a fine piece of Dostoevskian imagery he recalls waking up that morning to find a spider of "detrimentally large proportions" sitting on his chest. But he's recovered sufficiently to handle his dramaturgical assignments on the guitar. He drifts in and out. What is he "really after"? Forever displaced, he gives us a sense that if she would have him he might go off with Carlotta to work the vaudeville circuit as a song-and-dance team.

All the speeches from the outriders of the dramatis personae, as we might regard them, prepare the way for the theatrically more central news of self and more impassioned rhetorical flights to come. Their largely comic nature doesn't make them any less serious, for no such division exists in Chekhov. But they're further from the play's governing situation and its metaphysical or ontological issues. None of these speakers says anything about the orchard or the auction, for example. But they do send out tremors of uncertainty—about ego, position, and status—that anticipate in a minor key the concerns and anxieties of the dramaturgically larger personages, and so extend the act's range of feeling and dilemma.

In one of *The Cherry Orchard*'s pivotal speeches Liubov lays herself bare, amplifying our factual knowledge and, unless we're frozen in social theory and intent on blame, greatly quickening our appreciation of her humaneness, which spills past moral systems and is imaginative, idiosyncratic, and deep.

"All my sins," she begins, and launches into a history of people and circumstances, physical and moral events: her own improvidence and that of her alcoholic husband; his death and her subsequent affair; her son's death and her flight to Paris; her lover's following her and her nursing him through a long illness; his robbing and deserting her and her suicide attempt ("It was so stupid and so shameful!"—the language is that of someone entirely and admirably sensitive to the nuances of moral situations); her sudden yearning for Russia. And then, "Dear God, dear God, forgive me. . . . Don't punish me any more!" Immediately after this comes a wonderful Chekhovian sequence of feeling, inner perception, and behavior, as attention and morale rapidly change in response to successive awarenesses. Liubov takes out and, without reading it, tears up another telegram, saying, "He wants me back," and then, with no transition but an internal prompting of avoidance, asks, "Where's that music coming from?"

She has several other dramaturgically influential occasions. She berates Gayev for his behavior at lunch, one article of her indictment being especially shrewd. "Talking about the seventies, about Symbolism . . . to the waiters!" she says, which calls attention to Gayev's insensitivity to situations and his being more deeply fixed in the past than anyone in the play except Firs. She exasperates Lopakhin by refusing to "take in" the threat of the auction. When the tramp asks for money she has no small change and gives him a gold coin instead. She suggests to Lopakhin that he marry Varya, and in a curious speech denounces him and others for going to the theater: "You ought to stop going to see play-acting and take a good look at your own reality. What a boring life you lead!"

This is reminiscent of such charges in *Ivanov* and *Uncle Vanya*, accusations we've learned not to take always at face value. I think that what's intended here is a little epiphany of Liubov building up her own spirits. "*I* haven't led a drab life!" her implication goes; as such it's not her finest moment but it doesn't cost us a great effort to forgive her.

Lopakhin's response is to go off on a sally against his "idiot" peasant father and speak of his own status as an idiot too, one who "never did well in school" and whose handwriting is no better than a pig's. Otherwise he spars with Trofimov and discourses on how hard he works, deploring the scarcity of "decent, honest" people around him. (Almost everyone in *The Cherry Orchard* is active in promoting, defending, or explaining himself or herself; it's mostly rather amiable, though it does have some sharper edges, and it has to do, I think, with the flux they're all caught in, the erosion of old roles, the birth of new ones, and the consequent uncertainty of status and identity.)

Lopakhin also keeps prodding Liubov about the auction. In one revealing gesture he cheerfully offers to lend her money after Varya wails to Liubov that nothing's left to feed the servants "and you go and give him [the tramp] a gold piece!"

Firs is involved in several oddly disturbing occasions. When told that he looks much older he replies, "I've been alive a long time," then talks about the emancipation of the serfs (which took place in 1861, about forty years before the time of the play) and how he ignored it, choosing to stay with his former owners. After a strategic pause he says that "they got all worked up about it, but they never even knew what they were getting so worked up about." Lopakhin interjects a sarcastic comment on those "good old days," when the masters "had the right to beat you . . . remember?" Firs doesn't hear this and so goes on in his own world, saying that the "masters stood by the serfs" and the "serfs stood by the masters. Nowadays it's all mixed up, you can't tell who's who." From the margins Firs is offering his homely, naive comment on the painfulness of change.

After they hear the breaking string he again refers enigmatically to the distant past: "It's like just before the misery came. They heard an owl, and the samovar wouldn't stop whistling." Gayev asks, "Before what misery?" and Firs answers, "The day we got our freedom back." Firs continually, doggedly brings up the past, with its dubious victories and pronounced losses, and this supplies a tension to the question affecting everyone apart from himself: What kind of future am I likely to have?

Late in the act Trofimov seizes a platform and surrounds the tramp incident, the string, and diverse conversations with a couple of long monologues which might seem to carry the play's chief sociological arguments, if any such existed. He denounces the "theories and ideas" of intellectuals in light of the workers' degradation and deplores the "ignorance" that marks even the universities. "We have to . . . get down to work and work harder than we've ever worked before," he says, scoring Anya for her parasitic ancestors, for whom "other people slaved away." "We have to do something to make up for our past," he argues, "and the only way to do that is to make sacrifices" and to work. And he brings in the future with romantic ardor: "Human beings are constantly progressing, and their power keeps growing. . . . We are moving forward, toward the future! Toward one bright star. . . . I feel happiness. . . . I feel it coming, I can almost see it.—"

All this sounds impressive, but the moment Trofimov invokes work and summons the future we ought to go on the alert, not so much for outright insincerity as for a species of cant, or not even so much for that as for a peculiar hollowness, passion without a ground. As he goes through his oratory—for most of what he says certainly isn't conversation in any recognizable sense—we hear an echo of Tuzenbach, and of Vershinin as well. For all three men are concerned with the future as some sort of deliverance and with its ideological complement, the redemptive power of work. But their concern, their anxiety, we might call it, is almost purely verbal, abstract, since in the conditions of such didacticism it can't be otherwise.

By the end of Trofimov's sermons we should have remembered how in Chekhov the future *as a subject* is always ghostly, bodiless, and most often compensatory for a present felt to be oppressive, and that work is never a solution. The future as liberation, work as atonement: these are in no sense themes of *The Cherry Orchard* but notions expressed *within the play,* chiefly by Trofimov, who no more speaks for Chekhov than did Tuzenbach or Vershinin in their play.

We've so often seen Chekhov's mistrust of such rhetorical insistences that we can't fail to notice how he subtly (or sometimes not so subtly) undercuts Trofimov in several places and so partly devalues the oratory. After Trofimov excoriates intellectuals for their empty talk, for example, he says, "If that's all our talk's good for, I'd rather just shut up." Yet he goes on spouting! When he denounces the family for living "off other people" as landowners, Anya mildly reminds him that because of their debts the house "hasn't ever been really" theirs.

Indeed his portrait of the family comes largely from theory, congealed bias, for the exploitation he charges them with is a thing of the past, for which they surely have no responsibility, and his indictment totally ignores Liubov's generosity, Varya's industriousness and probity, and even Anya's innocence. And when he extols work, we're entitled—and meant—to ask, "What have *you* ever done?" On this point at least Gorky was right.

The language of Trofimov's hymn to the future feels borrowed, most likely from the kinds of novel he says he despises; it's banal, coerced, literary in the worst sense, the language not of Chekhov's own beliefs (as we've seen, his pronouncements about the future are full of acrid scepticism) but of Trofimov as an agency of ironic meaning. Nothing, furthermore, better exposes him as the high-minded, programmatic, and more than slightly ridiculous "progressive" intellectual he affects to repudiate than his declaration that he and Anya (not consulted in the matter, to be sure) are "above love." In Act Three Liubov will light into him for this and other aspects of his know-it-all bravado.

If I spend so much time on Trofimov it's because I think him a major source of misreading, like Serebryakov in *Uncle Vanya*. But I don't want to overstate the case. To reject Trofimov as a political or ideological surrogate for Chekhov doesn't mean he's nothing but a cautionary figure. No, Trofimov is more complex than that. For one thing, he's given too much to say; were he simply the butt of Chekhov's sarcasm, the master of economical expression would have managed it more expeditiously. The point to see is that for all his pomposity and borrowed zeal, much of what Trofimov says is objectively true: Russia *does* suffer from "dirt and ignorance and crime," the past *does* weigh stiflingly, there *is* a need to let go and move on.

And then, obeying the Chekhovian principle of never limiting a character's "reality" to his or her pet agenda, Trofimov is shown elsewhere to possess a gawky, long-faced sort of charm along with his humorlessness, and a degree of compassion when his self-righteousness momentarily collapses. And he's certainly persuasive at times. "Oh, Petya, you're so smart," Liubov tells him, and Anya is notably, if intermittently, moved by his rhetoric: "Oh, you talk so beautifully" and "How beautifully you put it!" and "I love the way you say things!"

But the pointer of meaning takes another half-turn. Liubov's "you're so smart" is followed by Lopakhin's more accurate sarcasm: "Oh, yes, very." Besides, nobody else takes much heed of what Trofimov says anyway. And even Anya, receptive as she is, is far from a consistently enraptured listener. When, for instance, he tells her he sees happiness coming, her response is to say ("dreamily"), "Look, the moon's rising." The stage direction and the change of subject tell us that even if she's been listening she doesn't exactly share his programmatic optimism at this point.

Something else remains. While refusing to swallow Trofimov whole, Anya does yield to him on one key matter. In a remark that goes very near the play's central action she says, "I don't know what it is you've done to me, Petya, but I don't love the cherry orchard . . . the way I used to."

Let us take an even closer look at Act Two: style as rhythm, statement, texture.

We can enter the play anywhere to analyze Chekhov's craftsmanship—I hope I've been doing this in some fashion all along—but I want now to visit a particular stretch for an even more careful study. In what follows I'll do some foreshortening and omit minor details (although what details in Chekhov are ever "minor"?), but I'll render the exact order of events and dialogue so as to try to show how supple the construction is, how intensities rise and fall and "meaning" is inseparable from evocation.

It's late in the act. Trofimov goes through his first long aria, a soliloquy bulging with invective and discontent. Next to speak is Lopakhin who, largely ignoring Trofimov, runs off a little number about his own industriousness, ending with "Dear God, you gave us this beautiful earth to live on . . . by rights we should be giants." The effect is rather to deflate Trofimov by stealing his thunder, but Liubov immediately deflates *Lopakhin*: "The only good giants are in fairy tales. Real ones would scare you to death."

Yepikhodov now passes by, playing his guitar. "There goes Yepikhodov," Liubov says "pensively." "There goes Yepikhodov," Anya repeats, also pensively. Notice that she doesn't say "Yes, there he goes" or some variation, as we would have expected. This mysteriously changes the episode from a conventional order of action and dialogue into a fragment of pure, unexplained, mutual sentience, as though Anya and Liubov are recognizing, *for us,* some aspect of the soul of the play.

Now, as if "reciting a poem," Gayev starts an apostrophe to "wondrous nature" and is cut short by Anya and Varya. The stage direction then reads, "They all sit in silence. The only sound we hear is old Firs mumbling." How long this is to go on depends, like so many other occasions in all the plays, on the rhythms already established, on stage or in the mind; what we can be sure of is that these "silences" are times when much is being internally weighed. All at once we hear "a distant sound . . . a sad sound, like a harp-string breaking. It dies away."

Explanations follow, all of them too specific for the unease we feel. Lopakhin: an echo from a mine shaft. Gayev: a bird, a heron. Trofimov: an owl.

Liubov says that it makes her nervous, and Firs deepens the disquiet by mentioning the sounds heard before the "misery"—the emancipation of the serfs. The ensuing pause is among the most uncanny in Chekhov.

Liubov then suggests they go in and embraces Anya, who has tears in her eyes. "It's nothing, Mother," she says, but we suspect that the eerie sound is involved. With no transition the tramp (or someone we'd now call a "homeless" person) appears. Much perturbation. Varya is scared, Lopakhin angry, Liubov flustered. She gives the man money. Varya scolds her. "Very much obliged," the tramp says as he goes off. "Everybody laughs." The tension subsides, yet hints of something somber hover in the air.

A swatch of partly discontinuous dialogue ensues. Liubov tells Varya they've "just gotten you engaged." Varya ("through tears") tells her not to make jokes. Lopakhin quotes *Hamlet*—"get thee to a nunnery"—saying "Amelia" for Ophelia. Nobody reacts. Gayev's hands are shaking; he needs a billiards game. Lopakhin again quotes *Hamlet*—"nymph in thy orisons . . . ," saying "horizons" instead; again no one reacts. Varya can still feel her "heart beating" from the tramp. As most of them go off Lopakhin reminds them again of the auction: "You've got to think about what to do!" Anya and Trofimov remain and he immediately speaks again about being above love and goes into his rhetoric about the future. The act ends with Varya off stage calling for Anya.

Character, atmosphere, theme. Delicate reciprocities, the whole producing its parts.

If the four acts of a Chekhov play seem to begin and end capriciously with no obvious logic of plotted events to connect them, the disjunction between the end of Act Two and the start of Act Three is especially striking in *The Cherry Orchard*. When the oddly matched couples come dancing in to the *grand rond* of the Jewish band, we see an exuberance for which the sober, pensive, and sometimes melancholy second act has scarcely prepared us. It takes a little while to adjust to the new rhythm and tone, to unlock the secret of the true relationship of the acts to each other and so become able to hold the play steadily in the mind as a thematic and lyrical unity.

Everything that's gone before, reaching back to the first moments, all the excitements and subsidings, the musings and expostulations, the innocent or calculated assertions, the flurries of encounter and withdrawal, the little enactments and disclosures of self, the tears and joys, the histories and prospects—all this flowers now into aesthetic logic; the end toward which these means have been moving is taking shape. The relative calm of Act Two with its incidental hints of danger, will be seen to have artfully prepared the way for this act's tensions.

We soon learn their source. The auction, we're told almost casually (though we might have divined it earlier from Varya's tears as she dances), is taking place this very day. The party, then, is a piece of bravado, an irresponsible act, and the gaiety is forced if not desperate. Or so we might think. But it might also have an edge of quixoticism, as a gallant gesture on Liubov's part. "I suppose it was a mistake to have a party," she tells herself, but adds, "Oh well, who cares." Then she "sits down and hums quietly." One thing we can't help noticing is that Chekhov puts the crucial physical action off stage, as he did in the three previous plays. The effect is to multiply speculation and heighten anxiety while at the same time, as always, keeping the event from becoming the nail-biting center of direct attention a melodramatist would unhesitatingly have made it.

The auction stays in the background before it bursts abruptly upon us near the end of the act. Seemingly forgotten for stretches, it sends out anxious reminders ("My entire life . . . it's all being decided today," Liubov says) before activity resumes under its tacit menace. Pishchik announces his high blood-pressure and rumored "descent" from Caligula's horse. Carlotta does her tricks, her sleight-of-hand at the abyss's edge. Varya says she'll marry Lopakhin but "I can't propose to him myself!" Small confrontations abound: Trofimov and Varya, Yasha and Firs, Dunyasha and Yepikhodov, Yepikhodov and Varya; and one huge one, Trofimov and Liubov.

Yasha's assault on Firs—"time for you to crawl off and die"—contrasts with the others' affection for the old man (yet prepares the way for the final scene) and adds to our impression of the young servant's callowness, his insensitivity to time as anything except a vehicle for his own "advancement."

Trofimov's running quarrel with Varya says things about both. His taunting her about Lopakhin betrays another aspect of his less prepossessing side. He too is callow but unlike the much narrower Yasha, who has no ideas, or Yepikhodov, who has only pretentious ones, Trofimov tries to vault over messy, complicated, unruly life by means of righteous theories. Varya irritates him partly, I think, because she actually works instead of talking about it and because she raises the possibility of seriousness in love, which, we remember, he's above. For her part, she sees him as irresponsible, aimless, a threat to her beloved Anya. But her stern uprightness, puritanism some might think it, is balanced by her basic kindness, demonstrated when in a soft voice, "almost crying," she tells him, "Oh, Petya, you used to be so nice-looking, and now you're getting old!"

A strange way to show kindness, it might seem. But many of Chekhov's characters display a hard but essentially loving truthfulness in their complex confrontations with one another. The kindness consists in refusing the *un-truthfulness* of evasion or sentimentality. We're convinced that Trofimov *has* grown ugly and hasn't aged well. Varya's gentle voice and tears when she's telling him this testify to the lovely delicacy of Chekhov's perception: when she speaks she's sharing the pain of these facts of mortality; for the moment she's not Trofimov's adversary but his fellow sufferer, one who will pass through the same disfigurements inflicted by time, or perhaps already has done so. Later Liubov will be "kind" to him in a way that calls upon even more consequential elements of candor and love.

(A note on callowness. From one rough perspective the characters of *The Cherry Orchard* can be divided into the mature and the spiritually adolescent, into those who have undergone and absorbed experience, for good or ill, and those who for reasons not entirely of age but also of undeveloped or embattled ego have held it off or missed its meaning. On one side, then, with no claim to precision, are Liubov, Varya, Firs, Carlotta, Lopakhin, and Pishchik; on the other Yasha, Dunyasha, Yepikhodov, Trofimov, and Gayev. Only Anya is neither developed nor immature but simply poised, we feel, at the edge of a possible self.)

Liubov's and Trofimov's face-off is one of *The Cherry Orchard*'s set pieces, if we can use such a mechanical term about writing like Chekhov's, which never builds methodically or incrementally to a climax but invariably springs excitement on us when we're least prepared. Their dialogue sways back and forth, alternating accusations and remorse, harsh words and placatives, revealing love behind anger on Liubov's part and on Trofimov's a struggle for warmth against his rigidities. It passes through a great range of consciousness and attitudes about the play's central issues and gives us, if we haven't yet possessed it, the fullest sense of Liubov's flawed, unprogrammatic, and irrepressible humanity.

We're reminded again of Henry James's remark that Ibsen's plays were about "the individual caught in the fact,"[20] which I earlier applied to Chekhov. Trofimov and Liubov are both caught—in circumstance, in time as a condition—but because she is dramatically the richer character, the locus of fuller meanings, her ontological entrapment reaches us more acutely. Trofimov acts in one capacity as the voice of reason, an accurate assessor: the question of the estate, he says, is settled. "You can't go back to the past. . . . You can't go on deceiving yourself." And again, about the Paris lover, "He robbed you blind! He's rotten!"

Liubov reaches the edge of despair; if the orchard has to be sold, she says, then "you might as well sell me with it." As for her lover, "He's a millstone around my neck . . . but he's my millstone." A moment earlier she had spoken of him as "sick . . . alone . . . unhappy. . . . Who has he got to look after him?" This recalls the piercing episode in Fellini's film *La strada* when the little clown Gelsomina is asked why she doesn't leave her paramour, the circus strongman who mistreats her, and replies, "If I don't stay with him, who will?" (Feminists aren't likely to think much of this or of Liubov's position, and in truth from a certain obvious perspective I don't like it myself. But I think that such loving concern as hers, such a demonstration of human solidarity, transcends gender and indeed all "right" ideas. Strict justice sometimes has to yield to what the spirit decides.)

Propelling everything is a question that spreads past them both, to touch on what's chiefly at stake in the drama. When Trofimov tells her to face the truth, Liubov replies, "What truth? You seem so sure what's truth and what isn't, but I'm not, I've lost sight of the truth. You're so sure of yourself . . . so sure you have all the answers to everything . . . you have more courage than my generation has, and better morals, and you're better educated, but for God's sake have a little sense of what it's like for me, and be easier on me." When he goes on, pressing her about the lover, she explodes: "At your age you ought to understand something about love. You ought to be in love yourself! . . . You're like a kid who doesn't know the first thing about it, you're probably a virgin, you're ridiculous, you're grotesque."

He is indeed a monster of rectitude and abstraction, reminiscent in this respect of Lvov, the self-righteous doctor of *Ivanov*. But just as Chekhov said of Lvov that narrow and "rectilinear" as such people are, they're nevertheless necessary, so *The Cherry Orchard* needs Trofimov to press on Liubov and Anya the recognition that the "way" that leads to the orchard is closed off and that something else awaits.

He tells this and other truths without grace or compassion; even when he says, "I pity you . . . from the bottom of my heart," she replies, "I wish you'd said that a little differently," a sly rebuke to what she senses as the tight spirit behind the slightly too conventional words. Still—and it can't be repeated too often—what he says of the orchard is true and she will assimilate it, though the truth will reside in her far more precariously and at a cost that Trofimov, with his moral and intellectual certainties, can never encompass or understand.

We should notice how Liubov's condemnations are interspersed with expressions of keen regard—"I love you like one of my own family"—and how, as in so many other Chekhovian clashes of personality and soul, nothing definitively judgmental is being imposed, no knock-out blow is being sought. The strategy in the scene is to say what needs to be said without pretending it's all that can be said.

Neither of them is conclusively "right" or "wrong," although we feel that the preponderance of spontaneity and felt life is on Liubov's side, so the great bulk of our sympathy goes to her. But Trofimov, the messenger of change, is necessary as, generously or not, with substantial love or a thin, pinched urgency, he points out to her the possible and the impossible in her life to come.

Along with some rather endearing physical specifications about Lopakhin (he "wears a white vest and yellow shoes . . . takes big steps . . . thinks while he walks and walks in a straight line"[21]), Chekhov told Stanislavsky that "he may be a merchant but he is a decent person in every sense; his behavior must be entirely proper, cultivated and free of pettiness or clowning."[22] Of all the blunders a production of *The Cherry Orchard* can commit, among the worst is to have its Lopakhin disregard this admonition.

Chekhov was ordinarily tight-lipped and cryptic when making recommendations about characters to actors and directors: "Astrov whistles";[23] Trigorin "wears checked trousers";[24] Masha "may be thoughtful."[25] But for this play he was direct and relatively expansive, offering solid pointers on Liubov, Anya, Varya, and Pishchik, along with Lopakhin. His apprehensions about things going wrong stemmed, understandably, in part from the dangers of melodrama, particularly of easy or shallow tears. Hence his warnings about weepiness, which had to do chiefly with the women.

But an even greater danger came from ideology, and here Lopakhin was the potential site of infection. If the play is seen as dramatized socio-history, as in one way or another it continues often to be, then Lopakhin will figure strongly as an agent if not a cause. Representative predator and vulgarian in this reading (the "ferocious entrepreneur," a reviewer in the *New York Times* called him not long ago[26]), he rides the winds of historical change: the triumph of money, the advent of the reign of abstract economics. And pitted against him in this view is the family as either elegiac "losers" in an exercise of social Darwinism or corrupt and active connivers in their own destruction.

The risk of distortion is present for Lopakhin throughout. (His name, by the way, has suggestions of "spade" in Russian, as well as of "raking in money" and "breaking" or "bursting.") His "get thee to a nunnery" can be delivered brutally instead of as rueful homage, his barbs at Trofimov can be made to seem snide, his describing himself as illiterate and uncouth can be taken at face value. Above all his repeatedly bringing up the orchard and the prospective cottages can be taken as evidence of his materialism and philistine lack of soul. The overwhelming locus of the peril of misreading, however, is unquestionably his speech, the longest in the play, after he reveals that it's he who has bought the estate.

Our first impression here has to be of Lopakhin's boastfulness, even cruelty. He crows, laughs loudly, stamps his foot. He smiles when he picks up the household keys Varya has thrown down because, as he says, "she knew she wasn't going to be running the place any more." He says he's "going to chop down every tree in that cherry orchard, every goddamn one of them." He says, "My God, the cherry orchard belongs to me! . . . the most beautiful estate in the whole world!" In a little follow-up speech he tells the band to "keep playing. Louder! It's my house now. . . . I can do what I want to!"

There's no question about it, he's an indecent, improper, uncultivated, petty, and clownish fellow, exactly what Chekhov said he mustn't be played as. Hold on, though; we can be sure Chekhov didn't list Lopakhin's virtues and then undercut them in action. Before we look at what his big speech actually reveals about him and how it functions dramatically, let's quickly run through some counterevidence to this scarifying portrait, evidence with which everything surrounding the famous aria is suffused.

I wrote earlier that both Liubov and Pishchik speak highly of Lopakhin; in fact the only ones who attack him are Gayev—and there we should consider the source—and Trofimov, but the young man will cancel his dispraise in Act Four when he tells Lopakhin, "I like you. . . . You've got nice hands. . . . You could have been an artist." Varya's put out by him a few times, but how significant it is that *after* he buys the estate (and after the Speech) she's still more than willing to marry him. His generosity shows itself on several occasions, as does his humor; his self-deprecation is a sign of real modesty, not a confession of weakness. And his concern for the family is utterly genuine; only the most cynical observer would think it a sham.

The Cherry Orchard

How is all this to be reconciled with the obnoxious Lopakhin who brags that he "can pay for everything"? What has happened to the "good" Lopakhin of the first two acts? Well, let's begin by remembering that the closer a Chekhov character is to the dramatic center, the more contrarieties or at least dissonances he or she is likely to contain. So it is with Lopakhin. He's drunk, true, but his behavior here more significantly issues, I suspect, from internal clashes, one of them between different eras of his history—what he once primarily was and in part remains, and what he now largely is and in part finds amazing—and another between different capacities—for egotism and vanity, for generosity and love.

A complicated hero, Lopakhin is unexpected, agile, evading our moral categories. He swoops past propriety and even, for an instant, decency, when he "rubs it in." He lets his worst side spill out, which is easy to see, but not so readily visible is the way he summons his best side as more than a balance. All through the aria Lopakhin shows himself as the creature of Chekhov the moral revolutionary who despised hierarchies, the epistemologist of dramatic life who knew that both strength and weakness are always provisional; Lopakhin *represents* nothing, no practice or value, no institution, but is his own wayward, contradictory, and mostly admirable self.

In the big speech Chekhov allows Lopakhin to surrender to the temptations of self-satisfaction or, so to say, to be overtaken by them. "Tell me I'm drunk, tell me it's all a dream"—we feel him being carried away . . . by himself. But just after those words his exultation takes on a new subject and we see—or ought to see, for it's most often disastrously missed—that his victory is in no sense over Liubov, who sits weeping, but over his own past, over *past time itself.* "If [they] could only see me now," he cries, and then speaks of himself as the "kid they used to kick around, the poor boy who never went to school," the boy whose father and grandfather "slaved away their lives" and were never allowed in the kitchen.

If they could see me now. We need to absorb the whole speech in the light of those words and of what we already know about Lopakhin having "made something" of himself. All this is a powerful reminder of Chekhov's well-known letter to Suvorin (which I quoted earlier in the book) in which he sketched out a tiny autobiography, a tale of his own transformation into a dignified "free" soul out of degraded origins, having "squeezed out" the slave's blood "drop by drop."[27] We're greatly moved by Chekhov's quiet pride, and even if Lopakhin's isn't nearly so quiet, we should be moved by it too.

That it isn't vanity or true braggadocio, that such ruthlessness as he displays is temporary and immediately chastised by himself, is swiftly demonstrated by what he says to Liubov right after the monologue: "Oh, why didn't you listen to me? You dear woman, you dear good woman, you can't ever go back." Then, with "tears in his eyes," he speaks a line that goes straight to one aspect of the soul of the play: "Oh, if we could only change things, if only life were different, this unhappy, messy life." He'll let himself swagger a bit again when Pishchik leads him off, but even there, when he says, "It's my house now," the stage direction has him saying it "ironically"; he will not bluster or pretend too far.

In Act Four all his kindness and good nature will reassert themselves. He will become reconciled with Trofimov and will reassure Carlotta that they'll "take care of" her. When Liubov complains about the tree cutting starting before they've left, he has it stopped at once.

Lopakhin isn't easy to play. The most useful thing I can think of to tell an actor is contained in a review by the critic Desmond McCarthy of a 1933 production in which he described Charles Laughton's performance in these words: "He was soft and hard, humble and overbearing, ruthless and sympathetically upset; he was triumphant and yet he felt that somehow it was all wrong."[28]

It should be clear that if, as I think, *The Cherry Orchard* is a comedy in Chekhov's meaning, it isn't a matter of comic characters and funny scenes: *Uncle Vanya* has them too, and *Three Sisters* isn't without laughs. No, the status of comedy (to sum it up a final time) rests on the question of fate or destiny: how it unfolds and whether or not it's free to some degree. Will something be possible, has some space remained open—or is it all closed—for some central figures of the drama? As we've come to see, at the end of Chekhov's plays it's chiefly his women in whom we sense the possibility of a future, active or static, beckoning, usually in the most fragile way, or blank. So it is with Liubov and Anya in *The Cherry Orchard*.

Mother and daughter. To know the play fully we have to see that unobtrusively, in only an economical few bits of dialogue and gesture, an exchange of roles takes place, a psychological and spiritual process whereby Anya in effect becomes the parent of her own mother. For as the play goes on it's the daughter who leads, comforts, instructs, and so can almost be said to give birth to the mother's new life. Under Trofimov's influence Anya has given signs of breaking free of the orchard's seduction. Then, at the climactic moment after Lopakhin's bombshell, she steps forward and lovingly helps Liubov into new consciousness and morale.

The Cherry Orchard

Lopakhin has just tried awkwardly to comfort Liubov and now she sits sobbing alone, as the band softly plays. Anya comes on, kneels, and addresses her in a speech whose language and tonalities have marked similarities to Sonya's comforting of Vanya, though the circumstances and intention are very different. "My lovely, kind, good mother," she says, "I love you. . . . The cherry orchard is . . . gone, I know, but don't cry. You still have your life to lead . . . with your . . . innocent heart." And she tells her they'll "plant another orchard, even better than this one, you'll see, and it'll make you smile again. . . . Come, mama. Come with me."

Liubov does go with Anya, which is to say she moves in the direction her daughter has pointed out. After her initial great sorrow, once the orchard is truly lost she tells the others that Gayev is right in thinking she "looks better than she has in a long time"; "my nerves have quieted down." Nearly everyone seems better. Gayev gives off an air of resolve, however temporary it may prove. Trofimov thaws into a condition resembling likableness. Pishchik has his lucky find.

Liubov will have a few more spasms of longing and nostalgia—there are no abrupt cures in Chekhov! Just before the curtain she and Gayev will weep in each other's arms and she will address the orchard as "my life, my youth, my happiness." But without questioning her sincerity we observe something slightly literary in her diction. It suggests a memorial to a completed emotional cycle rather than any present recognition.

She will say good-bye to everything without despair, passing with dignity through the "suffering of change" that Francis Fergusson wrote about. Earlier she had asked Anya if she was "happy, really happy," to which the reply had been, "Oh yes, mama, really! We're starting a new life!" Neither they nor we have any way of knowing what sort of life it will be, but what is clear is that the old life has been blocking the new.

Now as Liubov lingers for "one last long look" at the walls and ceilings of the house which, too, has become in effect a memory, Anya and Trofimov hurry her up from off stage, calling "joyfully" and "excitedly." She's being helped along by their enthusiasm, but there's no doubt that this unsubduable woman has her own sources of resilience.

Some implications of what I've been saying, some unfinished business, a few loose extensions, cleanings up, jottings, and answers to dangling questions. And something new.

Consider that Lopakhin never calls the family "parasites" or "decadents" or "idlers" or anything stronger than "scatterbrained" and "unbusinesslike," which are rather endearing faults, I should think. Why hasn't it been obvious all along that moral judgment simply doesn't enter into the matter? It's nobody's fault that the property is taken away. The point is that they have to give up the estate; its loss is as inevitable as the Prozorov sisters' failure to get to Moscow, since those outcomes are crucial to the respective plays' aesthetic designs. If *Three Sisters* is "about" living while not getting to Moscow, *The Cherry Orchard* is about living while having to give up the trees.

The orchard isn't a principle of beauty under attack by a mean, utilitarian ethic or simply a metaphor for a vanishing way of life, although it does partly function that way; it's a real object that happens to be beautiful but was once also useful (the lost recipe for jam!) and that reigns much more now as a locus of nostalgia, of feeling frozen in time, and so as a gorgeous prison for the past—"My childhood! My youth!" (the exclamation points are like cell bars)—than as a present joy.

To give it up is in part saddening, yes, but not in any way tragic and, what's more, the mourning is wider than for the trees alone. It's for what time itself does to us (so persistent a Chekhov theme), it's over the way nothing can be arrested, no pleasure made permanent. The sorrow also rises from the painfulness of having to change and from the knowledge that the unknown is a risk but the known is a risk too. The sadness is for mortality. At the same time the comic aspect, the narrow way out, the relief from inevitability, belongs to mortality too.

If the dramatic conflict has a historical (political) dimension, as the tale of a "refined" and outdated way of life opposed to the brutal (or simply inescapable) necessities of social and economic growth, that isn't where Chekhov's artistic sense or impulse lay. No dramatist (or novelist for that matter) worth anything writes out of a sense of "historical necessity" or *about* such a thing. (Or if it happens it's done badly, with strain and didacticism, as in so much of Tolstoy.)

History, in works of the imagination, even social history, is always in some sense what I call counterhistory; Georg Büchner's *Danton's Death* is one great and obvious model. What is life like beneath, beyond, and in defiance of the official version, the verifiable "facts" that time as an archive can be made to yield? How, really, does—or did—time *feel*? The family in *The Cherry Orchard*, which isn't "real," and those circling round them in the fiction undergo change not as a "historical process," which is an academic's or politician's term, but as suffering and liberation. The images are those of mortality, not "society in transition."

Yepikhodov's and Trofimov's pratfalls. A tumble down the stairs. The squashed hat box. Galoshes (the wrong ones) flying onto the stage. Carlotta's parlor tricks. Pishchik's bonanza. Varya whacking Lopakhin with an errant stick. Firs being left behind. The tramp. The breaking string. Lopakhin not proposing to Varya. Liubov drifting into the shock of the auction's outcome. Throughout *The Cherry Orchard* there's a strong sense of the accidental and inadvertent; of the casual, the unintended, unpredictable, and unforeseen; of the abortive and messy.

All this is an aspect or outcome of the play's almost complete plotlessness, its superbly hidden dramatic hinges. But it's also necessarily a thematic element, a view of life. More than in any of his other plays we get the sense in Chekhov's last one that this is *the way things happen,* this loose, unplanned, serio-comic behavior, without immediate discernible causes or explanations. This is Chekhov's true comedy, because of the release that we, and certain of the characters, get from absolute fate, from the ordained; a relief from inevitability, I called it before. The very "unbusinesslike" nature of the family is far better suited to the spirit of comedy than it is to any grave social agenda. Fatality as it's exhibited in this play has more to do with fumbling and bumbling than with "tragic patterns."

Some further notes on sorrow in this comedy. The words "sad" or "sadly" appear at only a handful of strategic times in the stage directions, although "tears," sometimes accompanying joy, are called for on other occasions. Anya "sadly" says that her mother bought the brooch Varya thinks looks like a bee. Yepikhodov is said to play "the same sad tune" he played earlier. Both times the string is heard it's described as a "sad" sound. And in the last scene we hear the "mournful" sound of an axe striking a tree.

Most of these ascriptions don't require much exegesis. Anya speaks sadly because the brooch reminds her of her mother's unhappiness. Yepikhodov's sad music is in keeping with the sometimes broadly melancholic mood of Act Two and especially with Liubov's and Anya's pensiveness as they watch him go by. The sound of the axe against the tree is self-evidently rather sorrowful. Peter Hall, who directed a notable production at England's National Theatre in 1978, has said that the "tree-cutting . . . is the most difficult sound in drama."[29]

If it isn't, the breaking string surely is. Why does Chekhov describe that sound as sad? What is it doing there?

No single detail of the text, maybe of any Chekhov text, has elicited so much comment, much of it highly ingenious. The reading that satisfies me most is by J. L. Styan (a clearheaded if not always inspired critic). The string, he writes, "suggests time in its most inscrutable mood; it is the passing of one order of life, with what seems like irreparable loss; but it is also the mark of change, ushering in the new order, both hopeful and frightening, because it is unimaginable."[30]

This seems intelligent, even if Styan is asking the string to carry a rather heavy load. At least there's no symbol mongering here; the sound "suggests," evokes, it doesn't *stand for* or replace. And time as a subject, a factor, is quite properly summoned to consciousness in every Chekhov play. Then, too, Firs's comment about it being "like just before the misery came" gives substance to the idea of the string as related to change. Still, we might also leave room for a response not quite so loaded with interpretation: the breaking string as a musical element, a sensuous detail of special efficacy.

Why is Firs left behind? I'm not at all sure, but it feels right. Everybody's gone, off to some new scene or phase, moving, however uncertainly, toward the *next thing*. But there's no next thing for aged Firs. He sums up an era, finishes it off. He'll die with the house, a victim technically of Yasha's thoughtlessness but really of time in its casual dispositionings. Throughout the play he's been composed almost entirely of memories; now they're used up. His being abandoned makes us think, all at the same time, of mortality, chance, the end of things, the beginning, change.

Why doesn't Lopakhin ask Varya to marry him? Because he really isn't interested in her, the ready answer goes. But is it as simple as that? Is it true? In Act Two he tells Liubov he's "got nothing against" the marriage, and just before the famous failure to propose in Act Four he doesn't disagree with Liubov when she urges the marriage as reasonable and desirable for both of them. "I'll do it," he says, "we've even got some champagne ready." But when Liubov sends Varya in, after "a few stifled laughs and whispers behind the door," they engage in evasive small talk and the opportunity passes.

Hints at what might lie behind his reluctance or inability to propose (and we remember that earlier Varya said that *she* couldn't ask *him*) are his remark to Liubov that "it's all a little funny" and, much more pointedly, that "I don't think I can propose without you." It *is* funny, this situation of relationship and feeling. Might it be that Lopakhin will never propose as long as Liubov is there?

My theory is as follows: Her presence might remind him of just how dependent on her he is for his self-esteem—not a favorable portent for a marriage to Varya. Furthermore, he has told Liubov that he feels closer to her than even as if she were family. In that "closer" might lie the source of his inertia. Is it that to marry Varya, adopted daughter though she may be, is to come too close, aspire too high, perhaps even violate a taboo? All of this unconscious, to be sure.

Something else is at work along with this possible psychological activity: sheer chance once again, the way things unpredictably unfold. A distraction—Varya, nervous, expectant, ruinously miscalculates by inventing a lost object; a stalling remark about the weather; pauses in which courage and consequences press to be weighed; the inopportune (for Varya) call to Lopakhin from outside; flight; collapse of a plan. Whatever one's reading of it, the scene is marvelously revealing of Chekhov's mastery of the drama of the undramatic.

In that regard I want to consider now a remarkable essay on *The Cherry Orchard* which appeared in the symbolist journal *Balances* in the same year, 1904, as the play's première and Chekhov's death.[31] In it the young avant-garde poet and novelist Andrei Bely (whose real name was Boris Nikolaevich Bugaev) wrote about Chekhov as a "realist." Although only about four pages long, the essay is uncommonly dense, with some thickets of literary jargon, and I can only hope to do its ideas rough justice here.

For our purposes Bely's central notion is that the conditions of contemporary consciousness—the triumph of the machine, the "mechanical organization of life," and the consequent loss of "inner experience"—resisted the conventional imagination, but under Chekhov's special genius the age was made to yield up a world beyond appearances or, precisely, beyond those mechanized surfaces presented to the mind.

Chekhov's drama (in its full range, not just this play) was one which passed through realism to what Bely called the symbolic without giving up its basis in the keen perception of actuality; the symbolic here is made up of that which the "real" world, having been debilitated by abstractions and repetitions of the already perceived, ignored. Descriptions of reality (literary and theatrical naturalism, that's to say) were thought to have reached completion, been exhausted, but "at the very point where everything once ended, everything has now become transparent, pellucid." I know of no better word than "transparent" to render the quality of Chekhov's imaginative truthfulness.

Bely doesn't identify Chekhov's method as a technical instrument but speaks of what we ourselves might call his "glance," as it falls, with unparalleled clarity, on the most minute particulars, on the extreme momentariness of our experience. It's this approach toward the humble, the casual and fragmentary, the scorned—the very basis of the revolution Chekhov brought about in the theater—which sets free the previously unknown, what we might call the music that hasn't yet been heard.

"An instant of life taken by itself as it is deeply probed becomes a doorway to infinity," Bely writes. "The minutiae of life will appear ever more clearly to be the guides to Eternity." And he adds, capturing Chekhov in his most exact procedure, that "seeing through banality . . . *seeing through anything* [Bely's italics] means being a symbolist." It means, too, being Meyerhold's lyric mystery writer. In *The Cherry Orchard*, Bely goes on to say, Chekhov, a symbolist in the meaning the essay has been advancing yet "remaining a realist," "draws back the folds of life, and what at a distance appeared to be shadowy folds turns out to be an aperture into Eternity."

Notes

Works frequently cited in the notes are identified by the following abbreviations:

ACLT   *Anton Chekhov's Life and Thought: Selected Letters and Commentary*, translated by Michael Henry Heim in collaboration with Simon Karlinsky; selection, commentary and introduction by Simon Karlinsky (Berkeley: University of California Press, 1975)

Note-Book   S. S. Koteliansky and Leonard Woolf, trans., *Note-Book of Anton Chekhov* (New York: B. W. Huebsch, 1921)

Letters   Avrahm Yarmolinsky, ed., *Letters of Anton Chekhov* (New York: Viking, 1968)

PREFACE

1. Vladimir Yermilov, *Anton Pavlovich Chekhov*, trans. Ivy Litvinov (Moscow: Foreign Languages Publishing House, n.d.), 170.
2. *ACLT*, 107.
3. Ronald Hingley, *A New Life of Anton Chekhov* (New York: Knopf, 1976), 109.
4. Ibid., 126.
5. Ibid., 209.
6. Thomas Mann, "Chekhov," *Last Essays*, trans. Richard and Clara Winston and Tania and James Stern (New York: Knopf, 1959), 181.
7. *Note-Book*, 103.

8. Hingley, *New Life*, 289.

9. Ibid., 318.

10. V. S. Pritchett, *Chekhov: A Spirit Set Free* (New York: Viking, 1989), x, xi.

11. Sally Fitzgerald, ed., *The Habit of Being: Letters of Flannery O'Connor* (New York: Farrar, Straus, Giroux, 1979).

CHAPTER 1

1. Ronald Hingley, *A New Life of Anton Chekhov* (New York: Knopf, 1976), 250.

2. Maxim Gorky, "Fragments from Reminiscences," *Chekhov: A Collection of Critical Essays*, ed. Robert Louis Jackson (Englewood Cliffs, N.J.: Prentice-Hall, 1967), 198.

3. Ernest J. Simmons, *Chekhov: A Biography* (Boston and Toronto: Little, Brown, 1962), 546.

4. Konstantin Korovin, "My Encounters with Chekhov," *TriQuarterly* 28 (Fall 1973), 562.

5. Simmons, *Chekhov*, 615.

6. *ACLT*, 109.

7. Ibid., 109.

8. Ibid., 85.

9. *Letters*, 107.

10. *ACLT*, 85–86.

11. Hingley, *New Life*, 271.

12. *ACLT*, 217.

13. *Letters*, 453.

14. Simmons, *Chekhov*, 545.

15. *ACLT*, 435–36.

16. Ibid., 36.

17. Ibid., 414.

18. Henri Troyat, *Chekhov* (New York: Dutton, 1986), 36.

19. Korovin, "Encounters," 562.

20. Simmons, *Chekhov*, 50.

21. Ibid., 254.

22. Ibid., 63.

23. Yermilov, *Chekhov*, 212.

24. *Letters*, 307.

25. *ACLT*, 475.

26. Nathalie Sarraute, "Ich Sterbe," *The Use of Speech*, trans. Barbara Wright (New York: Braziller, 1983), 5–6.

27. *ACLT*, 107.

28. Doris Vidaver and Maynard M. Cohen, "Dr. A. P. Chekhov," *American Scholar* 55 (Spring 1986), 228.
29. *New York Times*, Oct. 18, 1990.
30. *ACLT*, 159.
31. *Letters*, 189.
32. *ACLT*, 367.
33. Ibid., 269.
34. *Note-Book*, 68.
35. Korovin, "Encounters," 568.
36. Vladimir Yermilov, *Anton Pavlovich Chekhov*, trans. Ivy Litvinov (Moscow: Foreign Languages Publishing House, n.d.), 156.
37. *ACLT*, 117.
38. Ibid., 106.
39. Ibid., 104.
40. *Note-Book*, 112.
41. Simmons, *Chekhov*, 215.
42. *ACLT*, 302.
43. Ibid., 261–62.
44. Ibid., 203.
45. *Letters*, 227.
46. *ACLT*, 261.
47. Ibid., 261.
48. *ACLT*, 408.
49. *Letters*, 31.
50. *ACLT*, 104.
51. Ibid., 62.
52. Ibid., 118.
53. Hingley, *New Life*, 45.
54. Sarraute, *Use of Speech*, 5, 6.
55. *Letters*, 133.
56. Troyat, *Chekhov*, 207.
57. *Letters*, 37.
58. Ibid., 88.
59. *Note-Book*, 65–66.
60. Troyat, *Chekhov*, 294.
61. Ibid., 174.
62. Ibid., 141.
63. Hingley, *New Life*, 105.
64. Introduction to Virginia Llewellan-Smith, *Anton Chekhov and the Lady with the Dog* (New York and Oxford: Oxford University Press, 1973), x.

65. V. S. Pritchett, *Chekhov: A Spirit Set Free* (New York: Viking, 1989), 163.

66. Lewellan-Smith, *Chekhov,* 9.

67. Ibid., 38.

68. Ibid., 217.

69. Troyat, *Chekhov,* 30.

70. *ACLT,* 46.

71. *Letters,* 237.

72. Ibid., 206.

73. Ibid., 215.

74. Ibid., 251–52.

75. Ibid., 38.

76. *Note-Book,* 119.

77. Ibid., 28–29.

78. *Letters,* 48.

79. Ibid., 180–81.

80. Ibid., 190.

81. *ACLT,* 174.

82. *Letters,* 164.

83. Simmons, *Chekhov,* 225.

84. *Note-Book,* 125.

85. *Letters,* 255.

86. Ibid., 259.

87. Ibid., 263–64.

88. Ibid., 273–74.

89. *ACLT,* 258.

90. *Letters,* 319.

91. Ibid., 312.

92. Ibid., 315.

93. Ibid., 342.

94. Ibid., 348.

95. Ibid., 434.

96. Ibid., 389.

97. Ibid., 439.

98. *ACLT,* 2.

99. *Letters,* 406.

100. Ibid., 409.

101. Ibid., 426.

102. Ibid., 431.

103. Ibid., 468.

104. Ibid., 470.

105. *ACLT*, 18.
106. Eudora Welty, "Reality in Chekhov's Stories," *The Eye of the Story: Selected Essays and Reviews* (New York: Random House, 1977), 69.
107. Ibid., 80.
108. Ibid., 68.
109. *ACLT*, 316.
110. Simmons, *Chekhov*, 414.
111. *ACLT*, 250.
112. Ibid., 112.
113. Ibid., 165.
114. *Letters*, 112–13.
115. Troyat, *Chekhov*, 288.
116. *Note-Book*, 86.
117. Troyat, *Chekhov*, 154–5.
118. Simmons, *Chekhov*, 284.
119. Ibid., 284.
120. *Letters*, 244.
121. Simmons, *Chekhov*, 498.
122. *Letters*, 405.
123. *ACLT*, 221–22.
124. *Note-Book*, 116.
125. Ibid., 87.

CHAPTER 2

1. G. Berdnikov, "*Ivanov*: An Analysis," in *Chekhov: A Collection of Critical Essays*, ed. Robert Louis Jackson (Englewood Cliffs, N.J.: Prentice-Hall, 1967), 90.
2. Ernest J. Simmons, *Chekhov: A Biography* (Boston and Toronto: Little, Brown, 1962), 353.
3. Ibid., 428.
4. Louis S. Friedland, ed., *Letters on the Short Story, the Drama, and Other Literary Topics, by Anton Chekhov* (New York: Benjamin Blom, 1964), 130.
5. *Georg Büchner: The Complete Collected Works*, translated with commentary by Henry J. Schmidt (New York: Avon, 1977), 312.
6. Nikolay Gogol, "Petersburg Notes of 1836," *The Theater of Nikolay Gogol: Plays and Selected Writings*, ed. Milton Ehre (Chicago: University of Chicago Press, 1980), 166–67.
7. David Magarshack, *Chekhov the Dramatist* (New York: Hill and Wang, 1960), 67.
8. *Letters*, 100.
9. Ruby Cohn, ed., *Casebook on Waiting for Godot* (New York: Grove, 1967), 70.

10. Vladimir Yermilov, *Anton Pavlovich Chekhov*, trans. Ivy Litvinov (Moscow: Foreign Languages Publishing House, n.d.), 76.

11. *Six Plays of Strindberg*, trans. Elizabeth Sprigge (Garden City, N.Y.: Doubleday, 1955), 69.

12. *New York Times*, May 1966.

CHAPTER 3

1. Victor Emeljanow, ed., *Chekhov: The Critical Heritage* (London: Routledge and Kegan Paul, 1981), 139.

2. *ACLT*, 277.

3. Ernest J. Simmons, *Chekhov: A Biography* (Boston and Toronto: Little, Brown, 1962), 172.

4. Ibid., 353.

5. *ACLT*, 277.

6. "Dante . . . Bruno. Vico . . . Joyce," *Our Exagmination Round His Factification for Incamination of Work in Progress* by Samuel Beckett et al. (London: Faber and Faber, 1961), 14.

7. *Ibsen: Letters and Speeches*, ed. Evert Sprinchorn (New York: Hill and Wang, 1964), 100.

8. Robert Louis Jackson, "Chekhov's *Seagull*: The Empty Well, the Dry Lake, and the Cold Cave," in *Chekhov: A Collection of Critical Essays,* ed. Robert Louis Jackson (Englewood Cliffs, N.J.: Prentice-Hall, 1967), 99–111.

9. *Letters*, 310.

10. David Magarshack, *Chekhov the Dramatist* (New York: Hill and Wang, 1960), 177.

11. Ibid., 190.

12. *ACLT*, 277.

13. Albert Camus, *The Myth of Sisyphus and Other Essays* (New York: Knopf, 1955), 3.

14. *ACLT*, 285.

CHAPTER 4

1. S. D. Balukhaty, "*The Cherry Orchard:* A Formalist Approach," in *Chekhov: A Collection of Critical Essays*, ed. Robert Louis Jackson (Englewood Cliffs, N.J.: Prentice-Hall, 1967), 137.

2. Ernest J. Simmons, *Chekhov: A Biography* (Boston and Toronto: Little, Brown, 1962), 197.

3. *Letters*, 353.

4. Ronald Hingley, *A New Life of Anton Chekhov* (New York: Knopf, 1976), 110.

5. Vladimir Yermilov, "*Uncle Vanya*: The Play's Movement," in Jackson, *Chekhov*, 112.

6. Eric Bentley, *In Search of Theater* (New York: Vintage, 1953), 339.

7. David Magarshack, *Chekhov the Dramatist* (New York: Hill and Wang, 1960), 225.

8. Maxim Gorky, *Reminiscences of Tolstoy, Chekhov, and Andreyev* (New York: Viking, 1959), 84–85.

9. *ACLT*, 337.

10. Jean Cocteau, *The Eiffel Tower Wedding Party*, trans. Dudley Fitts, in *The Infernal Machine and Other Plays* (New York: New Directions, 1967), 156.

11. Yermilov, "*Uncle Vanya*," 115.

12. Hingley, *New Life*, 86.

13. Vladimir Yermilov, *Anton Pavlovich Chekhov*, trans. Ivy Litvinov (Moscow: Foreign Languages Publishing House, n.d.), 365.

14. Simmons, *Chekhov*, 111.

15. Ibid., 636.

16. Yermilov, *Chekhov*, 214.

17. *Letters*, 211.

18. Yermilov, *Chekhov*, 185.

19. Hingley, *New Life*, 271.

20. George Bernard Shaw, *The Quintessence of Ibsenism* (New York: Hill and Wang, 1957), 182.

21. Bentley, *In Search of Theater*, 328.

22. *ACLT*, 446.

23. Yermilov, *Chekhov*, 361.

24. Konstantin Stanislavsky, *My Life in Art*, trans. G. Ivanov-Mumjiev (Moscow: Foreign Languages Publishing House, n.d.), 272.

25. Maurice Valency, *The Breaking String: The Plays of Anton Chekhov* (New York: Oxford University Press, 1966), 190.

26. *Letters*, 213.

27. Bentley, *In Search of Theater*, 340.

28. Yermilov, *Chekhov*, 349.

29. Ibid., 355.

30. Hingley, *New Life*, 204.

31. *Note-Book*, 145.

32. Ibid., 118.

33. Nils Ake Nilsson, "Intonation and Rhythm in Chekhov's Plays," in Jackson, *Chekhov*, 171.

CHAPTER 5

1. Jean Benedetti, ed., *The Moscow Art Theatre Letters* (New York: Routledge, Chapman and Hall, 1991), 94.

2. David Magarshack, *Chekhov the Dramatist* (New York: Hill and Wang, 1960), 226.

3. *Letters*, 381.

4. Ibid., 380.

5. Ibid., 383.

6. Vladimir Yermilov, *Anton Pavlovich Chekhov*, trans. Ivy Litvinov (Moscow: Foreign Languages Publishing House, n.d.), 163.

7. Ibid., 212.

8. Ibid., 54.

9. *ACLT*, 338.

10. "Virginia Woolf in 'New Statesman,' 24 July 1920," in Victor Emeljanow, ed., *Chekhov: The Critical Heritage* (London: Routledge and Kegan Paul, 1981), 199.

11. Lyubov Vendrovskaya and Galina Kaptereva, *Evgeny Vahktangov*, trans. Doris Bradbury (Moscow: Progress, 1982), 152.

12. Henry James, *The Scenic Art: Notes on Acting and the Drama: 1872–1901* (New York: Hill and Wang, 1957), 250.

13. Ibid., 252.

14. Ibid., 255.

15. Samuel Beckett, *Proust* (New York: Grove, 1957), 1.

16. *Letters*, ix.

17. Ibid., ix.

18. Ernest J. Simmons, *Chekhov: A Biography* (Boston and Toronto: Little, Brown, 1962), 611

19. L. A. Avilova, *Chekhov in My Life*, trans. David Magarshack (New York: Harcourt, Brace, 1950), 145.

20. Konstantin Stanislavsky, *My Life in Art*, trans. G. Ivanov-Mumjiev (Moscow: Foreign Languages Publishing House, n.d.), 260

21. Brooks Atkinson, "The Three Sisters," *New York Times*, July 28, 1964.

22. Ronald Hingley, *A New Life of Anton Chekhov* (New York: Knopf, 1976), 310.

23. Yermilov, *Chekhov*, 324.

24. *Note-Book*, 130.

25. Yermilov, *Chekhov*, 382.

26. M. N. Stroeva, "*Three Sisters* in the Production of the Moscow Art Theater," in *Chekhov: A Collection of Critical Essays*, ed. Robert Louis Jackson (Englewood Cliffs, N.J.: Prentice-Hall, 1967), 125.

27. Stroeva, "*Three Sisters*," 122.

28. Stanislavsky, *My Life in Art*, 262.

29. Beckett, *Proust*, 4–5.

30. *Note-Book*, 26.

31. Roland Barthes, *Mythologies* (New York: Hill and Wang, 1972).

32. Quoted in "Alexander Woollcott in 'New York Herald,' 31 Jan. 1923," in Emeljanow, *Chekhov*, 239.

33. *ACLT*, 122.

34. *Letters*, 388.

CHAPTER 6

1. *The Cherry Garden, Anton Chekhov*, trans. M. Mandell (New Haven: C. G. Whaples, 1908).

2. "Pseudonymous Notice by 'Jacob Tonson' (Arnold Bennett), 'New Age,' 8 June 1911," in Victor Emeljanow, ed., *Chekhov: The Critical Heritage* (London: Routledge and Kegan Paul, 1981), 100.

3. Peter Brook, *The Shifting Point, 1946–1987* (New York: Harper & Row, 1987), 158.

4. David Magarshack, *Chekhov the Dramatist* (New York: Hill and Wang, 1960), 14.

5. Ernest J. Simmons, *Chekhov: A Biography* (Boston and Toronto: Little, Brown, 1962), 612.

6. Constantin Stanislavski, *My Life in Art*, trans. J. J. Robbins (New York: Theatre Arts Books, 1952), 420.

7. Konstantin Stanislavsky, *My Life in Art*, trans. G. Ivanov-Mumjiev (Moscow: Foreign Languages Publishing House, n.d.), 322.

8. *Letters*, 454.

9. Magarshack, *Chekhov the Dramatist*, 265.

10. Nick Worrall, comp., *File on Chekhov* (London and New York: Methuen, 1986), 68.

11. Joe Andrew, *Russian Writers and Society in the Second Half of the Nineteenth Century* (London: Macmillan, 1982), 178.

12. *ACLT*, 443.

13. Ibid., 443.

14. Vsevolod Meyerhold, "Naturalistic Theater and Theater of Mood," in *Chekhov: A Collection of Critical Essays*, ed. Robert Louis Jackson (Englewood Cliffs, N.J.: Prentice-Hall, 1967), 65.

15. Ronald Hingley, *A New Life of Anton Chekhov* (New York: Knopf, 1976), 20.

16. *ACLT*, 142.

17. Ibid., 459, 460.

18. Magarshack, *Chekhov the Dramatist*, 272.

19. *ACLT*, 466.

20. Henry James, *The Scenic Art: Notes on Acting and the Drama: 1872–1901* (New York: Hill and Wang, 1957), 255.

21. *ACLT*, 463.

22. Ibid., 461.

23. Worrall, *File on Chekhov*, 48.

24. Ibid., 39.

25. *Letters*, 388.

26. *New York Times*, May 24, 1990.

27. *Letters*, 107.

28. "Desmond MacCarthy on Charles Laughton and Athene Seyler, 'New Statesman and Nation,' 21 Oct. 1933," in Emeljanow, *Chekhov*, 382.

29. John Goodwin, ed., *Peter Hall's Diaries: The Story of a Dramatic Battle* (New York: Harper & Row, 1984), 336.

30. J. L. Styan, *Chekhov in Performance: A Commentary on the Major Plays* (Cambridge: Cambridge University Press, 1971), 337.

31. Andrei Bely, "The Cherry Orchard," *Russian Dramatic Theory from Pushkin to the Symbolists*, ed. and trans. L. Senelick (Austin: University of Texas Press, 1981), 89–92.

Index

Characterization (*continued*)
    in *The Seagull,* 77–78, 87–88, 97–98
    in *Three Sisters,* 162–68
    in *Uncle Vanya,* 120, 121, 132–33
Chekhov, Alexander, 20, 36, 107
Chekhov, Anton, 1–35
    appearance of, 10
    on artistic aims, 15, 33
    on characters in plays, 175
    on *The Cherry Orchard,* 203
    on comedy, 200
    condemnation of violence by, 31–32
    courtesy of, 17–18
    death of, 11–12
    on dissatisfaction with self, 142
    "faults" of, 33–34
    on freedom, 4–5, 32
    on health, 14
    idolization of, 1–3
    on intelligence and knowledge, 15–18
    and Olga Knipper, 27–29
    on literature, x
    and love, 21, 114–15
    and Maurice Maeterlinck, 111
    on marriage and family life, 26
    on Marxists, 122–23
    and medicine, x, 12–14
    on own hypocrisy, 6–7
    on religion and spirituality, 7–9
    on self, 3–5
    and serfdom, 6
    and sexuality, 21–26, 29–31
    on success and failure, 190
    on talent and inspiration, 18–20
    on *Three Sisters,* 141, 142, 191
    tuberculosis of, 10–11
    wit of, 18
    and women, 24–25
    and work, 136–37
    on writing plays, 36, 95, 217
Chekhov, Mikhail, xi, 8, 26, 45, 56
Chekhov, Mitrofan, 6
Chekhov, Nikolai, xi, 18

Chekhova, Maria, xi, xii, 14, 25, 34, 142
Chekhova, Yevgenia, xi
Chekhov Memorial Theater (Yalta), xvii
Chekhov Society, xii–xiv
Cherry Orchard, The (Chekhov), 143, 197–243
    arrival and departure in, 198–99
    autobiographical elements in, 208–9
    breaking string in, 241
    characterization in, 217–23
    characters in
        Anya, 199–202, 209, 213–19, 221,
            226–30, 232, 233, 237–38, 240
        Carlotta, 199, 215, 217, 219, 222–
            24, 231, 237, 240
        Dunyasha, 214, 216–19, 223, 224,
            231, 232
        Firs, 199, 214–16, 219, 220, 223,
            226, 229, 231, 232, 240, 241
        Gayev, 78, 216, 219–21, 223, 225,
            226, 229, 230, 232, 235, 238
        Lopakhin, 199, 205, 209, 212, 214,
            216, 218–23, 225–26, 228–32,
            234–42
        Pishchik, 216, 219–21, 232, 235,
            238, 240
        Liubov Ranevskaya, 198–200, 202,
            205, 209, 214–38, 240
        Trofimov, 198, 199, 205, 214, 215,
            219, 221, 223, 226–35, 237, 238,
            240
        Varya, 199, 205, 214–20, 225–27,
            230–32, 240–42
        Yasha, 217–20, 223, 224, 231, 232,
            241
        Yepikhodov, 214; 216, 218, 219, 223,
            224, 229, 231, 232, 240
    Chekhov on, 203, 208
    as comedy, 200, 237
    exposition in, 212–14
    future in, 227
    orchard in, 239
    productions of, 202–7

Index

Index